MR TOTTENHAM HOTSPUR

MR TOTTENHAM HOTSPUR

BILL NICHOLSON OBE

Memories of a Spurs Legend

Steve E. Hale

FootballWorld

First published 2005 by
Football World
Tel: 01708 379 877
Website: www.footballworld.co.uk

Printed by Biddles Ltd, King's Lynn, Norfolk

Cover Photography: Empics, Action Images

Distributed by Football World and Vine House Distribution Ltd
Waldenbury, North Common, Challey, East Sussex,
BN8 4DR, England.
Tel: (01825) 723398
Email: sales@vinehouseuk.co.uk

Set in Times New Roman

ISBN: 0-9548336-5-1

To my wife, Carol, and to my children, Matt and Sarah –
survivors of all my 'Bad Spurs Days'

Contents

Foreword

By Steve Perryman

Tottenham Hotspur Football Club has had some wonderful characters in the past, names who have played their part in the history of the club. But no single name or personality was ever more influential than that of Bill Nicholson, for everything he achieved as a player and a manager.

I, of course, do not have any knowledge of him as a player but, as a manager, he led by example. He was always first into the office or the training ground in the morning and the last out at night.

He was a totally honest, straightforward, direct man, with no mind games or trickery, and you certainly knew exactly where you stood with him. If he thought you had played well then he told you, a little begrudgingly sometimes maybe, and if he felt you didn't do so well, of course, you heard about that too.

Bill was a very hard taskmaster but, as a result, he produced some terrific teams and had phenomenal success, not only in England, but on European playing fields as well. He was responsible for so many great memories for all of us Tottenham people.

He was the forerunner for the success of English clubs in European competition and his list of honours for the Club is unrivalled.

With Bill at the helm, Tottenham were the first English club to win a major European trophy when they lifted the European Cup Winners' Cup in 1963, having previously become the first club in the last century to win the League and FA Cup Double, in 1960-61.

I was lucky enough to represent Bill in the League Cup Final twice, in 1971 and 1973, as well as the UEFA Cup in 1972.

And the great respect he commanded from all of his players was tremendous. When you played for Bill, you felt that you never wanted to let him down.

It wasn't just Bill Nicholson you were playing for, but Bill Nicholson of Tottenham Hotspur. He was the one who put us all on the right lines, the one who instilled into us that: "The most important people at the club are the supporters."

Discipline wise, he never had to fine anyone, ever, but if you were late you didn't want to meet his eyes! One glance from him and you certainly knew he was looking at you . . . and you definitely weren't going to be late again!

He laid all the basic foundations, not only in the way we should play our football, but also the manner in which we conducted ourselves – on and off the pitch. He gave you guidelines that were sensible, honest and correct.

About referees, he would say: "Before you start moaning at the officials, they are only human like you and, as a player, you will definitely make more mistakes in a match than they will. Bear that in mind when you start criticising them.'

His total honesty and integrity were unchallenged. If Bill said you were going to get something, you got it and he treated everyone equally. He promised my parents when I signed for the Club that, as a young apprentice, I would be treated the same as the most senior professionals.

No player was more special, we were all special, because we had the Bill Nicholson seal of approval when we signed our contract. He had decided that we were good enough to represent the club that he loved so much.

It was a stamp of honour, whether he had paid money for you or he had helped you to come up through the ranks.

He had an aura about him of discipline and straight-forwardness that you just wouldn't dream of going against. It sounds as though he was overpowering us all, but he couldn't have been like that to have produced the teams of flair and attacking purpose that he did.

He knew that we were all individuals, but that we had to have a core of stability and discipline. We were all treated the same but within that framework we could bring our own special talents to the team and he encouraged that.

Bill knew that Jimmy Greaves couldn't run 10 laps as well as Terry Naylor, for instance, and yet they were both in the same team to blend together and play.

Bill's enormous character absolutely shone out of him, without him having to make rash statements, big headlines or having to rant and rave at anyone. His amazing desire for his club to go forward and succeed was infectious.

Through him, we were so aware of the history of Tottenham Hotspur, how lucky we were to be part of that, the standards we had to attain and follow. And, invariably, we responded and produced for him.

In later years, I came to know Bill more as a friend. He was always great to speak to, I loved talking with him immensely. The football that he spoke about was as relevant when he was 80-years-old as it had been when he taught me 30 years before.

Bill Nicholson will always be Mr Tottenham. He put the club on the map and anyone who came into contact with him should be grateful that he had some role in their development. I am certainly very proud to have known him and will be eternally grateful for all that he did for me.

Steve Perryman, April 2005

Steve Perryman speaks at Bill Nicholson's memorial service.

Introduction

In the early hours of Saturday, October 23, 2004, an elderly gentleman passed away in a hospital in Hertfordshire. He was with family, and his passing was one of dignity and peace. To his immediate circle of family and friends, the end of this man's life came after his health had been deteriorating gradually over a period of a few months, and it must have come as some relief to know that he was now at rest. If the gentleman in question had been any ordinary man, his departure onto a better life would have raised an obituary in the local press, and a few well-intentioned platitudes from his immediate neighbours. But this was no ordinary man.

This was Bill Nicholson.

With the exception of obviously evil individuals, there is a tendency when somebody dies to gloss over the less salutary facts about their life. Misdemeanours get overlooked, the more unwholesome traits in their characters become mere irrelevances and even their whole life can become a kind of celebration of things that would otherwise be considered unpalatable had they still been alive. In compiling this book, I have no doubts in my mind that require that kind of analysis, because Bill Nicholson lived his life in such exemplary fashion that no amount of dirt digging, mud slinging or attempts at character assassination would make the slightest difference. To the supporters and many ex-players of Tottenham Hotspur Football Club, and to anyone who ever had anything to do with 'Bill Nick', the memories of this great man will be only good ones.

Not, of course, that he was a soft touch. Just ask anybody who had the honour of playing alongside him or under his leadership. Bill was an unashamed perfectionist – it was often said that if his side had won a game 6-1, he would want to know why the goal had been conceded.

He always wanted his teams to perform to a standard that he required, while all the time remembering that the very reason for the existence of professional football was as a means of entertainment. His ethos was simple: win, but win well. As his historic Double-winning captain, Danny Blanchflower, so eloquently put it: "The great fallacy is that the game is first and last about winning. It is nothing of the kind. The game is about glory. It's about doing things in style, with a flourish, about going out and beating the other lot, not waiting for them to die of boredom." Every side that Bill built, from the Double winners of 1960-61 through to the team which went all the way to the UEFA Cup Final in 1974, played with that simple but effective formula in mind. It was often to be deemed 'The Tottenham Way'.

In recent years, the application of that way has been at best sporadic, at worst non-existent. The reasons for this are manifold, and are so complex and open to personal interpretation that this is neither the time nor the place to delve into why the guidelines left to us by Bill appear to have been lost, at least for the time being.

Suffice to say, the outpouring of sentiment by long-suffering Spurs fans following the death of their mentor suggests to me that his passing has simply reminded them what they have been missing, and what Bill Nicholson himself would have loved to have lived long enough to see once again – open, attacking, winning football by a Tottenham team.

Eight trophies in 17 years, including two in Europe, is not to be taken lightly, and yet if League titles alone were the yardstick by which managers' success were measured, there were more successful bosses than Bill. Some would suggest that it was Spurs' brand of 'high risk, high entertainment' football itself that prevented more championship trophies from gracing the White Hart Lane trophy cabinet, and that may be true.

Shankly, Paisley, Busby, Revie, Clough – all were successful at landing more than Bill's single league title. Yet to a man, they all spoke in glowing terms of an individual who, like themselves, epitomised what they stood for – they all left their own indelible fingerprint on their clubs. Bill Nicholson was Tottenham, and Tottenham was Bill Nicholson. With his passing, a period of this club's history is consigned to the past. This book is a record of that glorious past and the memories it evokes, but it can also hopefully provide a blueprint for the future.

In recent years, Bill was often to be seen on match days at White Hart Lane, right up to the point where his failing health made it impossible for him to attend any more. The thoughts that must have been going through his mind were his own – to Bill's credit, he had never spoken a single word to the press about his feelings over any of his successors or their teams, even though there must have been many times when he had wanted to. Bill would never undermine a fellow manager of the club he loved for his whole life, and that is the strength of the character that was Bill Nicholson – integrity and honesty.

This is the record of the feelings of his people – the fans, staff and players of Tottenham Hotspur. This is Bill Nicholson.

Steve E. Hale, April 2005

PART 1
THE MAN WHO WOULD BE KING

Chapter 1

A Yorkshire lad, a long way from home

"If you get simple beauty and nought else,
you get about the best thing God invents."
Robert Browning

While it may be considered a truly memorable day in the history of Tottenham Hotspur Football Club, March 16, 1936 was not exactly a significant day in the context of world events. True, the Spanish civil war was boiling up, and at home, there was political unrest not 10 miles from White Hart Lane, as Oswald Mosley's fascist 'black shirts' fought pitched battles with socialists in the infamous 'Battle of Cable Street' in London's East End. The previous decade had seen a great deal of hardship as the depression had caused millions around the world to lose their jobs, and a few months later, in October, thousands of unemployed shipyard workers, miners and mill workers were to march on London on the famous 'Jarrow crusade'.

None of which, of course, would have meant much to the fresh-faced teenager from Scarborough who turned up at the door of Tottenham Hotspur FC hoping to make a half way decent career in football. He had just travelled through the night by train from York – the journey in those days was much more scenic, but not much fun in the dark – and had been referred to Spurs by a Mr. Nelson, a dentist from York. It makes one wonder if that man ever realised the significant effect he was going to have on the lives of so many people all those years later.

Young Bill Nicholson, the second youngest of nine children and son of a hansom cab driver, was born in Scarborough on January 26, 1919. The history of Tottenham Hotspur might have taken a very different course had Bill not been given a small rubber ball for his seventh birthday – because before that, with so much to occupy his time at the picturesque seaside town, he had little or no interest in football at all.

He later attended Scarborough Boys' High School, playing in the school team at centre-half. On leaving school he worked as a laundry assistant for six months and played for the Young Liberals side in a local league. Having been recommended by his manager to the aforementioned Mr. Nelson, who happened to be Tottenham's York-based scout, he was invited for a trial by chief scout Ben Ives in a letter dated February 29, 1936.

After arriving at King's Cross, bleary eyed but excited, he made his way on the Underground to Manor House – deep in Arsenal territory – and then took the bus to White Hart Lane. Although less developed in those days than it is today, the imposing stadium must nevertheless have seemed like a coliseum to a lad who had probably seen nothing like it before.

The *Tottenham Weekly Herald* dated Friday, March 13 announced his arrival in a six line paragraph: "On Trial – Spurs are giving a month's trial to an amateur, Wm. E. Nicholson, an inside-right of Scarborough Working Men's Club. He recently celebrated his 17th birthday. His height is 5ft 8ins and weight 10st 12lbs."

William Edward Nicholson's love affair with Tottenham Hotspur began in earnest on his trainee debut in a midweek fixture against West Ham. He must have made an immediate impression, because he was taken on as a groundstaff boy on £2 per week. Somehow the idea of that arrangement working nowadays is a non-starter, but Bill seemed to lap it up. He was a hard worker, and later claimed that he had painted just about every inch of every stand in the ground, including the impressive Archibald Leach edifice that Spurs fans would now know as The Shelf, or East Stand. By his own admission, Bill hated painting, but said that he felt a pang of sadness years later when the old West Stand was pulled down to replace the structure that stands in its place today.

In the course of a day's work, Bill and the other trainees used to pull a huge roller across the sea of mud that older fans may recall passed for a pitch in those days. Six feet across and weighing slightly less than an Amtrak locomotive, it probably did Bill's fitness no harm at all and may go some way to explaining his impressive stamina levels when he played.

With all the painting and working on the pitch, Bill and best friend Ron Burgess (later to feature significantly in the great Tottenham championship-winning side of 1951) still found time to roll up a bunch of rags and kick it around out of sight of the boss. With Bill still a trainee, things were a whole lot different for young players in those days, and it would be a full two years before he was to be signed as a full professional. In his 1984 autobiography 'Glory Glory, my life with Spurs', Bill Nick made it quite clear that, unlike today where youngsters are included in training schedules and are openly encouraged by older pro's, that rarely if ever happened in football clubs in the 1930s.

The Herald's first mention of Bill wearing the club colours was in a 3-5 defeat of our 'A' team at Guildford City on March 21. Bill scored a hat-trick on his second outing for our 'A' team, in a 7-1 victory over Brentwood Mental Hospital on November 19, 1936. He also featured for Northfleet Amateurs during 1937 and it was about this time that he switched from playing at inside-forward to left-back.

He made his debut for our London Combination reserve team in a 3-0 home win over Bournemouth & Boscombe Athletic on January 1, 1938 and was given a professional contract with the senior nursery club Northfleet United. On April 18, 1938 he gained a Kent Senior Cup winners' medal in the final against Dover.

The small Kentish club, now known as Gravesend and Northfleet, had a unique relationship with Tottenham that under current league rules would never be allowed today. While at the Thameside club, Bill quietly 'did his thing,' which was playing the game he loved whilst always looking, learning and listening.

Not the kind of person to disrespect his elders, he would take in all that he had learned, whether good or bad, and only later would he filter out what he felt was worth hanging on to. Several generations of Tottenham fans were later to thank him deeply for his attention to detail. Bill signed professional forms for Spurs during August 1938.

Bill, meanwhile, had become settled in the Tottenham area, after the club had found him lodgings at 23 Farningham Road, less than half a mile from the ground (I have often parked my car in the area on match days, and found that to my annoyance there is still no 'blue plaque' there to this day). Bill's landlady at the time, Mrs Lawrence, was to remain a friend of Bill's for many years afterwards.

Although he could not have known it way back then, a few doors away from him at number 17 was a family with three daughters. Bill later admitted he initially had a bit of a thing for the elder of the three, Winnie, but for some reason one of the two younger twin sisters, Grace and Ivy, later became a more attractive proposition. He started dating Grace shortly after but, because of her slightly darker complexion than her sister, who was nicknamed 'Fairy', she later became known to Bill (and almost every Spurs fan since) as 'Darkie'. For the record, she actually hated her real name. They were to see a lot more of each other over the course of the next 66 years.

Having made nine appearances for the second X1, the first team debut Bill longed for came on October 22, 1938, when regular left-back Billy Whatley picked up an injury, and Bill stepped in to play at Ewood Park against Blackburn Rovers in a Division Two fixture. Although Bill later said he could remember little about the game, Spurs lost it 3-1, with the young defender suffering a thigh injury and finishing the game at outside-right. As you might expect of Bill, he saw to it that he was fit to return to reserve team action the following week. At the time he was the tenth youngest player ever to have featured in Tottenham's league team.

It was probably not the start to his professional career that he would have wanted, but it didn't make a lot of difference to the league standings at the end of the season, because events elsewhere were to dictate that the 1938-39 season would fizzle out in a uniquely unpleasant way.

Bill had made a solid, if not spectacular, start to his footballing career with Tottenham Hotspur and, like many other young men of his age, he could have been planning the next few years with a fair degree of optimism, although he readily admitted that he was daunted by the amount of players ahead of him in the pecking order at White Hart Lane.

By September 1939, however, optimism was firmly off the menu – because a few hundred miles to the east of Tottenham, Adolf Hitler was making a few less wholesome plans of his own.

Chapter 2

Nicholson, W.E – Sergeant, DLI

"The British soldier can stand up to anything –
except the British War Office"
George Bernard Shaw

World War II didn't really arrive at a good time for anybody, but for professional sportsmen like Bill Nicholson it brought their flourishing careers to an abrupt halt. Bill wasted no time at all in enlisting and, unlike people from other fields of expertise, such as manual or office workers, it was almost impossible for an athlete to just take a six-year sabbatical and pick up where they left off, such was the level of physical conditioning at which they performed. Bill, like so many other professional sportsmen who 'took the King's shilling', must have wondered what was in store for him in the coming years.

After passing through his basic Infantry training, Bill was assigned as a Physical Training Instructor to the Durham Light Infantry. It was common practice for professional athletes to enter the armed forces as 'PTIs' – their level of fitness made them naturals for the job. Many of Bill's adversaries in games after the war were to have featured in matches involving army, navy and air-force units – men such as Stan Cullis, Tom Finney and Tommy Lawton, as well as several players who were to feature in the great Spurs side of 1951, such as Les Medley, Les Bennett, and Ron Burgess.

I worked with several hundred troops on 16-week courses and it was punishing work. I had no time for playing football except for the odd appearance for Newcastle and Darlington, the local clubs. My experience as a PE instructor proved invaluable because one of the prime requisites for coaching is being able to put your ideas over and I was used to addressing a large number of men.
Bill Nicholson

Posted to Brancepeth, County Durham, Bill, in common with many sportsmen serving in the armed forces, was invited to play for local clubs as a 'guest' player. With fuel rationing in force, there was no chance of clubs travelling long distances on a regular basis, so small leagues were set up that kept teams within a short hop of each other. Whilst many would feel that, with a war raging and the very future of the country in doubt, such novelties as football were an unnecessary adornment, the fact that life was to be seen as going on as normal was vital to public morale. It was, however, not unheard of for a game to be completed while air-raid sirens were sounding!

Bill spent time playing for Newcastle United and Darlington, and had less well-documented spells at Sunderland, Hartlepool, Middlesbrough and, curiously, Fulham and Tottenham themselves...

During the earliest part of the war, Bill played a guest match for Hartlepool at home against Darlington on March 30, 1940. This was during the so-called 'phoney war', at which time hostilities between the major protagonists were still at a relatively low key. The match ended in a 3-1 win for the home side.

The following two years saw a lot of hardship for the beleaguered people of these islands, and Bill, along with many other servicemen, probably had more important work to do. There are no recordings of Bill playing any football for local clubs in seasons 1940-41 or 1941-42.

Bill then appeared at Roker Park for Sunderland in 1942, playing a total of seven games with mixed results. The really curious thing is that, in the middle of that stint with the Wearsiders, he saw fit to play two very unsuccessful games for Middlesbrough, and also returned to London where he played twice against Portsmouth, for Fulham and Spurs. It must be taken as read that Bill was home on leave at the time. Even in the middle of World War II it seemed that Bill Nicholson and Tottenham could not be parted!

Bill then returned to the North-East, but this time chose the colours of nearby Newcastle United. The rest of the 1942-43 season saw Bill play three home games for the Magpies, resulting in two wins and a defeat.

I first met Bill Nicholson as a young lad when I was living in Wallsend. My father had taken me down to St James' Park to watch Newcastle play a game against Sunderland. It was just after Christmas 1943, and our lad Bobby was home on leave from the RAF. He came along too.

It was a good game, played on a frosty pitch and the Magpies beat the Black Cats – it was either 4-1 or maybe 4-2. I waited outside the players' entrance afterwards, and spoke to quite a few of them. One of them was Bill Nicholson.

My dad didn't have a clue who he was before the game, but said that he'd 'liked the way he got stuck in'. When we spoke to him, he said he was a Spurs player before the war. Dad said "You should come up here and play for Newcastle when it's all over," but Bill said he was quite keen on someone down there and that she probably wouldn't want to leave!

We could never have known how famous Bill Nicholson was going to become. I've still got the autograph somewhere, along with some other famous ones like Jackie Milburn, Denis Compton and Jim Baxter. Football will miss people like Bill Nicholson.

Albert Boswell

The following season found Bill Nick turning out for an improving United a further 16 times, of which they won eight, drew three and lost five.

On September 30, 1944, Bill appeared for Darlington in a 2-1 win at Huddersfield Town. Of the 20 games he played for the Quakers in that 1944-45 campaign, they won 12, drew two and lost six.

BILL NICHOLSON

During the war, Bill Nick (as he was known even then) helped Darlington to be one of the best teams in England along with other quality guest players like Jimmy Mullen. As kids we used to hang around outside the changing rooms kicking a tennis ball around, waiting for the players to come out and hoping they would join in. Bill Nick always did for a few seconds only, but it made our day. He was always in uniform going to get the bus back to camp. He also played for Northern Command.

John Noble

Bill eventually reached the rank of sergeant, which was also a very common occurrence in the Physical Training Corps. After the war, Bill was stationed in Udini, Italy, with the Central Mediterranean Forces HQ.

It was while there that the impressionable young Nicholson came into contact with a man by the name of Geoff Dyson, later to become a AAA athletics coach. It was the undeniable influence of Dyson that prompted Bill to consider a career in coaching.

After six years of war, Bill was demobbed and decided to travel to Birmingham University to gain his FA coaching badge. He passed it at the first attempt, although in his autobiography, Bill was the first to admit that it is harder in the modern age to gain that honour than it was then.

Tottenham themselves were part of a London league, with varying degrees of success. Quite remarkably, given all that was going on around them, people still flocked to watch football at White Hart Lane. No less surprising is that, after Highbury sustained considerable bomb damage during the blitz, Arsenal were put up as 'lodgers' at White Hart Lane for the remainder of the war!

The following season after the war, Bill was reunited with his team-mates at Spurs, on February 28, 1946. His weekly wage was recorded as £8. Bill played in a total of 11 games, of which Spurs won eight, drew one and lost two under the guidance of former Arsenal winger Joe Hulme, by now installed as manager at White Hart Lane.

The 'lure of The Lane' was to prove as irresistible in 1946 as it obviously was so many years later. This time Bill was in for a much longer stay.

THE FOOTBALL LEAGUE, Ltd.

Extract from Agreement between *Tottenham Hotspur Football* Club and *William Edward Nicholson* professional player.

Period of Engagement *28th Feb. 1946* to *4th May 1946*

Wages £ *8 : - :* weekly from *28th Feb. 1946* to *4th May 1946*

£ : : weekly from........to........

Other Special Clause :........

10. It is hereby expressly agreed that if the said Player be incapacitated and unable to follow his occupation as a Player through any Accident or any other cause whilst Motoring or Motor Cycling, the said Club shall not be liable for the payment of any Wages during the period of such incapacity.

11. It is further agreed that the said Player shall not play any other game as a Professional without first receiving the consent of the Board.

(Signed)........ Secretary.

Date *28/2/46*

Previous Service with League Clubs (including Scottish and Irish) :—

Club and Season *Tottenham Hotspur F.C. 3 Seasons (2 seasons as amateur).*

(Signed) *K Nicholson.* Player.

REGULATION 36 : "In the case of a professional player, a certified copy of or extract from the Agreement must also be forwarded to the League Secretary on the form provided."

12 1938.9.
5 1937.8
6 1936.7
29 1935.6

⊕ . MAR 1946

Chapter 3

The Shape of Things to Come

"I have seen the future, and it works"
Lincoln Steffens

With the war over, and Tottenham now increasingly intent on escaping the second division, Bill was becoming a regular fixture in the first team. His displays at half-back were earning him a reputation as a solid, dependable player who would not let the team down, and he was also featuring regularly in the England reserve line-up. Bill was to use his knowledge gained at Brancepeth, Spennymoor and Birmingham University to improve his game – to Spurs' great benefit. 'Push-and-run' was on the horizon.

It was apparent to many that while Joe Hulme was a competent manager, there was something that his teams were lacking, and the Tottenham board, in one of their more inspired moments, decided to appoint Arthur Rowe in his place.

Rowe, a former Spurs player of the pre-war years, was a visionary who had spent time in Hungary shortly before the war. It is open to debate whether or not he was influenced by the revolutionary coaching techniques employed in that country – Bill himself feels that in fact it was the Hungarians who learned much of their magic from English coaches, the most notable of whom was Jimmy Hagan. The English national team, for so long entwined in a sense of invulnerability born out of a reluctance to accept that they were not the football Gods of planet Earth, were to suffer a serious reality check in 1953 at the hands of the Hungarians– who were playing push-and-run.

Push-and-Run was simplicity in itself. The man with ball releases it, and runs into space, thereby making room for himself to receive the return pass. English players, for so long used to a more predictable style of play, initially had no answer to it. By the end of the 1949-50 season, Tottenham had landed the Second Division championship with a total of 61 points. Many felt that it was simply the beginning – they were right.

The basis for push-and-run was keeping possession of the ball by quick, short and accurate passes. It demanded great skill, particularly in movement off the ball, and fortunately Tottenham had the players on their staff at the time capable of playing it effectively.

"It also demanded maximum fitness because it was not possible to play that way unless 10 outfield players were one hundred per cent fit. In the 1949-50 season, when Tottenham were promoted with 61 points, the club used only 13 players and it was said we were lucky as regards lack of injuries. That may be so, but I believe

good players are injured far less than average or poor players. If they are playing in a good side, there is a continuity and flow about the play and they are supported to the hilt by their colleagues."
Bill Nicholson

My first impressions of Bill? Well, that was before I even met him – remember that before I was ever a Spurs player, I was a Spurs fan. I used to go and watch Bill play in the side that eventually became the push-and-run team. He and Ron Burgess were both great half-backs, very strong players. I remember Bill used to have what you'd call a great engine.

Then when I signed on as an amateur for the club, Bill would always find time for you, even if you were a young kid. Being one of the senior pros at the club, he'd have a good word to help you out . You always listened, because he knew what he was on about.

Bill often got portrayed as this dour Yorkshireman but that just wasn't right at all. That may have been what people thought of him but once you got to know him he was quite a jovial sort of fella really.
Tony Marchi

With Rowe's revolutionary new style sweeping almost all before it, Bill won a Second Division championship winners' medal as Spurs finally secured promotion on April 1, 1950.

Push-and-run had set the game alight. Crowds flocked to see this new style of football, but could it have the same effect in the first division? There was no reason why not. In the FA Cup they had met three first division sides. They had beaten a struggling Stoke City in the third round, followed that with a 5-1 hammering of Sunderland, and only went out to Everton at Goodison Park after a dubious penalty decision.
Bob Goodwin

Tottenham Hotspur's record in Football League Division Two, 1949-50
Promoted as champions
Played 42, Won 29, Drawn 7, Lost 9.
Goals for – 81, Goals against - 35.
Points: 61

Date	Att	H/A	Opposition	Result	Scorers
20-Aug-49	32,702	A	Brentford	W 4-1	Bennett, Duquemin, Medley (2)
22-Aug-49	41,882	H	Plymouth Argyle	W 4-1	Ramsey (pen), Bennett, Baily, Medley
27-Aug-49	53,016	H	Blackburn Rovers	L 2-3	Walters (2)
31-Aug-49	24,828	A	Plymouth Argyle	W 2-0	Bennett, Baily
3-Sep-49	42,649	A	Cardiff City	W 1-0	Medley
5-Sep-49	37,697	H	Sheffield Wed	W 1-0	Duquemin
10-Sep-49	48,274	H	Leeds United	W 2-0	Bennett, Baily

Date	Att.	H/A	Opponent	Result	Scorers
17-Sep-49	54,438	H	Bury	W 3-1	Nicholson, Duquemin, Baily
24-Sep-49	36,846	A	Leicester City	W 2-1	Walters, Duquemin
1-Oct-49	54,905	H	Bradford Park Ave	W 5-0	Ramsey (pen), Walters, Bennett, Medley (2)
8-Oct-49	30,240	A	Southampton	D 1-1	Walters
15-Oct-49	54,375	H	Coventry City	W 3-1	Bennett, Duquemin (2)
22-Oct-49	27,319	A	Luton Town	D 1-1	Walters
29-Oct-49	54,856	H	Barnsley	W 2-0	Duquemin, Baily
5-Nov-49	31,734	A	West Ham United	W 1-0	Walters
12-Nov-49	54,193	H	Sheffield United	W 7-0	Walters (3), Duquemin (2), Medley (2)
19-Nov-49	22,482	A	Grimsby Town	W 3-2	Ramsey, Bennett, Medley
26-Nov-49	62,783	H	Queens Park R	W 3-0	Nicholson, Bennett (2)
3-Dec-49	35,501	A	Preston North End	W 3-1	Bennett, Duquemin, Medley
10-Dec-49	50,758	H	Swansea City	W 3-1	Bennett, Duquemin (2)
17-Dec-49	49,297	H	Brentford	D 1-1	Baily
24-Dec-49	33,078	A	Blackburn Rovers	W 2-1	Scarth, Medley
26-Dec-49	41,879	H	Chesterfield	W 1-0	Ramsey (pen)
27-Dec-49	26,341	A	Chesterfield	D 1-1	Scarth
31-Dec-49	59,780	H	Cardiff City	W 2-0	Rees, Baily
14-Jan-50	50,476	A	Leeds United	L 0-3	
21-Jan-50	27,386	A	Bury	W 2-1	Walters, Bennett
4-Feb-50	60,595	H	Leicester City	L 0-2	
18-Feb-50	20,287	A	Bradford Park Ave	W 3-1	Duquemin (2), Rees
25-Feb-50	70,302	H	Southampton	W 4-0	Rees, Duquemin, Medley (2)
4-Mar-50	36,320	A	Coventry City	W 1-0	Medley
11-Mar-50	53,145	H	Luton Town	D 0-0	
18-Mar-50	22,346	A	Barnsley	L 0-2	
25-Mar-50	51,124	H	West Ham United	W 4-1	Walters (2), Bennett, Medley
1-Apr-50	29,771	A	Queens Park R	W 2-0	Baily, Medley
7-Apr-50	66,889	H	Hull City	D 0-0	
8-Apr-50	49,170	H	Preston North End	W 3-2	Walters, Bennett, Medley
10-Apr-50	38,345	A	Hull City	L 0-1	
15-Apr-50	41,419	A	Sheffield United	L 1-2	Medley
22-Apr-50	46,423	H	Grimsby Town	L 1-2	Duquemin
29-Apr-50	16,417	A	Swansea City	L 0-1	
6-May-50	50,777	A	Sheffield Wed	D 0-0	

Bill's style of play – effective but not given to attracting attention with acts of flair – meant that he simply got on with the job of making Spurs a great side without becoming a household name. But even when young fans found the opportunity to seek him out, they still found a man who gave very little away about himself...

It seems strange to imagine nowadays, but when I first started watching Spurs in the 40s, the players used to go home on the bus...that's the big red type buses you don't seem to see any more. As kids, if we wanted to get anyone's autographs,

Bill (far left), Ted Ditchburn and Alf Ramsey can't stop Wolves' Jesse Pye from scoring at The Lane in November 1951.

we'd hop on the bus, walk around and get as many as we could, and then get off.

Even back then, Bill Nick was a quiet, reserved man. He would be pleasant enough, he'd sign your paper for you and all that, but whereas some of the others might indulge in a little bit of chat, Bill never would.

Then when he became coach, and later manager, things didn't change much. There was always that distance between the hierarchy at Spurs and the ordinary supporter. I think it was something that Tottenham in particular actually encouraged – I don't know why, but they just did, and Bill seemed reluctant to change the way things were.

Mind you, I rather liked it that way. There was something mystical about the boardroom in those days. It was a bit like the Royal family, I suppose – they were a little bit untouchable, a little bit aloof, and I think I preferred it.
Morris Keston

Spurs – Champions of England

It had been 69 years coming but, finally, Tottenham Hotspur, from the humble beginnings of a few cricketers getting together to play football in the winter months, were officially the best team in the land. On April 28, 1951, Spurs defeated Sheffield Wednesday 1-0 with a Len Duquemin goal at White Hart Lane – and push-and-run was to enter the history books.

Tottenham's right-half in that league winning team was determined that it would not be the last that the British public would see of it.

Tottenham Hotspur's record in Football League Division One, 1950-51
Champions
Played 42 Won 25 Drawn 10 Lost 7
Goals for – 82. Against – 44
Points: 60

Date	Att	H/A	Opposition	Result	Scorers
19-Aug-50	64,978	H	Blackpool	L 1-4	Baily
23-Aug-50	21,745	A	Bolton Wanderers	W 4-1	Walters, Murphy, Duquemin, Medley
26-Aug-50	64,638	A	Arsenal	D 2-2	Burgess, Walters
28-Aug-50	44,246	H	Bolton Wanderers	W 4-2	og, Duquemin (2), Baily
2-Sep-50	61,480	A	Charlton Athletic	D 1-1	Ramsey (pen)
6-Sep-50	39,015	A	Liverpool	L 1-2	Medley
9-Sep-50	60,621	H	Manchester United	W 1-0	Walters
16-Sep-50	55,364	A	Wolves	L 1-2	Chatham og
23-Sep-50	59,190	H	Sunderland	D 1-1	Baily
30-Sep-50	36,538	A	Aston Villa	W 3-2	Murphy, Duquemin, Medley
7-Oct-50	46,518	H	Burnley	W 1-0	Medley
14-Oct-50	65,992	A	Chelsea	W 2-0	Walters, Duquemin
21-Oct-50	54,124	H	Stoke City	W 6-1	Walters, Bennett (2), Duquemin (2), Medley
28-Oct-50	44,543	A	West Bromwich A	W 2-1	Walters, Medley
4-Nov-50	66,402	H	Portsmouth	W 5-1	Walters, Duquemin, Baily (3)
11-Nov-50	47,125	A	Everton	W 2-1	Baily, Medley
18-Nov-50	70,336	H	Newcastle United	W 7-0	Ramsey (pen), Walters, Bennett, Baily, Medley (3)
25-Nov-50	36,519	A	Huddersfield Town	L 2-3	Nicholson, Walters
2-Dec-50	61,148	H	Middlesbrough	D 3-3	Ramsey (pen), Walters, Duquemin
9-Dec-50	44,367	A	Sheffield Wed	D 1-1	Bennett
16-Dec-50	22,203	A	Blackpool	W 1-0	Duquemin
23-Dec-50	54,898	H	Arsenal	W 1-0	Baily
25-Dec-50	32,301	A	Derby County	D 1-1	Murphy
26-Dec-50	59,885	H	Derby County	W 2-1	McClellan (2)
30-Dec-50	54,667	H	Charlton Athletic	W 1-0	Walters
13-Jan-51	45,104	A	Manchester United	L 1-2	Baily
20-Jan-51	66,796	H	Wolves	W 2-1	Walters, McClellan
3-Feb-51	56,817	A	Sunderland	D 0-0	
17-Feb-51	47,842	H	Aston Villa	W 3-2	Ramsey (pen), Baily, Medley
24-Feb-51	33,047	A	Burnley	L 0-2	
3-Mar-51	59,449	H	Chelsea	W 2-1	Burgess, Wright
10-Mar-51	26,236	A	Stoke City	D 0-0	
17-Mar-51	45,353	H	West Bromwich A	W 5-0	Bennett, Duquemin (3), Baily
23-Mar-51	47,391	A	Fulham	W 1-0	Murphy
24-Mar-51	49,716	A	Portsmouth	D 1-1	Uphill
26-Mar-51	51,862	H	Fulham	W 2-1	Bennett, Murphy
31-Mar-51	66,651	H	Everton	W 3-0	Walters, Bennett, Murphy
7-Apr-51	41,241	A	Newcastle United	W 1-0	Walters
14-Apr-51	55,014	H	Huddersfield Town	L 0-2	
21-Apr-51	36,689	A	Middlesbrough	D 1-1	Murphy
28-Apr-51	46,645	H	Sheffield Wed	W 1-0	Duquemin
5-May-51	49,072	H	Liverpool	W 3-1	Walters, Murphy (2)

BILL NICHOLSON

The most exciting happening to date was when, in November 1951, I was chosen by the London FA to play against a Berlin XI in the Olympic stadium, holding 80,000 people, in the German capital, the first representative match to be played between the English and German teams after the second world war. It turned out to be a most emotional and enjoyable experience. Our half-back line consisted of Bill Nicholson, Ron Greenwood and myself, and with inside-forwards Eddie Baily and Jimmy Logie, it was overwhelming. I wondered what on earth I was doing in the team – some of these players were gods to me, and only a short time ago I had paid to watch them.

That Berlin game was some occasion. The stadium itself was quite a spectacle, absolutely magnificent. We could not fault the hospitality of our German guests, and the 1-1 draw that was played out was probably the best result in the circumstances – we didn't want to be seen to lose against them, but didn't particularly want to beat them either in case we started another war!

The after-match dinner was something else too. We were led into this lavish banqueting suite, and when we looked at the table, there were the players' names – but oddly, in between each player's place was an empty seat. After we had all sat down, in walked a whole troop of very nice looking young ladies – quite respectable, they looked like students or something similar.

It turns out that a band had been laid on, and the young ladies were there in the event that any of us wanted to dance! Bill, not wanting to offend anybody, duly did his bit for King and Country, but I don't think he'd be too offended if I said he was no Fred Astaire!"
Jimmy Hill

The Cambridge Connection

Intelligence doesn't make you a good footballer. Oxford and Cambridge would have the best sides if that were true. It's a football brain that matters and that doesn't usually go with an academic brain. In fact I prefer it when it doesn't. I prefer players not to be too good or clever at other things. It means they concentrate on football.
Bill Nicholson

In the early 50s, and with an FA coaching badge to his credit, Bill was persuaded to take up a post coaching the Varsity side at Cambridge University under encouragement from England manager Walter Winterbottom. Bill was one of the gaggle of young coaches that had been heavily influenced by Winterbottom's ideas on expanding new ideas within the game, and the job at Cambridge seemed an ideal opportunity to put it to the test. To add spice to the job, his adversary at Oxford University was a team-mate from the push-and-run side, Vic Buckingham.

The Varsity match, played on the mud-filled public allotment that passed for a pitch at White Hart Lane in those days, did not provide the avalanche of goals both coaches were hoping for.

The game spluttered to a 0-0 draw, but with Bill and Vic Buckingham being good friends, I don't think either of these two usually fierce competitors 'did a Fergie'.

The result probably prompted an extended round of drinking by very-well educated young men in places like the Corner Pin and the Bell and Hare.

Push-and-Run – Bill's part in the well-oiled Tottenham machine

As Arthur Rowe understood the importance of team building, he knew that the relationship between right-back and half back was crucial. With Alf Ramsey's penchant for getting forward, the right-half had to restrict his own attacking instincts. Ron Reynolds is clear that 'what really made Alf so good at Spurs was playing with Bill Nicholson and Sonny Walters. The push-and-run style suited Alf perfectly. The number of times you'd see Alf with the ball, running back to his own goal, deliberately delaying the back-pass to Ted Ditchburn, to give the winger chasing him the feeling that he had an opportunity to get it. Alf would then play it back, peel off towards the touchline, and Ted would then throw it straight out to him, giving him yards on the winger to bring the ball away. Alf would bypass Nicholson, who would then slot into the right-back position, because that was Bill's strength, while Alf went on to feed Sonny.'

Though each was playing their part to the full, Nicholson and Ramsey did not always see eye to eye, as Ron Reynolds explains. 'There used to be out and out war between them on occasions, and there were times when Arthur used to leave them at it to argue among themselves. I think Bill was fed up with being by-passed so much and being left with the defensive responsibilities.'

Without Nicholson's grit, his tireless running, his biting tackling, Alf would have been a luxury the Spurs couldn't afford. Winger George Robb explained: "If you had Alf playing, there was always a possibility that a really good left-winger would use the space he'd leave behind by going forward. So Alf certainly benefited from having Bill Nick in the side as the dominating, forceful ball-winner who would cover for him. Alf did tend to leave space, so it was so useful to have Bill around."

Nicholson absorbed that lesson, for in management he teamed playmaker Danny Blanchflower with Dave Mackay, the man who made people play to similar effect.

That was Alf's game, as the BBC's Bryon Butler wrote in Soccer Choice: "Possession was everything to Ramsey. He hated wasting the ball, and the cold precision of his passing up to 30 yards meant that he rarely did." Always wanting the ball, he knew full well that without Nicholson he'd be sunk. Nicholson was a strong ball-winner; few forwards got much change out of him. But once Nicholson got it, Alf would want it, making it apparent that he considered himself better able to use it, his realistic view of things making the tactful approach redundant in his eyes. It's not hard to see how Nicholson resented Alf seeing himself as a cut above, but it was a fair assessment, however unpalatable.

Rowe was laid low by his shattered nerves and fell ill. He was forced to resign as Spurs manager, Jimmy Anderson stepping into the breach. That meant that there was a vacancy for a right-hand man and, since Nicholson's playing days were behind him, he was in the right place at the right time. Alf's hopes of staying at Spurs in the coaching capacity were dashed, for there was never going to be room for him and Nicholson. Instead, he had to look to play on and then make alternative arrangements.

The arrival of Blanchflower meant that Alf's playing days were up, too. A fixture in the team before Danny reached London, it was obvious that the balance between the two was askew, their styles too similar. As George Robb explains: "When Danny came, they were both attacking players, which did tend to leave a few gaps on the right-hand side. They just accepted that would be the case and that somebody had better come across and cover!"

To Nicholson, watching from the sidelines, that wasn't good enough. He knew Alf wouldn't change his game – he'd partnered him through five seasons and knew his game inside out – and that Blanchflower was also doing what came naturally. But Danny was the future, Alf the past. When Alf picked up an injury in March, he missed several games, including good wins against Sheffield United and Cardiff. His days were numbered.
Dave Bowler

Push-and-run caught everyone out when Spurs, under Arthur Rowe, started using this method not long after World War II. It was marvellous to watch and proved very successful. But opponents learned to counter it. They ran with the man and not after the ball: push-and-run's number was up.
Ron Greenwood

More Coaching experience –
England expects, Bill delivers

After Bill had proved more than adequate as a coach of Tottenham's first team, in the spring of 1957 the selection committee of the Football Association, under the advice of manager Winterbottom, invited him to take charge of the England under-23 team for several matches.

First on the agenda was a three-match tour of Eastern Europe, taking in Bulgaria, Romania and Czechoslovakia. Results were mixed but the experience gained in playing in those countries was no doubt invaluable when Spurs later returned to Europe in earnest a few seasons later.

In the autumn of the same year, Bill had what could only be described as a hectic month. First up was a game played at Stamford Bridge involving the England under-23s against Bulgaria on September 26. Ending in a resounding 6-2 win for the hosts, Bill was overseeing such blossoming talents as Johnny Haynes, Brian Clough and a rising star from Chelsea by the name of Jimmy Greaves. It's fair to say that young Jimmy must have made a favourable impression.

That match was followed shortly after by one in charge of an FA XI, against the RAF. Details of that fixture are hard to come by, other than the fact that the game was played in Nottingham on September 9, but the fact that he was shortly asked to take charge of the under-23s again suggests he must have done a good job.

On October 16, Bill oversaw the match between England under-23s and their Romanian counterparts at Wembley. The resulting 3-2 win saw Bill field a young player by the name of Duncan Edwards. In his autobiography, Bill describes Edwards as "a remarkable player, a powerful young man who could do almost anything on a football field. I doubt whether there has been a better all-round player in English football." Edwards, of course, was one of several members of the Busby Babes to perish so tragically in the 1958 Munich air crash a few short months later.

A week after the Romania game, Bill was in action again, this time taking charge of an England 'B' side against a combined Sheffield XI at Hillsborough on October 23. Included that side was John Bond, a young West Ham right-back later to become familiar with Spurs fans as the manager of Manchester City in our epic 1981 FA Cup Final clashes.

Only a week for Bill in which to put his feet up again before, on October 30 he took the reigns of another match involving an FA XI, this time against the Army. As with the previous game against the RAF, details are hazy but Bill must have relished the idea of putting one over on his previous employers!

Five matches in 21 days involving three different teams and, lest we forget, his efforts for England under-23s were in addition to his full-time duties as coach at Spurs. It is little wonder then, that Bill had by now acquired a reputation as something of a workaholic where football was concerned.

We seemed to do nowt else but put studs in. It was a job and a regular fascination. Boots were provided at Middlesbrough, as you might expect, but just one pair, which was news to Bill Nicholson. Bill eventually became Mi Tottenham Hotspur, and produced such a dazzling team at White Hart Lane that they won the Double and played the game in a way that was an object lesson to everybody. He was in charge of the England under-23s when I was picked, and he passed around expenses forms in our hotel in London. Hardly able to write anyway in those days, I hadn't a clue what an expenses sheet was.

"Put down everything that it's cost you to come and play," Bill told me.

"Including my boots?"

He clipped me on the ear and said: "I'll give you boots, you little bugger."

I spluttered and protested that I was telling the truth but he thought I was taking the mickey and trying to fiddle a tenner. Tottenham had probably been giving boots to their players by the boxful but at Middlesbrough, if we wanted an extra pair, we had to buy them for ourselves.
Brian Clough

Not one to rest on his laurels, Bill was 'back in the saddle' by May 1958 when he was again asked to take charge of a 'Young England' team against their full international counterparts.

It was not until September 24 of that year that Bill Nick was again called into 'international rescue'. It was again to manage the England under-23 side, who faced Poland in a match played at Hillsborough. Amongst the stars in a 4-1 win for Bill's young lions, there were appearances by Bobby Charlton, Maurice Setters and Jimmy Armfield.

The final match of Bill's stint with England saw his side take on Young Czechoslovakia on October 15 at Norwich City's Carrow Road ground. A resounding 3-0 win was a fitting way for Bill to round off his connections with the England youngsters – a few days later, and probably due in no small measure to his experience with the under-23s, Bill was to be offered the job that was to become the love of his life for the next 16 years.

October 1958 – the month that changed a club's history

I went to see vice-chairman Fred Wale in his offices at Brown's of Tottenham. He told me: "Jimmy Anderson isn't going to carry on as manager and would you like the job?" I had been coaching at the club for four years and I felt I could do it, so I accepted. He didn't mention a contract or pay increase, so I didn't either. I have never had a contract as a manager. I worked on the principle that if I was good enough, they'd keep me. If I wasn't, they'd sack me!
Bill Nicholson

As first games go, it could have been worse...

Tottenham Hotspur 10 Everton 4
Football League, Division One
October 11, 1958

Bill's first game in charge of the club was to give an indication of what was to be the ride of a lifetime. The crowd of just under 38,000 could surely never have expected to see 14 goals scored – just as the unfortunate Jimmy Harris of Everton could not have expected to score a hat-trick away from home and still end up on the losing side!

It was a big day for Bill Nicholson. He awoke on the morning with the knowledge that he was now the new Spurs manager with an official announcement due to be made before lunchtime.

At least Bill had the comfort of familiar surroundings having been a professional at White Hart Lane since 1938 and on the coaching staff since his retirement as a player in 1955.

As he walked along White Hart Lane from his home to his new office, Bill reflected on many things, not least that afternoon's game with Everton. It wasn't the most attractive of fixtures as we had managed just nine points from our opening 11 games and sat a point clear of a bottom three that included Everton.

But for Spurs fans it was an afternoon that was to go down in history.

Anderson had picked the team before departing and had recalled that genius Tommy Harmer, a brilliant ball player and crowd favourite. And this was to be Harmer's day as we won 10-4 and he was clearly man-of-the-match.

As Tommy recalls in the club's official history book: "I was feeling miserable that morning. I had been dropped for the previous four games and it was in the balance whether I'd get my place back."

We were ahead by the third minute when Alfie Stokes scored but Jimmy Harris equalised eight minutes later. Bobby Smith headed home from a Harmer cross on

15 minutes and George Robb then went through to make it 3-1.

Terry Dyson then set up goals for Smith and Stokes before making it 6-1 himself on the stroke of half time with a shot that went in off a post.

Harris pulled back another seven minutes into the second half but Danny Blanchflower then set up Smith for his hat trick.

With the injured John Ryden having to move to the left-wing – no substitutes in those days – we lost some of our momentum for a spell but that was just the calm before the storm as the game ended with five goals in the last 10 minutes. On 80 minutes Harmer found the net and what a cracker it was!

He recalls: "The ball just bounced towards me and I hit it first time, on the half volley from 20 yards, and it flew into the top corner of the net. I hardly ever scored from that range. It was just one of those days when everything goes in."

Harris then seized his hat trick – an amazing feat in such a one-sided game – but in the 85th minute Smith scored again from a Stokes corner. Within another minute Bobby Collins made it 9-4 before the hobbling Ryden rounded off the score with our tenth.

As they walked off, Harmer told his new boss: "We don't score 10 every week you know."

But Bill was already plotting Monday morning's training session. "I've got to sort out that defence," he thought. "It can only get worse!"

Danny Blanchflower

I played with Bill after being signed from Norwich City in 1955. I had been playing at centre-half for Norwich, but Spurs initially played me as a full-back. Bill was a dynamo, but he was getting on a bit by this time and it was no surprise when he decided to call it a day to concentrate on coaching. It was a good thing he did, because he had plenty of ideas that he had obviously stored up from his days playing under Arthur Rowe. He took what he had learned and took it a step further.

By the time Bill took over from Jimmy Anderson in 1958, he was more or less running the team anyway. Players often change a bit when they become managers – it's obvious, they have to. Bill was still approachable, and he would still have a bit of a laugh and joke with the boys, but not when it came to Tottenham Hotspur. That was the one thing he was deadly serious about. He was a born winner and he expected his players to be the same. Don't forget – this is the man who dropped Brian Clough from the England under-23 side, and young Clough was quite a prospect so it must have taken a bit of nerve to do that. Mind you, Brian was a whole lot quieter in those days. Maybe he was saving it up for later!

Just as we improved as players, I think Bill did as a coach and a manager every time he finished a game. The idea that people have about Bill is that he was fixed in his ways, but he was always looking for new ways of doing things, and he was open to new ideas. Quite often a player would suggest something, and you could see that Bill was thinking it over.

Maurice Norman

BILL NICHOLSON

When Ramsey was out, I played behind Bill against Sunderland. In that side was Len Shackleton. Bill was a solid, reliable sort of player. He was used to playing with Alf, who was a defender who spent most of his time going forward! He actually didn't like defending, really – I don't know why he ever played full-back, but he used to have the room because of Bill.

Eventually, I got a good run in the side – 30 or so games. When I played, I was more defensive than Alf. That must have been a little easier for Bill, because he was essentially a defensive player who was, let's face it, getting on a bit. But he was not what you would call an enterprising player – he was more of a terrier, keeping dangerous players quiet. If you were ever playing against him, he'd give you no room at all – just shutting you down all the time.

Then, of course, Danny arrived and everything changed again. He would be off, doing things, creating things, and I had to change my whole game plan. Bill and Danny would talk things through a lot after Bill got the manager's job. It would usually end up being what Bill had asked for in the first place, but with a few of Danny's ideas thrown in for good measure.

Bill would always talk to players – not just at work, but socially as well. As a result, they'd get closer and closer, and he kept it like that. I used to play golf with him – he was quite a good golfer, a four handicap, I think Danny was quite capable, too – we'd play up at Bush Hill. So the dour thing is a bit of a red herring.
Peter Baker

I was happy at Chelsea, and I'd been there quite a while, but I didn't like Ted Drake – he was a funny sort of man. I was in training one day, doing 'head-tennis', when Ted comes up and says: "Spurs have come to sign you.". My first reaction was: "No, I want to stop here." Drakey then let me know that he thought I wouldn't make it at Chelsea, but I reckon he thought that Tottenham would be too much of a step up for me.

Roy Bentley then took me to one side and said: "Bobby, don't take any notice of him. You go and sign for Tottenham – work hard, keep your head down and you'll never look back." So that's what happened.

It was obvious when I got there that, even though they had a few problems, there were some good players coming in, and it was only a matter of time before it all started clicking. Bill saw me as a big player, somebody strong up the middle who would get lots of goals who was good with the head and good with both feet.
Bobby Smith

Bill used to call me a few names, and once, following a 6-0 thrashing at Wolves, it was: "Brooksy, look, not a bit of sweat on your shirt. England player? ****ing rubbish." That was Bill, but next day it was forgotten.

He's still like that now (2001) when you sit in the stand with him. He criticises and used to hate Ginola, even though the fans loved him, because Bill liked people who put a bit of bite into it.

I always felt on tenterhooks and knew my time was getting near before I left.
Johnny Brooks

Bill Nicholson was a tough guy. He was a perfectionist and very fastidious in everything he did. He was the one who pushed me and he really knew his stuff. Even when Jimmy Anderson was the manager, Bill was the one who really controlled the team.

When he became manager he really tried to instil his own character on the team; he was tough, he was hard and he stood no nonsense. At training, you'd be out there for hours and we'd be working at free-kicks and getting behind defences.

He'd really work you and he was probably a bit like Sir Alex Ferguson now – everyone was terrified of him. I was a very shy person – probably too shy – and I found it difficult. I'd been playing the game for fun, then next minute it's deadly serious.

But it was exciting. People like Dave Mackay and John White arrived and they were wonderful players. Watching them train and play was like being in another world.
Eddie Clayton

I made no secret of the fact that I never wanted to leave Hearts. My only ambition as a lad had been to play for Hearts, who were my hometown club, and Scotland. So the idea of leaving never occurred to me.

Then it came to light that the club were looking to sell me, and that Tottenham were interested. We'd played a few pre-season friendly games against them, with half the Hearts team and half the Hibs team, and the fixtures alternating each year between Easter Road and Tynecastle, so I knew a wee bit about them. But it was only their international players that I would recognise – people like Cliff Jones and Danny Blanchflower. Other than that, I was pretty much in the dark about Tottenham – I probably couldn't even point to it on a map.

There had been a bit written by a few people about the fact that I had on three occasions broken a metatarsal bone in my foot – they seemed to be alluding to the fact that I was injury prone. That was complete nonsense. It was more to do with the fact that, due to the way I went in for tackles, I was more likely to hurt myself than perhaps other players were.

John Harvey, who was our manager at the time, had formerly not only been our club physio but also had served with Bill Nicholson in the army, so it was as much on his recommendation as anything else that I agreed to speak to Spurs. Once I had met Bill, however, there was no going back, because the first thing that came across was his honesty. Yorkshire folk are a bit like Scots – they'll tell you pretty much what is what and they've no time for fancy words that don't mean much.

Bill's knowledge of the game seemed boundless. It made an instant impression on me, because here was a man who knew his football, and who was a great thinker about how the game should be played.

Also, I was very impressed with Bill's ambition. He had already signed a couple of fairly talented guys, and it was clear that I wasn't to be the last. Every player wants to be a part of big things, and that was what I saw at Spurs – the start of something special.
Dave Mackay

BILL NICHOLSON

Tottenham Hotspur 13 Crewe Alexandra 2
FA Cup, Fourth Round Replay
February 3, 1960

You know when you go to places like Crewe that you could quite easily fall down. These clubs love to turn the big boys over, so they were going to be keen on getting one over on us. Up at their place, we had a right old scrap, and only just got through it. Bill had told us what to expect – and he wasn't wrong. We didn't particularly do much wrong that day, but they did as much as they could be expected to.

Once we got down to Tottenham for the replay, Bill didn't give us any special instructions. It was just sort of taken for granted that we'd got away with it, and now it was up to us to finish the job. We did that all right.
Ron Henry

Tottenham's haul of 13 goals in a senior FA Cup tie is a record that stands to this day. Rumour has it that Bill, whilst pleased with the manner of Crewe's destruction, had questioned the need for the replay in the first place!

But Bill Nicholson's apparently endless quest for perfection was to bear fruit soon. The wait was over.

The glory days were here...

PART 2
THE GLORY YEARS

Chapter 4
Top of the World

*"Those who believe they are exclusively in the right are
generally those who achieve something"*
Aldous Huxley

Outside the rather insular world of football, the 60s opened with a curious mixture of optimism and paranoia. Gone was the post-war austerity of rationing, although significant swathes of London, and the Tottenham area in particular, were remarkably still showing the effects of bombing from World War II. The wonderful and completely barking mad swinging-sixties had yet to materialise, but the charts were soon to be inundated with not only the 'Mersey Beat', but also the 'Tottenham Sound' – that of local group, The Dave Clark Five.

Overseas, there was trouble brewing between the USA and the Soviets, who seemed to use every minor territorial dispute around the world as a forum for flexing their military muscle, scaring the rest of us out of our wits in the process. But to the good people of North London (or half of them, anyway) none of that mattered much – because there was a feeling in the air that Bill Nicholson had finally assembled a team which could climb out of the shadows of Arthur Rowe's superb push-and-run side of 10 years before. History was in the making.

I cannot make the point too strongly, that it is no accident when Bill Nicholson produces a great team at Spurs; or Bill Shankly at Liverpool; or Matt Busby at Manchester United. A great football team is the product of many people, directed by the manager. To find the right players to blend into a team pattern is a long and laborious process, extending over many years.
Jimmy Murphy, Chief of Staff under Matt Busby at Manchester United.

Wolves were succeeded as England's leading club by Spurs, whose manager Bill Nicholson was similar in many ways to Stan Cullis – hard-working, disciplined and a good judge of players.

Football is about pairs, and Spurs had some exceptional pairings in their Double-winning side – Danny Blanchflower and Dave Mackay, Bobby Smith and Jimmy Greaves (author's note: Les Allen), and Terry Medwin and Cliff Jones. Nicholson shortened the game by reviving the short pass. It was exciting to watch. He was a gruff man who didn't bestow praise lightly, but knew what he wanted. He made some brilliant signings. Probably the best was Dave Mackay from Hearts for £30,000. Dave was an inspiration to everyone around him.

"Would that Spurs side have been as successful in today's conditions? I think so.

Of course the game is more compacted now. There is less space because the play is frequently pressed into a narrow strip of pitch, but I'm sure those fine players would have adapted. They would still be able to move the ball forward with accuracy and create chances for those sharpshooters Greaves, Smith and Cliff Jones. They were so good at using the width of the pitch, so economical in their passes. Arsenal's Double-winning side of 1971 cannot be discounted, but they lacked the artistry of Spurs and they failed to stay at the top for very long."
Sir Bobby Robson

Both Cliff (Jones) and I came from Swansea – Jimmy Anderson signed me a year or so before Cliff came. By that time Bill Nick had stopped playing and was involved with the coaching. What a difference that was – at Swansea we had done all sorts of things but nothing like the way Bill put things across – it was so much more advanced. I suppose the best way you could describe it was scientific. Apart from the physical side of things, which was punishing enough, Bill would spend hours drilling good habits into us – things that, when you sit down and think about them, are quite obvious, but at the time they were a bit revolutionary. With Bill in charge of the club, everything ran like clockwork.
Terry Medwin

I've got the utmost respect for Bill. He gave leadership, values and told us the club itself was important to the supporters; that it's a big part of the community and we must be aware of that and act accordingly.

He was the bloke that made everything tick and nobody knew more about the game. Nobody worked harder or put in more hours and he'd even have a day when he went round with Len Warren, the maintenance clerk. The saying was 'if a lightbulb needed changing in a toilet, Bill knew about it'. He managed everything from bootroom to boardroom and his training was superb. He was a great coach and motivator and he would never allow us to get into bad habits or become sloppy.
Cliff Jones

I was surprised to say the least when Bill signed me from Chelsea. Ted Drake, my manager, had been keen on Johnny Brooks for some time, and it suited both Tottenham and Chelsea when Bill came in for me. It was a straight swap – no fee involved at all.

Right from the off, I was impressed with Bill and how he sold the club to me. It was clear from early on that he had a vision of how he wanted his team to play, and he seemed to have the idea of exactly the kind of players he was going to get – and it was a question of when he got them, not if. He was that focused.

The training at Spurs was a world away from what I had been used to at Stamford Bridge. Lots of players often say that Bill was a hard taskmaster, but that's only half the story, because as well as the physical stuff, Bill would spend ages drilling tactics into us, and his preparation for games was second to none. It may have been something to do with his military training during the war, I don't know, but whatever the reason, Bill knew his stuff.

Bill never gave praise, or if he did I don't remember it. From pre-season, through to each game, his only concern was being better than the last game. I have played under some good managers in my time including Ted Drake and Alec Stock, but to try to compare Bill to anyone else is pretty pointless, because he was a one off.

Les Allen

The 11 Games That Shook The League

Spurs had won their last two games of the 1959-60 season, and many people were of the opinion that some kind of good start to the new campaign would give a few of the doubters food for thought. What nobody could not have foreseen was a run that, coupled with two games from the previous campaign, would stand as a record to the present day. 11 games – 11 wins. Noticed was served that Bill Nicholson's Spurs meant business.

TOTTENHAM HOTSPUR 2 EVERTON 0

August 20, 1960

Opening day of the season at White Hart Lane sees Spurs grab two late goals by Les Allen and Bobby Smith, after an entertaining game between two of the more fancied sides for the league title.

BLACKPOOL 1 TOTTENHAM HOTSPUR 3

August 22, 1960

Even the mercurial Stanley Matthews was not enough to stop Spurs dominating a match in which they could – and should – have scored a few more, as Bill was certain to have noted. Terry Dyson scored twice, Terry Medwin once, and the great John White was looking ominously good.

BLACKBURN ROVERS 1 TOTTENHAM HOTSPUR 4

August 27, 1960

Another trip to Lancashire saw Spurs hammer four first-half goals against an in-form Blackburn side to kill the game off. Bobby Smith grabbed a brace, while Terry Dyson and Les Allen finished the job. People up and down the country were beginning to take notice.

TOTTENHAM HOTSPUR 3 BLACKPOOL 1

August 31, 1960

A superb hat-trick from Bobby Smith helped Spurs not only do a double over Blackpool within the space of 11 days, but also elevated the big Yorkshireman into the realm of Spurs' top scorer of all time. More importantly, it was now eight points out of eight for Bill's impressive Tottenham.

TOTTENHAM HOTSPUR 4 MANCHESTER UNITED 1

September 3, 1960

United keeper Harry Gregg performed wonders in stopping Spurs running riot in the first half – but it was only a short reprieve. Bobby Smith (2) and Les Allen (2) took advantage of another virtuoso performance by White, Mackay and Blanchflower to completely eclipse United's emergent stars.

BOLTON WANDERERS 1 TOTTENHAM HOTSPUR 2
September 7, 1960

Starting slowly, Spurs fell behind to a powerful and physical Bolton side, and looked to be heading for their first defeat of the season. Les Allen and John White grabbed a goal apiece to take the game to a thrilling finale, but Spurs new-found grit saw them hold on until the whistle. 12 points out of 12.

ARSENAL 2 TOTTENHAM HOTSPUR 3
September 10, 1960

The home side harried, huffed and puffed, and denied space in a thriller of a game, but the sweetest of all victories saw Spurs edge it with goals from Frank Saul, Terry Dyson and Les Allen. Nicholson's passing geniuses put one over the neighbours to win the battle of North London.

TOTTENHAM HOTSPUR 3 BOLTON WANDERERS 1
September 14, 1960

An early Bolton goal was cancelled out by a Danny Blanchflower equaliser, before Spurs took the lead with a hotly disputed penalty. If Spurs were to go on to win the title, surely this was the kind of luck they would need. Once they had it, of course, they used it with deadly effect and Bobby Smith notched a winner at the end of a game that some said finally showed that Spurs could dig in when needed.

LEICESTER CITY 1 TOTTENHAM HOTSPUR 2
September 17, 1960

Leicester did their best to make a contest of this game, but in truth Spurs won it quite comfortably. The midfield trio of Mackay, White and Blanchflower yet again showed what Spurs had and most others did not, but it took another Bobby Smith brace to ensure Spurs maintained their impressive start to the season.

TOTTENHAM HOTSPUR 6 ASTON VILLA 2
September 24, 1960

A record was set by rampaging Spurs as they became the first club to win its opening 10 games. 61,356 lucky people saw Spurs win an eight-goal thriller with goals from John White (2), Bobby Smith, Les Allen, Terry Dyson and Dave Mackay. Most notable feature of the game was the scowl on Bill Nick's face as Villa pulled the game back to 5-2.

WOLVERHAMPTON WANDERERS 0 TOTTENHAM HOTSPUR 4
October 1, 1960

Wolves had been a revelation the previous season, but in this one-sided affair, the push-and-run influenced side of Bill Nicholson showed the world that Arthur Rowe's principles of 10 years before still held up. Goals from Cliff Jones, Danny Blanchflower, Les Allen and Terry Dyson saw Spurs sit proudly at the top of the league table.

After the game at Wolves, Bill Wright came into the dressing room. He was Wolves' captain, England's captain, and a man that people would always listen to. He walks into the centre of the room, stands on a table and says: 'Can I have a bit of order here, please!'

We all went quiet. Billy goes on: 'I'd just like to say well done, boys. If anybody's going to beat you lot this year, then I'd like to be there to see it.'

Coming from someone like Billy Wright, that is what you call a compliment. Wonderful.
Ron Henry

Forty-two days, 11 games, 22 points out of 22. Coupled with the two wins at the end of the previous season, that made 13 wins on the spin – a record which stands to the present day. The occasional slice of luck but, more than that, the application by great players of simple but effective principles. Spurs, of course, would lose or draw some games before the end of the season – but they were to win plenty more. Bill Nicholson had set the foundations for the greatest period in the club's history.

Any player coming to Spurs, whether he's a big signing or just a ground staff boy, must be dedicated to the game and to the club. He must be prepared to work at his game. He must never be satisfied with his last performance, and he must hate losing.
Bill Nicholson

Tottenham Hotspur 2 Sheffield Wednesday 1
White Hart Lane, Football League Division One
April 17, 1961
White Hart Lane was packed to the rafters as 61,205 very fortunate people turned up to watch Spurs lift the League Championship title for the first time since Arthur Rowe's historic 'push-and-run' season 10 years before – ironically, also against Sheffield Wednesday. But there was tension in the air…

I'd played with Ron Springett, the Wednesday keeper, for England a few days before, and on that occasion he'd said to me: "Bobby, please don't hit me any more in the next game. I'm black and blue already." It was legal in those days to charge the keeper.

Bill would have gone barmy if he thought for one second that I'd go easy on Ron just because he was a mate and a nice bloke. I said: "Ron, if you're there to be hit, I'll hit you."
Bobby Smith

MATCH REPORTS

Reprinted from the **Daily Express**

By Clive Toye

Tottenham Hotspur became champions of England last night. And the grey, gaunt, two-tiered stands of Tottenham can scarcely have gazed down on moments drawn so tight with nerve-tugging tension.

Or moments so filled with the magic impulse that makes Spurs the great team, the great goal machine, the great champions as 120 seconds of sheer, incisive, savage soccer which threw back the final challenge from Sheffield Wednesday.

The seconds of success started their brief life three minutes before half-time. Spurs, on their night of nights, were a goal down – scored after half an hour by Wednesday half-back Don Megson when a free-kick rebounded to him from Spurs' defensive wall.

And Wednesday were fighting grimly, gallantly to prove their worth as challengers in front of the 61,000 fans waiting only to hail the champions.

Then Bobby Smith hooked the ball past one England team-mate, Peter Swan, swung it viciously past another, Wednesday goalkeeper Ron Springett, and dived a whirling dance of delight into the arms of his own colleagues.

One minute later Maurice Norman leaped to head a free-kick down to the right foot of Les Allen. And the roof of the net bulged with the goal which took the title to White Hart Lane and turned the crowd's roar into a crescendo.

Those were the magic moments the crowd, the vast, demanding crowd, were remembering when they raced onto the pitch, chanting: 'We want Danny', and stayed on until the team came out for a proud parade of victory at the end.

Those goals…and the other glittering moments when Spurs rode to triumph…will never be forgotten. But oh, how taut the waiting for final, unassailable success!

The tension pulled Spurs away from their fierce flow of football. Gave a fraction's hesitation. A fractional inaccuracy.

A heart-lifting, blood-pounding period of fear for Spurs' hysterical fans as Wednesday fought and fought on, even when Springett, charged by Smith, was carried off on a stretcher and spent five minutes on the touch-line until he forced his way back on to the field.

Extracted from the **Daily Herald**, April 1961

Spurs are now just 90 minutes away from the greatest Double of modern soccer times.

Who can see Leicester stopping them in the Cup Final at Wembley on May 6? Certainly none of the joy-intoxicated 61,200 who saw Wednesday defeated in true champion fashion by a Bobby Smith and Les Allen arrogant two-goal burst in three minutes just before half time.

It was so appropriate that Spurs should clinch the title with a revenge win against rugged Wednesday, the first team to beat them this season – by 2-1 at Hillsborough on November 17.

That was a tough, bruising match in which the pure soccer skills were sacrificed in the fierce heat of a win-at-any-price mood.

So it was last night. It was no match for the soccer purists. It was 90 minutes of tension accompanied by some terrifying tackling.

Yet at the end, after the heat of the battle, came the pumping handshakes, those now-famous Spurs kisses and embraces, and the sincere congratulations from the weary vanquished.

This wasn't Spurs' match of the season. They have produced much more academic, scintillating soccer, but they have never equalled the fight and determination needed for their most dramatic success.

Reprinted from the **Daily Sketch**, April 1961

Five thousand crazy fans, drunk with success, brushed police aside and rushed to join the gigantic chorus in front of the directors' box at White Hart Lane last night.

"We want Danny! We want Danny! We want..." they yelled, until I felt my ears would split.

They kept it up for 10 thunderous minutes. Then their idol, carved from the Blarney stone itself, appeared with the rest of the conquering team – The Champions of 1961.

The crowd was delirious – the 5,000 on the pitch and the other 57,000 still rooted in the stands and on the terraces...they didn't care tuppence if they never got home.

When their heroes appeared, all the ear-splitting roar that went on before seemed but a whisper to what followed.

The players hurled their bath towels into the crowd and stood with smiles on their lips and tears of pride in their eyes.

Only now the lights are switched out and the crowd has disappeared into the countless back streets of North London is it possible to remember the facts about a game I'll never forget.

Spurs are eight points up with three to play. This not only wins them the Championship but leaves them needing only three more points to set an all-time First Division record.

Now the champagne has stopped bubbling in the dressing room I must report that, if this was a vintage occasion, it was not a vintage game.

How could it be when men were gambling for the highest stakes in English football?

Now only Leicester stand between mighty Spurs and a Double that hasn't been achieved since Villa in 1897.

Wednesday, for so long Spurs' most dangerous challengers – they were the first team to tame Tottenham this season – were fighting like tigers. And fighting tigers don't always stick to the rules.

Referee Tommy Dawes, like most of us, seemed affected by the occasion and made some strange decisions, one of which led to Wednesday taking the lead in the 29th minute.

This was shining White Hart Lane's one black spot for it resulted in not only a storm of booing but things including a bottle being thrown on to the pitch.

As players tensed up tackles became tougher. Men were hurt. And Wednesday, who seemed to me to be the first to start mixing it, finished the worst off – as so often happens.

Their England keeper Ron Springett, charged into the post by goal-hunting Bobby Smith, badly hurt his back.

For four minutes he had to be replaced between the posts by full-back Peter Johnson while he was given first-aid on the touchline.

Centre-forward Keith Ellis came off worse. He was ko'd late in the second-half and had to be led off the field, unable to hear the thunderous shouts for the buzzing in his own aching head.

Worst of all, Cliff Jones had two stitches clipped in his knee during the interval. Wednesday didn't know it. Nor did the crowd. Cliff lasted the game but he'll miss Wales's World Cup match against Spain in Cardiff.

Dave Mackay, victim of a couple of vicious tackles, had his name taken and most of the Spurs forwards suffered some hard knocks from trips and crash tackles.

Wednesday's golden goal was the biggest bit of night-light robbery I have seen.

John Fantham had fallen down before Maurice Norman was within two yards of him. But for some mysterious reason referee Dawes thought otherwise.

From that unjust kick left-back Don Megson got the goal that kept the hunters in the hunt.

From hell let loose we swiftly moved into a soccer heaven within 50 fiery seconds. That was the time it took Spurs to score the two greatest goals in their long soccer history, just on the interval.

Bobby Smith, pulling down a high ball – a back-header from Dyson – as if he had glue on his boots, turned and in one fantastic move volleyed the ball past the helpless Springett.

And while the echoes were bouncing around the back streets Maurice Norman headed back the ball for Les Allen to score the winner.

Tottenham Hotspur's record in the Football League, Division One, 1960-61
Champions
Played 42, Won 31, Drawn 4, Lost 7.
Goals for – 115, Goals against – 55
Points: 66

Date	Att	H/A	Opposition	Result	Scorers
20-Aug-60	50,393	H	Everton	W 2-0	Smith R, Allen
22-Aug-60	27,656	A	Blackpool	W 3-1	Medwin, Dyson (2)
27-Aug-60	26,819	A	Blackburn Rovers	W 4-1	Smith R (2), Allen, Dyson
31-Aug-60	45,684	H	Blackpool	W 3-1	Smith R (3)
3-Sep-60	55,442	H	Manchester United	W 4-1	Smith R (2), Allen (2)
7-Sep-60	41,565	A	Bolton Wanderers	W 2-1	White, Allen
10-Sep-60	59,868	A	Arsenal	W 3-2	Saul, Allen, Dyson

BILL NICHOLSON

14-Sep-60	43,559	H	Bolton Wanderers	W	3-1	Blanchflower (pen), Smith R (2)
17-Sep-60	30,129	A	Leicester City	W	2-1	Smith R (2)
24-Sep-60	61,356	H	Aston Villa	W	6-2	Mackay, White (2), Smith R, Allen, Dyson
1-Oct-60	52,829	A	Wolves	W	4-0	Blanchflower, Jones, Allen, Dyson
10-Oct-60	58,916	H	Manchester City	D	1-1	Smith R
15-Oct-60	37,248	A	Nottingham Forest	W	4-0	Mackay, Jones (2), White
29-Oct-60	51,369	A	Newcastle United	W	4-3	Norman, Jones, White, Smith R
2-Nov-60	47,605	H	Cardiff City	W	3-2	Blanchflower (pen), Medwin, Dyson
5-Nov-60	56,270	H	Fulham	W	5-1	Jones (2), White, Allen (2)
12-Nov-60	53,988	A	Sheffield Wed	L	1-2	Norman
19-Nov-60	46,010	H	Birmingham City	W	6-0	Jones (2), White, Smith (pen), Dyson (2)
26-Nov-60	39,017	A	West Bromwich A	W	3-1	Smith R (2), Allen
3-Dec-60	58,737	H	Burnley	D	4-4	Norman, Mackay, Jones (2)
10-Dec-60	21,657	A	Preston North End	W	1-0	White, Allen
17-Dec-60	61,052	A	Everton	W	3-1	Mackay, White, Allen
24-Dec-60	65,930	H	West Ham United	W	2-0	White, Dyson
26-Dec-60	34,351	A	West Ham United	W	3-0	White, Allen, Brown og
31-Dec-60	48,742	H	Blackburn Rovers	W	5-2	Blanchflower, Smith R (2), Allen (2)
16-Jan-61	65,535	A	Manchester United	L	0-2	
21-Jan-61	65,251	H	Arsenal	W	4-2	Blanchflower (pen), Smith R, Allen
4-Feb-61	53,627	H	Leicester City	L	2-3	Blanchflower (pen), Allen
11-Feb-61	50,786	A	Aston Villa	W	2-1	Smith R, Dyson
22-Feb-61	62,261	H	Wolves	D	1-1	Smith R
25-Feb-61	40,278	A	Manchester City	W	1-0	Medwin
11-Mar-61	45,463	A	Cardiff City	L	2-3	Allen, Dyson
22-Mar-61	46,470	H	Newcastle United	L	1-2	Allen
25-Mar-61	38,536	A	Fulham	D	0-0	
31-Mar-61	65,032	H	Chelsea	W	4-2	Jones (2), Saul, Allen
1-Apr-61	46,325	H	Preston North End	W	5-0	Jones (3), White, Saul
3-Apr-61	57,103	A	Chelsea	W	3-2	Norman, Smith R, Medwin
8-Apr-61	40,961	A	Birmingham City	W	3-2	White, Smith R, Allen
17-Apr-61	61,205	H	Sheffield Wed	W	2-1	Smith R, Allen
22-Apr-61	28,991	A	Burnley	L	2-4	Baker, Smith R
26-Apr-61	35,753	H	Nottingham Forest	W	1-0	Medwin
29-Apr-61	52,054	H	West Bromwich A	L	1-2	Smith R

Spurs' Road to Wembley, 1961 FA Cup

Third Round, White Hart Lane
January 7, 1961
Tottenham Hotspur 3 Charlton Athletic 2
An entertaining game saw Spurs win a London derby against spirited Charlton. As league leaders, it was no more than many people were expecting of Tottenham, and Bill made sure they did not 'believe their own publicity' without being able to back it up.

Scorers: Les Allen (2) Terry Dyson

Fourth Round, White Hart Lane
January 28, 1961
Tottenham Hotspur 5 Crewe Alexandra 1
Having been on the business end of a cup-record 13-2 drubbing at the same ground the previous season, Crewe must have feared the worst. They were right to – despite conceding eight goals less, they still left with a mauling.
Scorers: Dave Mackay, Cliff Jones, Bobby Smith, Les Allen, Terry Dyson

Fifth Round, Villa Park
February 18, 1961
Aston Villa 0 Tottenham Hotspur 2
A stunning performance from Bill's side saw off the Villa, just seven days after beating the same side on the same ground 2-1. If the pressure of being league-leaders was there at all, there was no sign of it.
Scorers: Cliff Jones, Neil (og)

Sixth Round Replay, White Hart Lane
March 8, 1961
Tottenham Hotspur 5 Sunderland 0
After a full-blooded drawn cup-tie against second-division Sunderland at Roker Park, in which Spurs players heard first hand the mighty 'Roker roar', it was the turn of 64,797 at The Lane to cheer their team to victory, proving that passionate support counts for little without a team to finish the job.
Scorers: Dave Mackay, Bobby Smith, Les Allen, Terry Dyson (2)

Semi-Final, Villa Park
March 18, 1961
Tottenham Hotspur 3 Burnley 0
Two of the top sides in the country went head-to-head at a ground where Spurs had come to grief three times in semi-finals since WW2. This time, there was to be no heartache for those travelling from London – a Cliff Jones goal killed off a late Burnley revival to make it 3-0, and, with an apparently 'easy' tie against Leicester City in the final, the Double was definitely on.
Scorers: Bobby Smith (2) Cliff Jones

Tottenham Hotspur 2 Leicester City 0
FA Cup Final
Wembley Stadium
May 6, 1961
Spurs: Bill Brown, Peter Baker, Ron Henry, Danny Blanchflower, Maurice Norman, Dave Mackay, Cliff Jones, Les Allen, Bobby Smith, John White, Terry Dyson
Scorers: Bobby Smith, Terry Dyson

BILL NICHOLSON

Bill would get us to study players for ages. When it came to the cup final, I'd been marking Harold Riley, the Leicester outside-right. I thought: 'I don't want to be making a muck-up at Wembley', and having studied him, I said to myself: 'If I let him have the ball he'll make his own mistakes,' because I'd remembered that from our league games against them. He'd put it too far in front of him, or run it over the line. I got man-of-the-match for that game, and it was all down to the good habit of watching your opponents.
Ron Henry

You would think that, having just won the Double, Bill would have been all over us. Obviously he was pleased with what we had achieved, but he let it be quite well known that he thought the performance against Leicester in the final was below par. He had been as pleased as punch when we beat Sheffield Wednesday to win the league, but this had been a Wembley final, shown all over the world, and maybe he thought that his Spurs side should have put on a bit of a show.

I often wonder whether, with a little more praise for small achievements, and perhaps a little less criticism, that Bill could have got a bit more out of some of us for a bit longer, but we'll never know, because Bill was Bill and if you had changed the man, you may have changed whatever it was that made him tick.
Terry Dyson

Leicester had lost Len Chalmers through injury and were down to 10 men — remember, there were no substitutes in those days. The lad had tried to carry on, but he was in a bad way and as soon as he went off, I reckon Bill must have expected us to really take Leicester to the cleaners. But with so much at stake, I suppose it's human nature to be a bit cautious, and when we eventually ran out 2-0 winners, I think Bill saw it as a bit of an anti-climax. Some of the stuff we had

Leicester City keeper Gordon Banks dives in vain as Terry Dyson (out of picture) hits Spurs' second goal in the 1961 FA Cup Final. Bill didn't approve of the performance but his team still made history.

*played that season had been out-of-this-world, but in many people's eyes there
was no way we were going to jeopardise the chance of being the first club to
achieve the Double in the 20th century, even if it meant we weren't our usual
selves.*
Dave Mackay

*Yes, Bill was quite annoyed about the performance at Wembley that day, but he
still knew we'd done something a bit special. I've often heard it said that Bill was
gruff and not very tactful, but that's not strictly true, in my opinion. I mean, people
like Cliff Jones and myself were the kind of players Bill could bawl out in front of
the others if we were playing below ourselves – he'd say things like 'and as for you
two buggers, it's about time you got moving out there!' and we'd just take the
criticism on the chin and get on with it. But there were others who took things a
bit to heart, and this is where the contradiction comes in – Bill would often take
them to one side and let them know what they were doing wrong, but he'd make
sure it was out of earshot of the others. There was more to Bill than many people
gave him credit for.*
Terry Medwin

*Leicester losing Chalmers the way they did was possibly the worst thing that
could have happened to that final. How many times have we seen this down the
years, where a team goes a man down and everyone thinks the game is a foregone
conclusion? What so often happens is that the team with the man down juggles
things around a bit, and a manager's plans go out the window.*

*I honestly think that's what happened that day. There was no way that Leicester
were going to beat us, because we were the better side. But they had their pride,
and they wanted to make things difficult for us. I suppose we could have gone at
them hell-for-leather to make the extra man count, but there was just too much at
stake, I reckon. That's why Bill felt it was a bit flat. When we had played our
league games that year, Spurs had taken people's breath away, and I think the
whole world was waiting for it to happen at Wembley.*
Maurice Norman

*I think we wanted the Double too much to play well at Wembley. We were too
pent up – the thought that we could be the first team to do it this century, especially
when everybody expected us to – it was just a burden, really. Everyone knows we
didn't play well that day. What many people, including Bill himself, didn't know
was that I should never have played at all. I could hardly walk the Friday before.
My knee was just gone.*

*In those days there were no substitutes, and there was no way I was going to miss
the final – it was the whole world to me. The only one who knew was Maurice
Norman – we used to room together, and I said to him: 'Maurice, you've got to
promise to keep your mouth shut.'*

*He said: "Yeah, all right." We both knew Bill. He wouldn't have played anybody
if he thought it would put the team at risk. I was with the doctor on the Friday*

morning, and he put two injections into the knee. He said: "Try that, and give me a ring back at about three o'clock and we'll see how it is."

Well, I gave him a ring back about three and said it felt lovely, no problems at all. He said that I would have to come back Saturday morning at eight o'clock, and again at twelve o'clock. Well, he put another two injections in at eight o'clock, and another two at twelve, and we got right through almost to half-time.

Then a couple of minutes before the break, it really started to go. I got into the dressing room and the club doctor took one look at it and said to me: "What's that? Have you been having something on that?"

I said: "No, I've just been rubbing it." Well, he put another two jabs in and said: "That should get you through to full time."

I know Leicester were down to 10 men, but so were we in a way. We were doing things we wouldn't normally do, instead of just letting it go and playing.

I'm forever grateful to Maurice for keeping quiet about it. If people had seen me indoors on the Thursday night – I couldn't move. But at Wembley I scored, got a winners' medal – and did a lot of running about.
Bobby Smith

After the game I went over to Bill and stuck my hand out. I said: "Well done, Bill – we've done it." He forced a smile and said: "Yes, I know, Ron – but we were bloody awful. That wasn't like our team."

I said: "Well, aren't you satisfied, Bill?" He said: "No, I am not."
Ron Henry

It's a joy for English football. At last we have a team of our own we can copy. Spurs' triumph is the vindication for Billy Nicholson's hard work.
Ron Greenwood, manager, West Ham United

Spurs are worthy of the Double. I told Billy Nicholson after the game that we are right behind them in the European Cup, because I am convinced the best football talent in the world can be found in Britain and Spurs can prove it.
Matt Gillies, manager, Leicester City

So 10 years after Arthur Rowe's Spurs had lifted the league trophy for the first time in Tottenham's history, Bill Nicholson's wonderful team had firmly poked in the eye all those critics who said that 'push-and-run' was simply a flash in the pan. They had said that was limited, and that with the right application of coaching, it was beatable. But when Bill had assembled such an array of talent as graced the football fields of England in 1961, all the coaching in the world would have done little to resist it.

The trick now was how to top it…

£99,999? He'd better be bloody worth it!
Spurs fan Doug Fraser's initial reaction on the arrival of Jimmy Greaves from AC Milan, December 1961.

The Double was won, and Spurs, although beset with injuries to key players, had a reasonable start to the new season up to the start of December, having played 18, won nine, drawn three and lost six. Many Spurs fans wondered why Bill Nicholson had flown to Milan in December '61 and landed a promising young striker by the name of Jimmy Greaves, for a staggering fee just under a hundred thousand pounds. The next few years would answer those questions comprehensively.

I was really grateful to Bill for bringing me to Tottenham. I'd had a successful, but largely unhappy time in Italy and just wanted to get back to England. The fact that I'd come back to the biggest side in the land was even better.

I had no trouble fitting in. You obviously worry a bit that here is a settled side, and where do I fit in? But Bill knew his plan.
Jimmy Greaves

Some months before moving to Italy, Jimmy had met Tottenham boss Bill Nicholson while they were both attending a football function. It was then that the idea of Greaves becoming a Spurs player first arose, as he recalls: "Bill actually asked what I was doing and I said: 'Well, it looks as though some Italian club are coming in for me,' and I said that I would be interested in joining any other club. Bill said: "All right, leave it with me." I think he knew what I meant by that conversation – that I'd be keen to join Tottenham. But of course he couldn't do it there and then because I had just been transferred to Italy. When Bill first came over to Milan to sign me he knew full well that he didn't have to sell Tottenham to me as an individual. He knew I was prepared to join the club without even asking the question.

On arriving home from training with AC Milan one afternoon Greaves found Nicholson sipping a cup of tea in his living room. Jimmy knew a dream transfer to Tottenham and a return to English football was on the horizon.

However, with further interest from his old club Chelsea, AC Milan saw the opportunity to force the two London clubs into a bidding war for the England international.

Nicholson, wise to the Italian club's plans and fully aware that Greavsie only wanted to join Tottenham, met with Chelsea secretary John Battersby and they both agreed to table identical bids.

Chelsea eventually realised there was no way Greaves was going to make a return to Stamford Bridge and dropped out of the chase, while Nicholson was forced to increase the offer to £99,999. The fee was specific because he didn't want Greaves saddled with the burden of being the first £100,000 player.
Chris Curry

Defeat at home by Alf Ramsey's Ipswich Town in March 1962 proved a bitter blow to Spurs' hopes of achieving back-to-back League championship wins. But there was precious little in it at the end of the season, with Tottenham finishing just four points adrift of champions Ipswich and a point behind runners-up Burnley. But for Burnley, there was a double disappointment...

Spurs' Road to Wembley, 1962 FA Cup

Third Round Replay, White Hart Lane
January 10, 1962
Tottenham Hotspur 4 Birmingham City 2
After surrendering a three goal lead, and almost losing, in the first leg at
St.Andrews (one wonders if there was any paint left on the dressing room wall
after Bill had spoken), Spurs won the replay quite comfortably.
Scorers: Terry Medwin (2), Les Allen, Jimmy Greaves

Fourth Round, Home Park
January 27, 1962
Plymouth Argyle 1 Tottenham Hotspur 5
Incredibly for a third division ground, a crowd of 40,040 saw an exhibition of
flowing, irresistible football from the reigning league champions as any hope of a
cup giant-killing soon disappeared down the river Tamar.
Scorers: Terry Medwin, John White, Jimmy Greaves (2), Cliff Jones

Fifth Round, The Hawthorns
February 17, 1962
West Bromwich Albion 2 Tottenham Hotspur 4
There was to be no repeat of the scare Spurs suffered on their previous visit to
the second city, with a resounding win which spared Spurs an unwanted replay;
they had their minds firmly on Europe by now.
Scorers: Bobby Smith (2), Jimmy Greaves (2)

Sixth Round, White Hart Lane
March 10, 1962
Tottenham Hotspur 2 Aston Villa 0
For the third time in four ties, Spurs were up against Brummie opposition.
Despite Villa's somewhat physical approach to the game, Bill's players had
enough in the tank to see them off.
Scorers: Danny Blanchflower, Cliff Jones

Semi-Final, Hillsborough
March 31, 1962
Tottenham Hotspur 3 Manchester United 1
With the European Cup semi-final against Benfica just days away, Spurs players
could perhaps be forgiven for having their minds elsewhere. Bill would see to it
that they didn't. Gaining a two-goal lead before half time, they resisted a brief
United comeback to reach their second final in as many years.
Scorers: Terry Medwin, Jimmy Greaves, Cliff Jones

It makes me laugh when I hear about modern players moaning about playing too

many games. We couldn't get enough – we would have played seven games a week if Bill had let us – which of course, he wouldn't have.
Ron Henry

Tottenham Hotspur 3 Burnley 1
FA Cup Final
Wembley, May 5, 1962
Spurs: Bill Brown, Peter Baker, Ron Henry, Danny Blanchflower, Maurice Norman, Dave Mackay, Terry Medwin, John White, Bobby Smith, Jimmy Greaves, Cliff Jones
Scorers: Blanchflower (pen), Smith, Greaves

That was a cracking game. I can remember walking out with Jimmy, and he said to me: "It's all right for you, Ron – you've already got a medal from last year. Tell you what – I'm going to score in the first minute." Well, he got that wrong – it was three-and-a-half. Burnley at that time were as good as we were, and at 2-1 I thought we were hanging on a bit. I was bloody relieved to see that third goal go in."
Ron Henry

Burnley and Spurs had been the two top teams of the early 60s. The Clarets had won the league in 1959, had lost to us in the semi-final of the FA Cup in '61 and had just come second in the league behind Ipswich. So really, it was a face-off.
Dave Mackay

After the disappointing final against Leicester the year before, our match with Burnley was an absolute cracker. We were without doubt the two best sides of our day, and the public weren't disappointed. Bobby Smith was just about unplayable that day.
Maurice Norman

That game was like the 'Manchester United v Arsenal' of the day. It was the final that most neutrals would have wanted to see, and it really could have gone either way. But on the day, we did the stuff and Burnley couldn't live with us. It was a cracking final – much better than the Leicester game.

It's a shame that we hadn't put on that kind of show 12 months earlier. Bill would have been a lot happier if we had.
Cliff Jones

At the end of my first full season at West Ham I went to watch Spurs play Burnley in the 1962 final. I arrived late and stood just behind the players tunnel, and as Bill Nicholson and Harry Potts led their sides out I felt tears in my eyes. I knew them personally, I identified with them, I shared their pride.
Ron Greenwood

Spurs' jubilant supporters pack the streets to see Bill Nicholson and Danny Blanchflower hold the FA Cup aloft in 1962.

England? Bill stays put

I enjoyed my experiences with England, but there was no question of my seeking Winterbottom's job when he departed in 1962. I was a Tottenham man through and through, and the winning of the Double the year before was as good a reason as any for wanting to stay at White Hart Lane. The FA never sounded me out. I would have rejected any overtures.
Bill Nicholson

FA Charity Shield, Portman Road, August 1963
Ipswich Town 1 Tottenham Hotspur 5

Just as the Tottenham side of the early 50s was quite revolutionary, and we had been 10 years later, other sides with clued-up managers devised ways of playing us. The prime example of this had been one of Bill's old team-mates in Arthur Rowe's side, Alf Ramsey. He had built a good Ipswich side, played with three up front and had got his players used to working that way. It really baffled a lot of managers that year, and Bill Nicholson was no exception. To their credit, Ipswich had plenty of good players and were worthy of their League Championship in 1961-62. Eventually, however, Bill and a few others worked it out.

In the Charity shield game at Portman Road on the opening day of the '62-63 season, Spurs devised a way of dealing with Ipswich, and we ended up beating the league champions 5-1 on their own ground. At that stage, many people couldn't see any way we wouldn't go straight back to the title.
Dave Mackay

Within a couple of months, Ramsey the alchemist looked more like a con man who had beaten the rest with a football version of the Emperor's new clothes. Starting their defence (of the league title) with the traditional Charity Shield game, against Tottenham, Ipswich were soundly beaten 5-1. Bill Nicholson had brought his full-backs inside to pick up Phillips and Crawford and let the half-backs take care of Leadbetter and Stephenson. It was a ploy that was to be repeated up and down the country.
Dave Bowler

Ipswich slumped to 17th in the final first division table for 1962-63 and though Tottenham remained serious title challengers, they had to settle for second place behind new title winners Everton, who finished six points clear.

The season would end with the wonderful, unforgettable triumph in Rotterdam, with Spurs becoming the first club from the British Isles to win a major European trophy. The following year, however, finishing fourth in the league, dumped out of the FA Cup in the third round, and, as holders, eliminated from the Cup Winners' Cup at the first hurdle (3-4 on aggregate by Manchester United), it was not looking quite so good. Bill was no fool. He realised that many of his ageing gladiators

On their victory lap of honour at Wembley after beating Burnley in the 1962 FA Cup Final.

would not be able to last many more seasons under the punishing physical demands of top-flight football.

The time had clearly come to put sentiment aside and make some tough decisions.

Bill ponders his next move...

Chapter 5

Nights in White Passion

"And gentlemen in England now a-bed, shall
think themselves accursed they were not here"
William Shakespeare, From 'Henry V'

There are things that are simply beyond the explanation of ordinary people. A scientist can explain what causes the Aurora Borealis but how would he go about describing the effect it has on those who see for the first time? Any grade 'A' biology student could explain how taste buds work but where would they begin to describe the taste of chocolate? Or the effect that watching Tottenham Hotspur playing in Europe has on fans of the club?

There have been many memorable days in the history of the Spurs. The wonderful 1951 triumph of push-and run, in which Bill figured so prominently; Bill's own memorable Double side; later on, the glorious triumph at Wembley in 1981, where Ricky Villa scored a wonder goal that nobody will ever forget. And yet it is in Europe where the true soul of Tottenham Hotspur lives in the minds of many people.

There was something about the sight of Bill's players, clad all in white, heading onto the field in front of a packed White Hart Lane. Nights when the air itself seemed to crackle under the weight of expectation, and where no matter what the playing surface, legends would be born as another set of interlopers from foreign shores were put to the sword. They were the nights where you had to be there to *really* be there.

And just for the record, none of Bill's sides ever lost a home tie in European competition.

1961-62

The Boss sounds out life in Eastern Europe as Spurs look for a good start to their European campaign against Gornik Zabrze in Poland…

There were no quick spying missions to that part of the world in those days. I remember flying into Warsaw and the train journey down to Katowice took four hours.

It was a very depressed place. You had to feel sympathy for those people. It was a cole mining area. Everything was grey. They tried their best for us.

I remember going to the stadium and seeing women down on their hands and knees with scissors cutting every blade of grass. The pitch was in immaculate

It all started so well against Gornik Zabrze of Poland. Terry Dyson and Les Allen celebrate as Bobby Smith (out of picture) heads Tottenham's fifth goal in the Preliminary Round, second leg victory at The Lane in September 1961.

Eusebio, under pressure from Maurice Norman, gets in a shot for Benfica in the European Cup semi-final at Tottenham in April 1962. The Portuguese were very fortunate to go through to the final. But Spurs' day would come...

condition.

There was a pattern running from corner to corner of the ground. It was an example of how they were determined to put on their best face. However it was obvious in some cases that the best in Poland was just not good enough. The hotel standards were a prime example.

It was supposed to be one of the best in that part of Poland. I was not happy, though, and we had a bit of an 'up and downer' about it. But to show how wonderful those people were, when we returned the whole place had been given a facelift.

The whole place had been painted, the restaurant area had been vastly improved, there had been general spring-cleaning of all the rooms and the curtains were replaced.

It was not exactly the Ritz but it was still a great deal better than before.

(Nicholson actually had a league game of Gornik's watched).

We knew nothing of them. The league game did not tell us anything that was remotely useful either. We knew they had a good player in Pohl but we were not expecting anything more unusual than a normal English league game.

What a shock we got. We had practised normally. We worked very hard and we were convinced that our European preparation was as thorough as it could be.

We had decided that we would adopt the same sort of principles and philosophy that had won us the Double.

We were convinced that we had nothing to worry about unduly. We were a very good side and we knew it. What we did not know was how to play in Europe.

We did not know how to play games over two legs. We had to learn quickly, though. At 4-0 down in the first leg we were in danger of being tossed out of the competition at the first time of asking.

We had tried to play our normal attacking football. We threw caution to the wind and we paid the price. They hit us hard. It made us realise that some teams in the continent prepare for the European ties very differently. They played a much more containing game.

We had to learn to eradicate the other team's strengths without losing our own strengths. Gornik did it to perfection and, but for our ability to play outstanding football, we would have been out.

Bill Nicholson

Tottenham Hotspur 8 Gornik Zabrze 1
European Cup, Preliminary Round, second leg
September 20, 1961
Spurs won on agg. 10-5

Nicholson had feared, watching the game from the Gornik dug-out that his side would be caught in the 'whirlwind' effect. He said: "It happened to Gornik at White Hart Lane. They were crushed 8-1. They were not that bad but they were caught in a domino effect. When one goal goes in it is difficult to halt the flood. It was an amazing start to a period that has covered 25 years. Maybe we learned more in that 90 minutes than we had in 90 years before. Europe was certainly a different place."

Taken from 'The Glory Glory Nights'

We were still a bit naive about European football at this stage, still learning, and we had gone to Poland uncertain of what we would expect. Well, we soon found out.

At half-time we came in 3-0 down, and Bill was worried. He said that it was important that we got something to take back to Spurs with us. Well, just after half time, there was another goal – for Gornik, and at 0-4, things looked pretty much up. Then we grabbed two late goals, and everything changed. We went back to The Lane knowing that they were beatable.

The atmosphere at Tottenham in those days was just electric. Anyone who knew those days will tell you what it was like. As soon as we ran out onto that pitch, it was like a goal start for us, and the opposition must have felt the same. We hit Gornik off the park, and that just summed up Spurs in Europe in the early 60s, really. We were amazing.

Terry Dyson

Their keeper had been spitting at me in the first leg, almost right from the first whistle to the last. I said to him: "By the time we play back at our place, I'll have the flu."

So we set it up at our place, where, it if was our kick I'd push the ball to John White, he would give it to Danny, and Danny would chip it into the box. The keeper would see me coming in out of the corner of his eye, and he knew that he'd be going in the net with the ball. I hit him – he went in the net, the ball went in the net, and as he laid there I said: "Get up – you've got more to come yet!"

Dave Mackay said afterwards "Bobby, I've never had so many shots at goal." See, the Polish lad was looking for me all the time instead of doing his job.

Bobby Smith

It's amazing how people always look back to that night when they talk about Spurs in Europe. We'd let ourselves down a bit in Poland – I think Bill might have drawn our attention to it in the dressing room beforehand – but we got two late goals out there, and I can remember as we came off the pitch after the away game, some of our lads were saying things to the Poles like: "Just wait till you get back to Tottenham, you won't know what's hit you."

I know there was a bit of a language barrier but the message seemed to have got across, because the roar that greeted them when they came out at Spurs was enough to make the hairs on the back of your neck stand on end, and it must have scared the life out of them. Bill knew they wouldn't fancy it too much, and he just told us to go out and remind them where they were.

Maurice Norman

In my formative years I spent a lot of time on the White Hart Lane terraces watching that great Spurs side of Danny Blanchflower, Dave Mackay, Jimmy Greaves and Bobby Smith, The players worked together so well. Smith was the ideal foil for Greaves. Blanchflower complemented Mackay. The blend was sensational and that, in my opinion, is one of the basic ingredients of a truly great side; blend. You can have good players but they won't necessarily make a good side unless they fit each other like pieces of a jigsaw.

I used to get off the bus at Seven Sisters and practically run to White Hart Lane. The atmosphere at the ground almost dragged you there. It was like a powerful stimulant. To me, there was no thrill in football to match it. I was there the night they outclassed Gornik in the European Cup after losing in Poland. What a night that was!
Sir Bobby Robson

Benfica 3 Tottenham Hotspur 1
European Cup Semi-Final, first leg
March 21, 1962

It must be difficult, or nigh on impossible, for younger Tottenham fans to ever imagine how close Bill was to making Tottenham Hotspur champions of Europe. And yet, for a few magical weeks in the early part of 1962, the dream was so close to becoming reality you could almost touch it...

We had gone out to Portugal with a bit of a mind to keeping things tight at the back. Terry Medwin was used as a sweeper, and it seemed to be working quite well. Then we had two disallowed, and we were as mystified as their players as to why. Bill always drummed it home to us that there was no point arguing with referees – they rarely changed their minds, and they were only human. In fact, he would often use the old adage that a referee was likely to make fewer mistakes in a match than any player. But the Benfica semi-final was a choker, and I think even Bill was amazed at us having those two chalked off in Lisbon.

Offside? Not on your life – everybody in the stadium knew it except the officials, but Bill wasn't the kind of manager to rant like many of today's would – I think the phrase he used was 'disappointed', which, considering that this was the semi-final of the European Cup, was as much of an understatement as you could get.
Terry Dyson

I've said it before, and I'll say it to my dying day, there was absolutely nothing wrong with our two disallowed goals in Lisbon. I never actually said as much at the time, but I'm convinced there was some kind of skulduggery going on there.

I honestly believe that it was never intended for Spurs to be there. I actually ran between two defenders to score my goal, and they give it offside. Then Big Bobby Smith scores, and there are two Benfica defenders on the line. And they give it offside. It's not rocket science, is it?

I'm not doing the old 'hard done by' bit here – I've had my share of goals given down the years that shouldn't have stood – every player has. But whereas I believe

they were genuine mistakes by the referee, what happened in Lisbon – and at White Hart Lane – in 1963 was anything but.
Jimmy Greaves

We should have beaten them 3-1 over there. Jimmy Greaves beat three men, passed the ball to me, and he gives Greavsie offside! It's little things like this that kills a game. We should have been winning 3-1 but in the end we're 3-1 down.

You just don't know what the referee's mind was doing, do you? I mean, it just wasn't known then, an English team winning the European Cup. I'll never forget the guy – he was only a little fella, and I can remember saying to Jimmy: 'I'd love to put him in the net!'

We had so many good through balls given offside that weren't. Bill was always telling us not to get into the referees but even he was a bit puzzled by what went on.
Bobby Smith

Benfica were a very good side – but I would have loved the chance to have played Real Madrid in the final. Over the course of the two legs of the semi, the record would show that they scored one more goal than we did. Bill, of course, was a gentleman and just put the goals that Jimmy had disallowed in Lisbon down to being one of those things that happens in football. At least, that's what he showed to the world. But those decisions were so poor that I think he was a bit annoyed and bothered about it for quite a while afterwards. When you think about it, that was the ultimate prize for any club in European football, and we could have won it before Manchester United did in 1968, even before Celtic did the year before.
Terry Medwin

Tottenham Hotspur 2 Benfica 1
European Cup, Semi-Final, second leg
April 5, 1962
Benfica won on agg. 3-4
Tottenham had returned from the first leg in Lisbon feeling very aggrieved that they had not got the reward their efforts had deserved. Now was the chance to set the record straight. Memories of crushing victories against Gornik and Dukla Prague fuelled the atmosphere at White Hart Lane to fever pitch. But Benfica were an almighty obstacle to overcome. The stage was set – but for what…?

It was bad enough losing out in Lisbon when we had the two goals disallowed. Then when we got back to Tottenham, I reckon just about all of us were as nervous as hell. You could almost taste it.

We should have beaten Benfica. They were a great side with some fine players, but the atmosphere that night was so tense, so electric, that it was hard to get our natural game going.

Bill, as a manager, could say and do all the right things in the dressing room but

once you're out there, you're on your own. When the lad Aguas scored their goal, it should have sunk us, but we came back and nearly tied it late on when Dave Mackay had a shot against the bar. I reckon if he'd scored then we'd have gone on to win it, because the crowd would have raised the roof. Most people in football agree that Benfica were worthy winners of the final against Real Madrid, but we'd given them every bit as much of a game. But what memories . . . what fabulous memories.
Maurice Norman

After having two chalked off in Lisbon, we couldn't believe it when Jimmy was given offside again. He scored a brilliant goal, and there were three men in front of him, but he gets it disallowed. People can make their own minds up about why it was, but it makes you wonder.
Bobby Smith

It is better to fail aiming high than to succeed aiming low. And we at Tottenham have set out sights very high – so high, in fact, that even failure can have in it an echo of glory.
Bill Nicholson

Spurs' Route to the Semi-Final of the European Cup, 1961-62

Date	Round	Att	H/A	Opposition	Result	Scorers
13-Sep-61	Pre 1L	70,000	A	Gornik Zabrze	L 2-4	Jones, Dyson
20-Sep-61	Pre 2L	56,737	H	Gornik Zabrze	W 8-1	Blanchflower (pen), Jones (3), Smith R (2), White, Dyson
01-Nov-61	1 1L	61,719	A	Feyenoord	W 3-1	Saul (2), Dyson
15-Nov-61	1 2L	62,144	H	Feyenoord	D 1-1	Dyson
14-Feb-62	2 1L	38,000	A	Dukla Prague	L 0-1	
26-Feb-62	2 2L	55,388	H	Dukla Prague	W 4-1	Smith R (2), Mackay (2)
21-Mar-62	SF 1L	70,000	A	Benfica	L 1-3	Smith R
05-Apr-62	SF 2L	64,448	H	Benfica	W 2-1	Smith R. Blanchflower (pen)

1962-63

Tottenham Hotspur 5 Atletico Madrid 1
European Cup Winners' Cup Final
Rotterdam, May 14, 1963
Spurs: Bill Brown, Peter Baker, Ron Henry, Danny Blanchflower, Maurice Norman, Tony Marchi, Cliff Jones, John White, Bobby Smith, Jimmy Greaves, Terry Dyson. Scorers: Greaves 2 Dyson 2 Blanchflower (P)

This was a team triumph, as much for the off-field tactics of Bill Nicholson as for the on-field magnificence of his players
Ralph L Finn

BILL NICHOLSON

On a spring night in 1963, more than 2000 fans travelled over to Rotterdam from England to cheer on Tottenham Hotspur. It was an almighty exodus, the like of which had never been witnessed in British sport before. For the lucky ones who made the journey, it was a night none of them would ever forget. In what has often been called by many the greatest performance by any English team in Europe, Spurs annihilated Atletico Madrid 5-1 to become the first British side to lift a major European trophy. For Bill, it was the crowning glory to the kind of football he had always insisted his teams played.

Bill Nick and two directors were in the toilets, and they didn't know that I was in one of the cubicles. I heard one of the Wales's, I think it was the son, say to Bill: "I reckon we've got no chance against this lot, Bill."

*When I walked out of the toilet, his face went as white as our shirts. I said: "We'll make you eat your words," and I walked away. I heard him say to his dad: "F****** hell, that's done it!"*

Later on, before we went onto the pitch, Bill was going round the players and he said to me: "Bobby, I don't often give you warnings, but I will now. This centre-half, if you get a ball in the air, he'll come in like a big bull and bang you. But then you should be used to that." I said: "Thanks Bill, that's handy to know."

Anyway, he came in the first time and knocked me flying. Well, I thought, I'd better get one in, so as he came in the next time, I just left an elbow out a bit, and it landed right in the pit of his stomach. He went down like anything.

The referee, a Dutchman, came up to me and said: "I'm glad you didn't retaliate the first time when he did that to you." I replied: "I didn't do anything to him this time.". But of course I had – I'd bowled him over. But the ref said to me: "Well, they go down like that." But I did hit him with my elbow.

So this bloke says to me: "I'll have you again." I said: "I'm here any time you want it, I'll be happy to oblige so it's up to you." He never did get me after that, because I was giving him the needle all the time. He spent so much time looking out for me, he didn't know what was going on half the time.

But it was a team game – we were very good, and every one of us played out of our skins that night. That was Terry Dyson's best game. I told him afterwards to retire – because he was never going to have another game like that!
Bobby Smith

It was the first time I can remember when Bill had no negative thoughts or criticism after a game. It was almost as if that was the absolute peak performance for his team, the one that he had been working towards, and in a way it was. Most journalists of the time and many since have said that it was probably the finest performance of any English club side in Europe. I don't think any side on the planet would have lived with us that night, and that includes most of the great club sides since. And when you think that we had lost Dave (Mackay) through injury not long before, it was an amazing feat. Bill was absolutely ecstatic.
Terry Dyson

Tonight, Terry Dyson, son of a jockey, who has never ranked with the gifted elite of this star-spangled team, scored two goals and was the architect of the third. He played, in the words of overjoyed manager Bill Nicholson: "The best game of his life. I never thought he could play so well."
From Spurs Go Marching On by Ralph L Finn

Dyson was delighted to see that even Bill Nicholson joined the celebrations that night. "It was about the only time that Bill came out with the team. I don't think that I've ever seen him looking so pleased."

It is not surprising that Bill looked so proud. Dyson recalled his last words before the team went out that night. He said: "Bill took myself and Cliff Jones to one side and said: 'This will be your night. Take on the full-backs as often as you can'.

He was not wrong.
From The Glory Glory Nights

I know it sounds a bit odd, but the way we were winning things at home about that time, the European games came as a bit of a break to the routine. Even in that final in Rotterdam, we were cruising.

People always said of that game: 'Well, you didn't even look like you were breaking into a gallop.' But that's because we were doing what Bill had drummed into us all those days on the training pitch – making the ball do the work. You still have to put the effort in, running off the ball and such like, but it's much easier when the other side are the ones chasing shadows.
Peter Baker

We suddenly went two goals up but then the penalty by Collar changed the whole face of the match. From being in a clear lead we were battling to survive.

For 10 minutes Atletico threw everything they had at us and we were fortunate to hang on. Then on another attack the ball broke free to their full-back, Rivilla.

Dave Mackay was not playing in the game because of an injury but when the full-back broke through I wondered what Dave would do.

I remembered that he got so many of his injuries by lunging in just throwing himself at people. So I decided to try the same. I launched myself in just as the player shot.

The ball hit me on the knees and it really hurt but it was worth it. In that moment, I think the match changed. If the ball had gone in and made it 2-2 who knows what might have happened?

I remember John White putting the ball inside the full-back and I kept thinking how close he was to me.

Spurs making British club history in Rotterdam, 1963.

BILL NICHOLSON

I rushed the cross a little bit and was disappointed. I thought that it was way too close for the goalkeeper.

My great memory was of the goalkeeper crying when the ball went into the net. From that second there was no doubt we were going to win the game.
Terry Dyson

That night in 1963 was a great occasion. It's Tottenham folklore nowadays – everyone knows about Bill having a sort of panic attack before the game, and Danny saying his piece, and about the fact that we won 5-1 – without Dave Mackay.

All these years down the line, people tend to just say: 'Oh yeah, Tottenham – first team to blah, blah, blah.' They point out what Liverpool and Manchester United achieved in later years. But back then, it was unheard of for British teams to take on the continentals and come out on top – it just didn't happen. It was pioneering sort of stuff, and when you look at it in that light you see it for the great achievement that it was.
Jimmy Greaves

It was one of those nights when everything just went our way. The goals just sort of flew in, like 'whack, whack, whack' – and you could see it in the faces of the Madrid team after the third one went in, they were gone.

A lot has been made of the dressing room talk between Bill and Danny beforehand, where Bill had been going through each of the Madrid players one by one, praising them to the rafters, and then Danny stands up and says something like: "Hang on, we can play a bit as well. These guys aren't world-beaters, we're every bit as good as they are, so let's get out and have a go at them."

It's been said that it was Danny that got us going but I don't think any of us were unduly worried by what Bill had said. We were used to him. Bill would always be completely thorough before each game, and of course he knew his opponents probably better than they knew themselves. He would brief us on who their good players were, who their bad players were, what tactics they would play and so on.

In all honesty, I reckon Bill was more nervous than we were.
Tony Marchi

The penalty? Bill always said to us that your goalkeeper is entitled to receive cover from his fellow defenders. On this occasion, their centre forward has gone through, and Bill Brown has come out. So, seeing the forward go round him, I've gone the other way and stood on the line. As he hit it, I've just stuck out my arm and punched it over the bar.

I know it gave away a penalty but if I hadn't used my instincts there, Bill Nick would have wanted to know why. Of course, today that would have been a red card – but it's just a defender's instinct to stop the ball going in. But it was a terrific game, probably the best I've ever been in, and Bill said to me afterwards: "Ron, in 20 years time you'll realise what you've done here tonight."
Ron Henry

We went into that game without Dave Mackay and the Spanish papers were making the most of it. They were saying things like: "So and so is such a big strong player," drawing attention to the fact that a couple of our lads were a bit on the slight side. Bill just got straight back at them, saying things like: "Have you seen the size of Maurice Norman?" But it was all quite good-natured – there was no malice in things Bill said.

He knew we would be missing Dave, and that famous quote about wanting us all to go out and play like Dave Mackay seemed to work. As to the final itself, I thought Atletico were actually quite poor. Not that we gave them the chance to be anything else, but they folded like a pack of cards and, while I honestly thought that we were as good a side that night as you're likely to see, it would have been interesting to see what Bill would have done if they'd caused us a few more problems.

After the game, a few of the lads went out to a local nightclub, but my wife and I just went down and spent the evening by the sea. I like the quiet life!
Maurice Norman

You could send this side anywhere in the world and be proud of them. This was the best performance I have ever seen from an English club. Why can't your national team play like this?
Leo Horn, top Dutch referee, after watching the game

Headline news – what the papers had to say

Dyson's devotion puts Spurs back on top
Spanish defence torn to shreds in first British triumph
Donald Saunders, Daily Telegraph

Spurs' night of glory
Danny's boys fought like ten mad Mackays
Laurie Pignon, Daily Sketch

Madrid Mauled 5-1
Greaves sparks off the great goal riot
Ken Jones, Daily Mirror

Spurs recapture their glories of old
Power and rhythm in attack baffles Spaniards
Association football correspondent, The Times

Glory Glory Hallelujah!
Wave The Union Jack we are on top of the world
Peter Lorenzo, Daily Herald

BILL NICHOLSON

Yes…it's Spurs 5-1

A 63-inch tornado named Dyson rips through Spanish aces to win Britain's first major European soccer title

Desmond Hackett, Daily Express

The master planners – Bill and Danny

Victor Railton, Evening News

Spurs' Greatest Triumph

…but we had to chase illusions away before the match

Danny Blanchflower, Sunday Express

Spurs' Route to the European Cup-Winners' Cup Final, 1962-63

Date	Round	Att	H/A	Opposition	Result	Scorers
31-Oct-62	1 1L	58,859	H	Glasgow Rangers	W 5-2	White (2), Allen, Norman, Shearer og
11-Dec-62	1 2L	80,000	A	Glasgow Rangers	W 3-2	Smith R (2), Greaves
5-Mar-63	2 1L	15,000	A	Slovan Bratislava	L 0-2	
14-Mar-63	2 2L	61,504	H	Slovan Bratislava	W 6-0	Greaves (2), Mackay, White, Smith R, Jones
24-Apr-63	SF 1L	45,000	A	OFK Belgrade	W 2-1	White, Dyson
1-May-63	SF 2L	59,736	H	OFK Belgrade	W 3-1	Jones, Mackay, Smith R
15-May-63	Final	40,000	Rot	Atletico Madrid	W 5-1	Greaves (2), Dyson (2), White

Defence of the ECWC

Tottenham Hotspur 2 Manchester United 0
European Cup Winners' Cup
First Round, first leg
December 3, 1963
Scorers: Dyson, Mackay

"DUNNE'S BOOB BOOSTS SPURS"

Daily Herald, December 4, 1963

By Peter Lorenzo

Three minutes from time an amazing blunder by Manchester United right-back Tony Dunne teed up Spurs' second goal in this tremendous European Cup Winners' Cup duel.

It might so easily signal Spurs' survival when they trek to Old Trafford for the second leg of their first round clash next Tuesday.

No danger threatened. No score seemed possible as Dunne gathered a long cross from John White.

Calmly he swept the ball under control, then turned and hit it softly towards goalkeeper Dave Gaskell.

But Dunne hadn't noticed the darting figure of little winger Terry Dyson speeding up on his blind side.

In a flash Dyson zipped in between the two United defenders and cracked the ball in so hard that it rebounded back onto the field before anybody had realised what had happened.

It was a masterly opportunist effort by Dyson. But he would be the first to admit that he should never have been offered the chance.

So Spurs go north with a two-goal lead, instead of the one they had just earned.

And that goal could make all the difference, for the big problem hovering over United is the doubt of Denis Law's availability.

At Leeds today the FA disciplinary committee will adjudicate on the incident when Law was sent off at Villa Park two weeks ago.

Law has gone on record as saying that he must accept the blame and will, of course, mean his absence from the return game.

It restores the balance slightly, and I do mean slightly, in Spurs' favour.

Until Dunne faltered, United had thrown up a superb defensive barricade. Skilfully, confidently and aggressively they had contained Spurs' attack.

They allowed Spurs to do most of the pressing. They even allowed them unrestricted midfield control – until they reached the United penalty area.

The red wall seemed impenetrable. Even when Spurs did pierce their way through, there stood the stubborn, flying figure of Gaskell to foil their best efforts.

Spurs piled on the pressure. The tension mounted. The crowd roared. But still United's tactics and defence stood solid – until the 67th minute.

Then dynamic Dave Mackay, moving like a human rocket, powered his way through to score a brilliant goal. It had to be brilliant to penetrate this superb defence.

Cliff Jones started the move with a cunning back-heel to the feet of the onrushing Mackay. From a difficult angle Mackay took aim – and smashed in a thunderbolt shot.

The delighted Scot did a double somersault in celebration as the crowd roared their approval of a magnificent effort.

United clearly had one major intent for this match – not to concede goals, rather than try to score themselves.

Often they had eight or nine men crowding their goal area. Inevitably, they were in attack only in breakaways.

Yet they were always dangerous. When he wasn't back helping his defence, Law operated almost as a one-man forward line.

Three first-time shots from the Scottish international had Spurs' goalkeeper Bill Brown stretching desperately to tip the ball over the bar.

One goal was all that should have separated two fine sides. But now United face the decisive second leg with towering doubts instead of stirring confidence.

I'm not satisfied but three goals will take a lot of getting by United at Old Trafford. There was no middle in our team, and little cohesion.
Bill Nicholson

Spurs suffer double blow

Manchester United 4 Tottenham Hotspur 1
European Cup Winners' Cup
First Round, second leg
December 10, 1063
Manchester United won on agg. 3-4

"DAVE MACKAY BREAKS LEG"
Daily Express, December 10, 1963
By Desmond Hackett

Spurs are out of the European Cup Winners' Cup. But, by the glowing glory of football, they were never down in the greatest man-to-man duel I have ever seen.

Sixty seconds at dynamite-charged Old Trafford last night were enough to switch this cup-tie of cup-ties.

It came after six minutes. It brought a goal to Manchester United and a crash that sent Dave Mackay, the iron man of Spurs, off to hospital with a broken leg.

Spurs, who had come here with a challenging two-goal lead, found themselves on the panic line of a one-goal margin.

Mackay and his merry men had been pounding away with all the threat of a conquering confident team. Sadly, two of United's boy reserves changed the course of it all.

Twenty-year old Phil Chisnall aimed a through pass so close to goal that goalkeeper Bill Brown was compelled to come out.

But Brown was beaten by 17-year-old David Sadler, the Kentish lad who had been pitched in to replace banned £116,000 Denis Law.

Sadler crossed the ball with the calm of a veteran and David Herd, unchallenged, scored a goal to send 48,000 fans erupting.

In the next minute Mackay was going through to hurl his dangerous power into a Spurs raid when he clashed with United captain Noel Cantwell.

There was a hush as the sickening crack sounded above the cheers.

Mackay, defiant to the last, was sitting up leaning on one elbow as he was carried off the field for the first time in his fighting football life.

In the 53rd minute the ball was bounding almost out of control among a surge of players outside the Spurs goal and Herd scored.

Within seconds there was an admiration-compelling burst by Spurs with John White centring for Greaves to head home superbly.

Manchester United were reduced to 10 men just before the hour mark when Maurice Setters collided in mid-air with John White.

Setters went off with a sponge over his forehead, but came back after 11 minutes. Later, he had six stitches put in a cut over his right eye.

Again the tumult bayed to a frightening roar as Charlton, a crimson ghost, beat the entire Spurs defence.

Charlton drew goalkeeper Brown out to meet him, but then earned only a mighty groan as he shot high over an empty goal.

Then at 78 minutes, Charlton the villain became Charlton the hero as he hammered the ball in off the far post to tie the overall score for the second time in this heart-bursting match.

Two unbearable minutes from time came the greatest goal of this game.

Herd, going at full speed, back-heeled to Crerand, who put the ball forward and Charlton racing forward incredibly turned the ball into goal to send the crowd into a crazy victory roar.

This was a night when men played with all their power, without the tarnish of a vicious tackle or petty abuse of the rules.

We are terribly sorry about Dave Mackay. It was a tragedy for Spurs and they played splendid football even without him. In fact it was a great tragedy that both clubs couldn't have met at full strength in what has been a great European Cup Winners' Cup tie.
Sir Matt Busby

It was just one of those things. Two of us went for the ball. I got there first and the thing just happened. I knew my leg was broken. I heard it break.
Dave Mackay

Spurs' Record in The European Cup Winners Cup, 1963-64

Date	Round	Att	H/A	Opposition	Result	Scorers
03-Dec-63	1 1L	57,447	H	Manchester United	W 2-0	Mackay, Dyson
10-Dec-63	1 2L	59,597	A	Manchester United	L 1-4	Greaves

Spurs and Manchester United had served up a treat of typically honest, dramatic English-style football in a European tie. But it was to be four more seasons before Spurs once again trod the European trail. And this time, they were to find that European football could be as ugly as it could be mesmerising.

1967-68

Olympique Lyonnaise 1 Tottenham Hotspur 0
European Cup Winners' Cup, Second Round
November 29, 1967
Agg. 4-4 – Spurs out on away goals)
Spurs fans had enjoyed the long, hot summer of 1967 with an FA Cup win over London rivals Chelsea firmly tucked under their belts. Now, as the nights drew in and the evenings got colder, it was back to business for Spurs in Europe.

It had been four years since the finest night in the history of Tottenham Hotspur. Bill had made no secret that he wanted more of the European adventure and,

BILL NICHOLSON

following a 6-3 aggregate win over Yugoslavia's Hajduk Split, Spurs were paired against French challengers Olympique Lyonnaise in the second round.

Bill had always impressed upon his players the need to maintain their discipline, and to accept the decisions of referees and linesmen. But 90 minutes of the first leg in France were to put that noble ethic firmly to the test . . .

Spurs, one of the least muscular or mean-tempered of English sides, found themselves involved in a riot here tonight. Uproar came when Alan Mullery was kicked in the face by French forward Andre Guy. Fans poured on to the pitch to support their team in an overall attack on Spurs.

Mullery was lying unconscious throughout, a victim if ever I saw one. He got groggily to his feet to be sent off with Guy as Czech referee Krnavek's gesture to good order.

At half time, Spurs manager Bill Nicholson was struck as he tried to prevent Guy attacking Gilzean.

Nicholson said later: "Some of their tackling was a disgrace, they were body-checking from the start. I can only assume that Mullery was sent off for retaliating in that scuffle."

Brian James, from the Daily Mail, November 30, 1967

It was probably about the only time I can recall Bill ever actually 'losing it'. We had been drawn to play the first leg in France and none of us were quite prepared for what we were going to get.

I don't know if they had been told to go out and get into us by their coach, but the long and the short of it was that we were getting kicked off the park. I had been caught by one of their players quite badly, and eventually needed 10 stitches in my shin.

What really got Bill, though, was that all through the game, a section of the French fans behind the dug-out were throwing stuff at our bench. Then, as we were going off at half-time, Bill actually got hit in the eye by the Olympique striker Andre Guy as he went to clobber Gilly. The tunnel was pitch black, and Guy could probably claim he didn't actually mean to hit Bill. All the same, Bill went potty.

"That sort of set it up for the second leg. Now, anybody who ever knows Bill will tell you how he feels about losing games – he's man enough to shake his opponents by the hand and tell them 'well done', but he really hates it. I got the impression, though, that this one had a bit of spice to it. Unfortunately for us, even though we won 4-3 at The Lane, Lyon got through on away goals.

Jimmy Robertson

The referee was responsible for the match getting completely out of hand. French manager Louis Hon said: 'He lost control altogether at times', and Bill Nicholson, who I have never seen so angry, made veiled hints about the official's eyesight.

"I think the match was a disgrace," stormed Nicholson, "and this Lyon side played more like Rugby League than Football League. They pulled and shoved all the way through the game, yet the referee let them get away with it. Guy should

have been sent off on his own. Mullery was, perhaps, not entirely blameless but he was heavily provoked."

Nicholson had good cause to criticise Guy. For the Olympique forward carried on the war at half-time in the tunnel leading to the dressing rooms. Guy went to attack Gilzean and Nicholson was struck in the eye by the Frenchman's elbow as he intervened.

Nicholson, having simmered down, made light of the matter but he was bitterly disappointed at losing the game. "We had enough chances to have won easily," he said, "and I am upset to think that we lost to such a bad team as this."

Nicholson agreed that the main trouble with these European games is the differing idea of what is fair play.
John Oakley, Evening News, November 30, 1967

The second leg against Olympique at White Hart Lane was absolutely amazing – I've never experienced atmosphere like it. We won 4-3 but those away goals did for us. It was a shame we couldn't put them out, because Bill was really annoyed about the way things had been handled in the first leg in France – he wanted us to win even more than usual. But sadly it wasn't to be.
Dennis Bond

Spurs Record In the European Cup-Winners Cup, 1967

Date	Round	Att	H/A	Opposition	Result	Scorers
20-Sep-67	1 1L	25,000	A	Hajduk Split	W 2-0	Robertson, Greaves
27-Sep-67	1 2L	38,623	H	Hajduk Split	W 4-3	Robertson (2), Gilzean, Venables
29-Nov-67	2 1L	10,997	A	Olympique Lyon	L 0-1	
13-Dec-67	2 2L	41,895	H	Olympique Lyon	W 4-3	Greaves (2, 1pen), Gilzean, Jones

1971-72

Rapid Bucharest 0 Tottenham Hotspur 2
UEFA Cup, Third Round, second leg
December 15, 1971

In December 1971 Tottenham travelled to Bucharest, the capital of Romania, which at the time was under the iron-fisted rule of dictator Nicolai Caucescu, for a UEFA Cup third round tie. Already leading 3-0 from a one sided-game at White Hart Lane, Spurs nonetheless needed to be cautious – Rapid had rolled over two previous sets of visitors by large scores, so nothing could be taken for granted. However, none of the Tottenham players, training staff or officials could have imagined in their wildest dreams was what was to follow. It was a brawl of a match, in which Bill's steely nerve and patience would be tested to the full by the worst intimidation he had ever witnessed in Spurs' 11 years in Europe . . .

"Above all," said Bill finally, when there were only five minutes to go (before kick-off). Looking up and looking round at everyone: "I want no retaliation.

BILL NICHOLSON

You've got to keep your tempers. It'll be hard, but you'll be penalised if you step out of line. So no retaliation."

Eddie (Baily) was up and shouting from the first kick, screaming at the ref for fouls he'd spotted. Bill just hung his head in silent fury. Five minutes later he himself was on his feet, tearing towards the touchline, shouting and screaming. Gilly had been brutally and openly punched in the kidneys by the Romanian number four, unseen by the referee, who was 50 yards away.

Bill and Eddie were hysterical. I thought they'd both have heart attacks. The powerlessness of their position was making them froth at the mouth. It had been a brilliant back-header from Gilly in the first minute of the match at Tottenham which had led to Rapid's downfall. There had obviously been instructions this time to get him.

In the dressing room at half-time, Bill and the doctor examined Steve (Perryman). Terry Naylor was told he was going on instead.

Bill said they were doing well, keeping cool, but they must keep the game quieter and give nothing away. He told them to watch out for the quick one-twos near the penalty area.

Bill's criticisms were mild, nothing compared to what he and Eddie had been shouting from the bench in the heat of the game, unheard by the players on the pitch. Peters, Coates and Chivers had all come in for unprintable abuse as each in turn had made some mistake or failed to take a chance which Bill thought they should have done. Bill finished his talk by complimenting them for not retaliating.

It was (Jimmy) Pearce who got the first and vital goal of the match. Chivers was put through by Pratt, but the goalkeeper blocked his shot. Jimmy hooked in the rebound.

Once again Jimmy had come on as a substitute late in a game and scored a vital goal. But this time he went off just as suddenly, sent off after only 12 minutes on the field. He got into a tussle with Rapid's number two out on the wing. They both aimed blows at each other, though neither connected. Immediately they were surrounded by other players all tugging and pushing at each other.

Bill and Eddie joined in from the touchline, shouting and screaming at the referee, an action which would have had them severely punished in an English league game. Jimmy was given a red card, and so was his opponent, and both left the field.

Just before the end, Chivers scored, a brilliant and typical Chivers shot.

When the final whistle blew, Bill and Eddie ran forward onto the pitch to help the team off, putting their arms round them, congratulating them, asking them if they were in pain.

"Now be careful with the press," said Nicholson, going to the middle of the room. "They're bound to ask you what it was like, just be careful what you say." There was a pause as everyone stopped talking and listened. "But as far as I'm concerned," Bill continued, "it was the dirtiest team I've seen in 30 years. If this is European football, I'd rather have a combination match. Diabolical. I've never seen such dirty fouls."

Even the players were taken a bit aback. There was nothing any of them could *have possibly said which was stronger than that.*

Bill later went round inspecting the injuries as the players began to undress.

"What about that miss then, Ralph?" Bill said to Coates, going back to his normal self, unable to forget the chances missed despite all the achievements.

"What?" said Ralph, obviously hurt. "What about that penalty I got you? You forget that, don't you?"

"Never mind," said Bill, playfully punching him. He went to the middle of the room and told everyone he was proud of them. That was the phrase he used: proud of them. The players looked amazed. It was the first time he'd used such words all season. "Yes, I'm proud of you. You showed them how to do it. You didn't retaliate. We've had the last laugh. Well done."

From The Glory Game by Hunter Davies

As a kid growing up in Hoxton, I didn't support any one club as a rule, although if anything I did look out for Leyton Orient's results, so I didn't have any great ideas about what Bill Nick would be like. My first recollection of Bill was when I was an amateur youth player at the club. We were playing Arsenal over at London Colney, and it was one of those games where nobody wanted to give an inch. I went into a slide tackle on Eddie Kelly, and it was a slippery old pitch, but even allowing for that I went in making sure that I not only got the ball but a fair old slice of the player as well. Eddie and I both ended up by the side of the pitch, and as I got up to run back on, somebody stopped me. It was Bill. He said to me: 'Son, if you want to carry on wearing that shirt, I don't ever want to see you do anything like that again.'

That was fair enough – although a few years later we were playing in Romania against Rapid Bucharest, and the lads were getting the s*** kicked out of them. It was well documented in all the papers – they were absolute animals, and even Bill himself said afterwards that he thought they were the dirtiest side he had ever seen, which was something coming from Bill. Anyway, Bill decided that I was to go on as a sub, and as I did, he said to me, pointing at one of the biggest culprits in the Romanian side: "Pratty – if you don't go on and kick him right up in the air, I'll kick YOU right up in the air!"

Just goes to show how things can change in football!

John Pratt

There is no reliable video evidence of the events that took place in Bucharest that day. The Romanian Television Service 'lost' the tape.

Tottenham Hotspur 2 AC Milan 1

UEFA Cup Semi-Final, first leg

April 5, 1972

Scorer: Perryman (2)

There were 42,064 people packed into White Hart Lane for the first leg of a European semi-final against one of the continent's premier clubs. Expectations were high, but of course Bill as much as anyone would have been aware of that age-old chestnut of European football – don't concede a goal at home . . .

'HATCHETS OUT FOR SPURS'

Daily Mail, April 6, 1972

Spurs – shamefully brutalised by the hatchet men of Milan – somehow kept enough of their limbs and their football together to sustain some hope of reaching the UEFA Cup Final.

It was no accident that one of their bravest players, young Steve Perryman, volleyed the two fine goals which give Tottenham a slender lead to defend in Italy in a fortnight.

This was a night when only a hero would go looking for goals in the face of the cynical chopping with which Milan sullied the good name of football.

Milan, who had Sogliano sent off in the 61st minute, were delighted with the result for their away goal counts double.

Milan were a downright disgrace and their coach Nerro Rocco stands accused as an accomplice to the soccer crimes his team committed.

So, too, does the Spanish referee Iglesias. He was so out of touch that he awarded 38 free-kicks against Tottenham, 22 against Milan.

Never has an international defender been so inaptly named as Baby Face Rosato, who tried so hard to eliminate Martin Chivers, but hurt his own back in the process.

Never before has a man with Benetti's violent nature been credited in a match programme with such an unlikely hobby as keeping pet canaries.

Benetti personified the split personality of his team. He burst on to Terry Naylor's 25th minute half-clearance to strike an opening goal full of skill and power.

No-one after seeing that, and some of the other talents, will argue that these are great players, even though they were misguided last night.

It was to Tottenham's credit that they raised their game after the sickening blow of Benetti's goal. The way they battle was also a tribute to the returning Alan Mullery, who gave Spurs renewed drive and direction.

It was much to do with Mullery's urging that Spurs forced surprising cracks in one of the world's greatest defences.

Alan Gilzean and Martin Peters combined to lay the ball into Perryman's path for the first of his 20-yard goals in the 33rd minute.

Immediately before the interval, Gilzean was booked for arguing, and Milan's great German, Schnellinger, for time-wasting. Both trivialities amongst last night's mayhem.

Sixteen minutes after the break, Sogliano was sent off for the last part in his hour-long running feud with Mullery.

Milan were left to survive half an hour with 10 men and they got through four minutes. Then they fumbled an attempt to clear Mullery's corner and Perryman buried his second goal to the right of Cudicini.

Milan sent on Zazzaro for Golin and Tottenham substituted Neighbour for Coates in the last stages of the battle.

Milan had a fabulous team with players like Gianni Rivera and Romeo Benetti. Being one goal down at home, bearing in mind we had to go to the San Siro and face a hostile crowd, was far from ideal. We were fully aware that the Italians would relish a defensive job of holding onto their lead, particularly an away goal.

I'm not exactly noted for my goals. Certainly, not for scoring from outside the box, but that was the only way through their well-drilled defence. I scored my first from the edge of the box, and the second from 25 yards!

The Italians feared the aerial ability of Alan Gilzean, and marked 'Gilly' very tightly. They were shocked by my goals. It was just my night, perhaps my best in Europe – certainly for scoring!
Steve Perryman

AC Milan 1 Tottenham Hotspur 1
UEFA Cup Semi-Final, second leg
April 19, 1972
Spurs won on agg. 3-2
With Spurs just 90 minutes away from another European final, hopes were high that the nine-year wait for more glory would soon be over; but with the talented Italians grabbing a vital away goal from the first leg, it would be tough. In the intimidating San Siro stadium in Milan, there was a need for strong hearts and clear minds. Just 90 minutes…

Back in the dressing room, Bill started his last-minute rites. John Pratt, in place of Gilly, was going to play his first match since his broken nose. He and Steve were told to keep tight hold of Rivera and Benetti. Peters wasn't to play his usual midfield role, but to move up front and try to take Gilzean's place, linking with Chivers and being ready to flick on free kicks or back-head corners.

"You'll be Martin Gilzean tonight," said Bill, as he went over what he wanted him to do. Even Bill was still in surprisingly light-hearted mood. The corner-kickers, Steve and Mullery, were told to try short corners when possible. This was Eddie's idea. He'd been to Italy to scout the Milan team, and was convinced it would work. Their man-marking system wasn't suited to short corners. If a man went out, it still left Spurs with a two-against-one situation. And if Cyril and Joe were coming up on the flank, that would mean three-to-one.

Bill then went very serious and said on no account must anyone argue with the referee. "I want you all to go back 10 yards on every free kick. You don't have to rush back, but give the referee no chance to take your name. Everybody hear that? I want no dissent of any sort."
From The Glory Game by Hunter Davies

We had just drawn with the mighty AC Milan in the San Siro in the semi-final of the UEFA Cup, and Bill was being interviewed by the TV guys beside the pitch. It had been the game of my life and, true to form, Bill had provided me with a complete dossier on the AC captain Gianni Rivera. You know, what he had for breakfast, when he went to bed – everything. So I was his shadow for 90 minutes, did a real job on him and was well chuffed. So as I'm going off the pitch, I caught a bit of the interview, and the commentator says to him: "Bill, what about John Pratt? He had a massive game," or something like that, and Bill response was: "Yes, he was amazing today. If he could pass he'd be the greatest player in the world."

Now, I'd been at Spurs for a few years at that point, and if any player on Bill's books couldn't pass, they wouldn't be there for long. What I think he was getting at was that I couldn't pass like, say, Glenn Hoddle, but then who could? It was typical of the standards Bill expected from his players.
John Pratt

The long wait was finally over. Spurs had survived the cauldron of the San Siro with a battling display, and after 11 long years, a team all in white from North London was to grace a European final once again. But any thoughts Spurs fans may have harboured of a trip to exotic lands soon fell away. They were more geared up for a trip from Euston or up the M1. Their opponents in the final were to be Wolverhampton Wanderers.

Wolverhampton Wanderers 1 Tottenham Hotspur 2
UEFA Cup Final, first leg
May 3, 1972
Scorer: Chivers (2)
The first (and, to date, only) all-English European final found Spurs paired up against Wolverhampton Wanderers. In the early 70s, the final of the UEFA Cup was a two-legged affair. Spurs had been afforded the luxury of playing the away leg first, with the apparent psychological advantage that could be gained with an away win, and the prospect of winning the cup in front of a home crowd.

But Bill Nicholson had not spent several seasons learning valuable, if sometimes painful, lessons in Europe without knowing that nothing could be taken for granted.

Wolves, being another English side, could at least allow Spurs the luxury of playing in a major final against opposition with whose style they would be familiar.

Both clubs had been impressive in their respective paths to the final, but now it was down to the wire. Ironically, the last time Wolves had appeared as a viable force in Europe had been in 1960, a couple of years before Tottenham themselves had shown the world how it should be done . . .

That was some night. Wolves had beaten a fair few good teams themselves on the way to the final, so they weren't just going to roll over for us. After Martin headed the first of our goals, Jim McCalliog scored while we were moaning about the free-kick.

That was the cue for Wolves to have a right old go at us, and we were under it a bit. Then big Chiv hit that goal. It seemed to come out of nothing really – he picked it up from just inside their half, took three or four strides, then let go. I don't remember seeing a ball hit so hard before or since. He hit is so hard that when it hit the net, the spray flew off the net and soaked the supporters standing behind the goal. I don't think they were too fussed about it, though!

I can remember that huge bank of Spurs supporters in the South Bank. And the rain . . . it was chucking it down but the fans were magnificent. They didn't stop singing all the way through, and gave us a real lift.

We played reasonably well that night, but you could say we rode our luck at times. But you often make your own luck in football.
Alan Gilzean

"It couldn't be better," said Bill, all smiles. "It just couldn't be better. We set out our stall as best we could, and look what happened. There's no justice in football. If I were the Wolves manager now, I'd be in tears. That first goal came at the perfect time, just as we were going under."
From The Glory Game

Tottenham Hotspur 1 Wolverhampton Wanderers 1
UEFA Cup Final, second leg
May 17, 1972
Spurs win on agg. 3-2

We didn't play too well that night. Bill being Bill, he came into the dressing room and had a wee moan at us, nothing too outrageous. He was an unashamed perfectionist, of course. But underneath it all you could see he was pleased. In fact, he was delighted.
Alan Gilzean

Spurs Road to the UEFA Cup Final, 1972

Date	Round	Att	H/A	Opposition	Result	Scorers
14-Sep-71	1 1L	11,000	A	Keflavik	W 6-1	Mullery (2), Coates, Gilzean (3)
28-Sep-71	1 2L	23,818	H	Keflavik	W 9-0	Knowles, Coates, Perryman, Chivers (3),Holder, Gilzean (2)
20-Oct-71	2 1L	20,033	A	Nantes	D 0-0	
2-Nov-71	2 2L	32,630	H	Nantes	W 1-0	Peters
8-Dec-71	3 1L	30,702	H	Rapid Bucharest	W 3-0	Chivers (2), Peters
15-Dec-71	3 2L	12,000	A	Rapid Bucharest	W 2-0	Chivers, Pearce
7-Mar-72	4 1L	20,000	A	UT Arad	W 2-0	England, Morgan
21-Mar-72	4 2L	30,253	H	UT Arad	D 1-1	Gilzean
5-Apr-72	SF1 1L	42,064	H	AC Milan	W 2-1	Perryman (2)
19-Apr-72	SF 2L	68,482	A	AC Milan	D 1-1	Mullery
3-May-72	Final 1L	38,362	A	Wolves	W 2-1	Chivers (2)
17-May-72	SF 2L	54,303	H	Wolves	D 1-1	Mullery

BILL NICHOLSON
1972-73

After the heroics of Martin Chivers and his team-mates in the final in 1972, the following year was looking like a repeat performance. Another monumental European campaign looked on the cards. Spurs stormed their way through Europe as their predecessors had done years before. Only mighty Liverpool stood in their way…

Alan Mullery, held aloft by Mike England and Pat Jennings, lifts the UEFA Cup after victory over Wolves.

Liverpool 1 Tottenham Hotspur 0
UEFA Cup Semi-Final, first leg
April 10, 1973

'LINDSAY FREAK CHECKS SPURS'
Daily Mail, April 11, 1973
By Jeff Powell

The trainloads of Londoners who cavorted away from Anfield last night would do well to remember that Spurs are no longer the irresistible force at White Hart Lane.

Liverpool strove frenziedly for the insurance of a second goal to take them into the second leg of this semi-final in a fortnight.

But one freakish rebound off the shins of Alec Lindsay may yet prove enough to end Spurs' ownership of the UEFA Cup and send Liverpool into their second European final.

In a courageous performance by Spurs there is special praise for another, if less extravagant, performance by Pat Jennings.

There are honourable mentions in this despatch for the desperate heroics of men like Mike England and John Pratt who, as Liverpool fragmented their defence, resorted to putting their bodies painfully in the way of many thunderous shots.

There was some chagrin in the judgment by Liverpool manager Bill Shankly, who said: 'We never stopped. We should have had a lot of goals. I thought the referee was good, but we should have had a penalty when Keegan was tripped.'

That late and justified penalty claim for England's foul on Keegan was the last of the major incidents on a frantic night which happened too fast for the Swedish official.

Jennings, the Irish goalkeeper whose phenomenal performance in a league game on this ground 10 days ago established him as a favourite to succeed Gordon Banks as Footballer of the Year, made three more outstanding saves to justify the Kop's appreciation of his talent.

All came after the almighty 27th minute scramble in which he was beaten. Jennings had blocked Smith's free-kick and one of a cluster of Spurs defenders saw his attempted clearance ricochet of Liverpool full-back Lindsay and deep into the corner of the net.

Spurs not only refused to lie down under pressure from Liverpool and the weight of the Anfield roar but also created fleeting chances of their own.

Chivers volleyed wide as he swept onto a marvellous pass from Peters. Coates fired over from an even better chance fashioned by Chivers and Gilzean.

The two forwards who missed those chances were taken off five minutes from time as manager Bill Nicholson sent on substitutes Evans and Pearce to relieve his beleaguered troops.

After watching his reshaped team survive the last perilous moments without further disaster Nicholson said: "I had hoped for a goal because away goals are so important in these competitions. But it is always hard at Liverpool and I suppose that in the circumstances I have to be happy with this result."

Long before Liverpool became the most dominant English club force ever in Europe, they approached this game with a view of establishing themselves by vying against the team who, more than any other at the time, symbolised what it was possible to achieve in Europe. The Anfield side, while qualifying for European football year after year in the 60s and early 70s, still seemed unable to land that elusive first trophy in Europe.

Bill Nicholson meanwhile, as was widely acknowledged, was the manager of the first team from the British Isles to win a major European trophy in 1963. What was not so readily recognised was the fact that he was also the first British manager to win two trophies in Europe.

So in the UEFA Cup semi-final of 1973, when Bill Shankly's side was paired up against that of his old adversary and long-time friend Nicholson, it was possibly a part of the learning curve that would eventually see Liverpool sweep all before them a few years later...

BILL NICHOLSON

Tottenham Hotspur 2 Liverpool 1
UEFA Cup Semi-Final, second leg
April 25, 1973
Agg. 2-2 – Liverpool through on away goals

The highlight of my career was the night Liverpool won the European Cup in 1977.

I can remember little about the UEFA Cup semi-final, apart from the fact that Steve Heighway had a habit of scoring at Tottenham in those days, and he did it again. That proved the vital away goal that took us through.

Spurs won the trophy the previous season and had a bigger reputation in Europe than ourselves.

The last thing on my mind when we played Spurs in that semi-final was that one day I'd be joining them. I'd only been at Liverpool about six years, and only the past three in the first team. I enjoyed a great time at Anfield, but I've also had my memorable moments at Tottenham.

When both clubs were at their height, the atmosphere was on a par. Night matches are always special, and European games are that bit more special. In fact, there is really nothing to compare.
Ray Clemence from The Glory Glory Nights

'STEVE STUNNER KO'S SPURS'
Daily Mirror, April 26, 1973
By Harry Miller

Two goals by Martin Peters and victory from a marvellous match were not enough last night to send Tottenham forward to a second successive UEFA Cup Final.

Like so many fine sides before them, they became victims of the rule that says away goals count double.

So the one that Steve Heighway sandwiched between Peters' double blast puts Liverpool in sight of a famous Double.

League champions in all but name, the Merseysiders now have a chance to win their first European trophy tackling Germans Borussia Moenchengladbach in the two-legged final next month.

They were cheered on the pitch for this semi-final second leg by a sporting 46,919 crowd and cheered off after going to the centre circle to salute the fans.

Somehow their gesture symbolised the four tremendous cup games these clubs have played this gruelling season.

Tottenham won the League Cup tie in a replay and Liverpool will regard this triumph as ample revenge.

But Tottenham should emerge from defeat with heads held high.

They went into the match seeking an early goal to wipe out the 1-0 lead Liverpool brought from Anfield.

The leveller for which they fought so hard came in the 48th minute. A long Chivers throw to the near post was headed across goal by Alan Gilzean and in zoomed Peters to hook the ball wide of Ray Clemence.

As they kept going forward with a frenzied wave of attacks, Mike England was caught upfield unable to cut out an Emlyn Hughes clearance.

Kevin Keegan raced onto the ball and his low cross into the goalmouth was carefully side-footed in by Heighway.

Joe Kinnear limped out of the action in the 70th minute to be replaced by Ray Evans and Tottenham came alive again with Peters' second goal one minute later.

A Gilzean header and a Pratt shot were blocked following a Cyril Knowles cross before Peters crashed the ball into the roof of the net."

Spurs' Road to the UEFA Cup Semi-Final, 1973

Date	Round	Att	H/A	Opposition	Result	Scorers
13-Sep-72	1 1L	10,777	A	Lyn Oslo	W 6-3	Peters, Pratt, Gilzean (2), Chivers (2)
27-Sep-72	1 2L	21,088	H	Lyn Oslo	W 6-0	Chivers (3), Coates (2), Pearce
25-Oct-72	2 2L	27,860	H	Olympiakos	W 4-0	Pearce (2), Chivers, Coates
8-Nov-72	2 2L	40,000	A	Olympiakos	L 0-1	
29-Nov-72	3 1L	23,958	H	Red Star Belgrade	W 2-0	Chivers, Gilzean
13-Dec-72	3 2L	75,000	A	Red Star Belgrade	L 0-1	
7-Mar-73	4 1L	30,469	H	Vitoria Setubal	W 1-0	Evans
21-Mar-73	4 2L	30,000	A	Vitoria Setubal	L 1-2	Chivers
25-Mar-73	SF 1L	46,919	H	Liverpool	W 2-1	Peters (2)
10-Apr-73	SF 2L	42,174	A	Liverpool	L 0-1	

1973-74

FC Cologne 1 Tottenham Hotspur 2
UEFA Cup, Fourth Round, first leg
March 6, 1974
When a side remains unbeaten on their own turf for two seasons, most 'experts' would say that any visiting team would stand little or no chance of coming away with a result. Bill Nicholson was too determined to reach another European final to have his mind diverted by the opinions of experts.

'TOTTENHAM LIVE UP TO THEIR MOTTO'
The Times, March 7, 1974
By Geoffrey Green
The match was probably won on the drawing board of room 108 in the Bad Godesberg Hotel on the banks of the Rhine – the room where the Fuhrer did much of his planning. Let's hope that Mister Nicholson's planning will have a happier ending.

Bill could field sides sometimes that other people wouldn't understand, and they'd work. We were playing Cologne, and there was me, Ralph Coates, Johnny (Pratt) and Stevie in midfield. They hadn't been beaten at home for two years, and were everybody's bet to win the UEFA Cup. We've gone over there and Bill set us out.

At one stage, a guy called Overath did a number on Johnny, nutmegged him. Well, I swear I nearly started laughing. The dummy Overath did on him, John had to buy a ticket to get back in - they were that good.

But Bill had told us that we had to stick together, to work for each other. As soon as one player got beat, bang – there was another right behind him. We knew we would be daft to get into a 'party tricks' contest with them but we were a better team. There were no Hoddles or Gascoignes that night but what we had was a heart as big as a lion, and there was no way we were going to lose.

We beat a top European side 2-1 in their own back yard, and when we got them back to The Lane, we beat them 3-0, but it just could just as easily have been seven or eight. We got two early goals and they just chucked the towel in. If the same thing had happened in the first leg to us, there's no way we would have folded like that. Bill would have gone apes***.

That night in the second leg we were what everyone thinks Tottenham are all about – the swagger, the cockiness, that sort of thing. But sometimes you have to dig in and set the stage for the second leg, and Bill Nick had been there, seen it and done it all before, and he made sure we knew that.
Terry Naylor

I return to room 108, where Mister Nicholson planned his campaign. He did it by reverting to a 4-4-2 formation, bringing in Dillon with a figure 11 on his shirt, yet drafted into defence as a further reinforcement.
Geoffrey Green, The Times

It takes a lot of bottle to put a relatively inexperienced player like I was into a game like that. Sure, we were hit by injuries a bit but Bill obviously had seen enough of me in training to know that I could play out of position and still do a job for the team.

It was an incredible experience to play in a major European competition, and one I will never forget.
Mike Dillon

Locomotiv Leipzig 1 Tottenham Hotspur 2
UEFA Cup Semi-Final, first leg
April 10, 1974

'BRILLIANT SPURS LAND A GREAT GAMBLE'
Daily Mail, April 11, 1974
By Jeff Powell
Spurs screwed up all their courage here yesterday to put one foot firmly into yet another European final.

Two goals inside half an hour were a glorious vindication of manager Bill Nicholson's decision to gamble Tottenham's UEFA Cup lives on attack.

Nicholson had reasoned that the best chance of taking goals from the notoriously defensive East Germans was to surprise them on their own pitch.

He was brilliantly right. Tottenham have a lead of one goal and the extra insurance of two away goals should surely guarantee their progress through the second leg of this semi-final in London in a fortnight.

Nicholson scorned caution by selecting winger Jimmy Neighbour in place of injured striker Chris McGrath. And Spurs were not to be deterred from their optimism…not by 75,000 banner-waving, klaxon-blowing fans, or the suffocating heat.

Martin Peters and Ralph Coates scored the early goals which launched Spurs towards a remarkable achievement in distant Europe. It is extraordinary the way Spurs rise to the UEFA Cup challenge.

Tottenham might have had even more goals in their opening burst. They then defended heroically to limit Locomotiv's enraged second-half comeback to one goal.

Wales' centre-half Mike England stood firm through the frenzied closing stages despite having had treatment for a gash sustained on his forehead late in the first half.

Tottenham's attacking gamble made for an exhilarating match rich in chances at both ends. And Peters had shot against the outstretched leg of German goalkeeper Friese in between menacing shots by Lowe and Macoul before he opened the scoring in the 15th minute.

England drove the ball forward from the half-way line, and Neighbour chested it down but too far away from him. But Peters cut commandingly across the path of his own winger to half-volley an almighty left-foot shot high into the corner of the net. Ten minutes later, Neighbour's through-ball launched Evans into a run and battle to reach the by-line and hammer over a cross at which Martin Chivers swung and missed, but which Coates was able to drive in off the crossbar.

Spurs were then denied a third goal in the most freakish circumstances. Chivers met a cross from Evans with a firm header which hit the post and then rebounded into play off the unknowing head of goalkeeper Friese.

Chivers put his hands to his head and fell back onto the turf in amazement.

Locomotiv were transformed in the second half when Spurs were required to take increasing punishment.

The Germans pulled a goal back in the 58th minute. World Cup striker Lowe meeting Geisler's free-kick with a decisive header at the near post.

Coates, who had carried his injured ankle through his vital contribution to the Tottenham performance, limped off in favour of substitute Phil Holder for the last 15 minutes, which saw Matoul hit a post and Lowe hit the legs of Pat Jennings.

But Tottenham survived.

Tottenham Hotspur 2 Locomotiv Leipzig 0
UEFA Cup Semi-Final, second leg
April 24, 1974
Spurs win 4-1 on agg.

BILL NICHOLSON

'SPURS IN FINAL!'

Daily Mirror, April 25, 1974

By Harry Miller

Tottenham last night walked away from a season of domestic mediocrity and towards a glorious European finale.

Goals from Chris McGrath and Martin Chivers at White Hart Lane enabled them to clear the hurdle at which Wolves and Ipswich fell, and reach the UEFA Cup final for the second time in three years.

If Tottenham did it with a performance which made the old 'Glory Glory' anthem the most muted of sounds around North London, the facts still speak for themselves.

This win, built on the firm foundations of a 2-1 first-leg semi-final success in Leipzig, means that Tottenham have qualified for a two-leg summit clash against Feyenoord on May 22 and 29 without losing one of their 10 games on the way.

To that fact must be added the impressive statistic of 29 goals scored, and only seven conceded. The East Germans are left to concede that with better finishing in both legs they might have knocked Tottenham off a road they now know better than any side in Europe.

Tottenham, in the first half, were sometimes forced to resort to tackling that was uncharacteristically crude. But Phil Beal and Mike England steadied them up at the back.

And as Locomotiv began to leave large gaps through their anxious rushes forward to bridge the 2-1 deficit, Beal nearly surprised them with a low 35-yard drive that keeper Friese nearly lost as he finished on his backside.

It was the sort of night where Chivers suffered anguish and enjoyed admiration in equal parts. He had a penalty appeal turned down when Grobner appeared to handle his shot early on.

He later rounded Grobner and, with a clear opening, lashed the ball high over the bar. And he got in at the far post for a fine header from McGrath's cross, but Sekora cleared off the line.

Yet East German World Cup star Wolfram Lowe missed a chance just before half-time that surely changed the course of the evening's proceedings.

A badly-placed Joe Kinnear clearance was headed down to him by Liciewicz. He raced forward, made the mistake of trying to take the ball around Pat Jennings, and lost it.

The tide really began to turn Tottenham's way early in the second half. An England right-foot shot seemed certain to find the net, until Martin Peters somehow got in the way and diverted the ball over the bar.

Then in the 55th minute came the goal that delighted the 41,280 Tottenham fans and marked the beginning of the end for Locomotiv. The busy Ralph Coates went wide on the right, crossed – and McGrath was there at the far side of the six-yard box to beat Friese with a dipping header.

It was the fifth goal in five UEFA Cup games for the talented teenager from Belfast.

Locomotiv, even as the end drew near, refused to accept that Tottenham were about to achieve what Wolves and Ipswich could not. Jennings, who has saved Tottenham so often in recent months, needed to be at his most agile and alert to divert a firm header from Matoul.

Finally, four minutes from the finish, Chivers set the seal on Tottenham's march to the final. Steve Perryman set him up with a fine run and pass, and Chivers bore in from the left to score with a low left-foot shot."

And so to Rotterdam...

When football historians look back on the 1974 UEFA Cup campaign of Tottenham Hotspur, they will doubtless overlook the fact that a British team reached the final of a European competition twice in three seasons, and that they were narrowly defeated by an away goal in the semi-final of the same competition in the intervening season. They will skip over the fact that this was done with skilful use of tactics, and with several young players, many of whom were inexperienced at top-level football. They will also neglect to mention the fantastic resolve shown by all of Bill's players in their march to the final.

What they will surely highlight will be the scenes of violence and mayhem witnessed in Holland, yet again overlooking the fact that, during the rest of the three consecutive European campaigns, not one meaningful act of disorder from Spurs fans was reported on their travels.

Bill Nicholson and his players deserve much better than that.

Tottenham Hotspur 2 Feyenoord 2
UEFA Cup Final, first leg
May 22, 1974
Spurs: Pat Jennings, Ray Evans, Terry Naylor, John Pratt, Mike England, Phil Beal, Chris McGrath, Steve Perryman, Martin Chivers, Martin Peters, Ralph Coates. Scorers: England, Van Daele (og)

We could have kicked ourselves for letting that game slip. We were the better side, and even conceding a goal at home, at 2-1 we would have fancied out chances in Rotterdam. But conceding a late goal like we did was a sickener.
Martin Peters

'SPURS ON THE BRINK'
Daily Mirror, May 22 ,1974

Feyenoord 2 Tottenham Hotspur 0
UEFA Cup Final, second leg
May 29, 1974
Spurs: Pat Jennings, Ray Evans, Terry Naylor, John Pratt, (sub Phil Holder) Mike England, Phil Beal, Chris McGrath, Steve Perryman, Martin Chivers, Martin Peters, Ralph Coates

BILL NICHOLSON

'HOOLIGANS SHAME SPURS'
Daily Mirror, May 30, 1974

To be honest, I think we lost the final in the first leg at The Lane when we allowed a lead to slip, although the referee didn't do us any favours in Rotterdam when he chalked off a perfectly good goal by Chris McGrath when it was still 0-0. Then Feyenoord scored, and it went nuts in the stand. As players, you do your best to ignore it, but lots of us had friends and family out there, so it was difficult because we had no idea whereabouts in the stadium they all were.

So half-time comes, and we all troop into the dressing room. We had only been there for a short while, when a UEFA official walks in and whispers in Bill's ear. He nods, picks up his coat and walks out, leaving Eddie Baily to go round to us all, giving advice and trying to build us up. Then, about five minutes later, Bill came in, chucked his coat on the floor and said: "They're tearing the f****** place to pieces out there."
John Pratt

No way would I condone any kind of stuff that went on in Rotterdam but, personally, I think the press went way over the top on our fans. I know a lot of them were out of order but an equal amount of them got a right going over from the police out there when they hadn't even done anything. It was indiscriminate.

As for the game – well, we knew beforehand that Feyenoord were a good side, but with two goals against us from the first leg, the last thing you want is to see a perfectly good goal disallowed. Paddy McGrath was onside when he put the ball in the net. That would have really given them a thing or two to think about.

As it was, when Feyenoord did score, it seemed to give them a lift, and it hurt us. Then, of course, it all kicked off on the terraces and most of us, whether we would care to admit it or not, had half an eye on what was going on, because we all had people out there and it's only human nature to worry about what's happening.

The sad part of it all is that we'd done so bloody well to get there, and now it all seemed to be for nothing.
Terry Naylor

It's a crying shame that the final of '74 will be remembered for all the wrong reasons. We had just played three brilliant seasons in Europe, in which we had only lost narrowly to a very good Liverpool side, and with a bit of luck we could have landed three UEFA Cups back-to-back. That kind of achievement would have stood up to anybody's record; and yet all people seem to remember from 1974 is the trouble in Rotterdam.

I know a lot of our people were in the wrong but they weren't fighting themselves, were they? Personally, I think the Dutch fans should have taken their share of the blame as well.
Martin Peters

*We had a such a good relationship with the Feyenoord club. The stadium, such
a lovely place, was just smashed to pieces. It proved to football that there is a
certain section who, if hell bent on trouble, will cause trouble. It is something that
had been proved all too regularly since those days.*

*I cannot understand why people should do such things. I don't know why they
don't respect law and order. In the old days we had respect for that sort of thing.*

*But that night in Rotterdam was so bad. I don't think I have seen anything like
it. I remember the days of battles during the depression but this was much worse.*

*My daughter went over on the boat and coach and they said the fans were so
drunk, they had to lock themselves in the cabin. There was so much drinking going
on and so much trouble.*

*We knew nothing of what might happen while we were preparing for the match.
It was never an excuse for our defeat but they were not ideal conditions in which
to play a match. I still cannot forget the scenes of the seats spinning down from the
stands. It was fortunate that a lot more people did not get hurt.*

Bill Nicholson from The Glory Glory Nights

Rotterdam, 1974 – A fan's perspective

*That whole Rotterdam thing, it's been a nightmare ever since, really. Each time
I see or hear about the way Bill reacted, with the resignation and the words he
used and all that, I shudder. The worst of it is, people must think when they hear
me talking like this, 'the guy's just gone out there for a ruck', but I swear that
wasn't the case. My mate got me a ticket and the two of us went out there with a
view to watching Tottenham land another European trophy – that's all we went
for.*

*Anyway, it all sort of blew up from the first leg at The Lane, because the
Feyenoord fans in the top tier of The Paxton were bang out of order that night. We
were just doing the usual fan stuff, you know, chants and that – and then they start
topping up empty beer bottles and cans with pee and lobbing them at the people
in the lower tier, all Spurs fans. Well look, that doesn't exactly make for a good
atmosphere, know what I mean? The Old Bill over here have got it well sorted, and
the Dutch boys went home just thinking they'd had one over on us, and I knew a
few people who weren't too chuffed with the idea of that.*

*So come the day of the return leg, we got down to the ferry and got on board,
and then the fun and games began, because the bar staff were serving anyone, and
I mean anyone – there were lads of about 14 or 15 getting rat-a****. A couple of
the bar staff had a right stand-up row with each other about serving us, and I can
remember one of them saying: "Look, there's about a thousand of them on here –
if we start getting shirty about who we do or don't serve, this ship will look like
it's been hit by a f****** missile. Give it an hour or two, they'll be in Rotterdam,
then they'll be someone else's problem." And so they just kept serving.*

*The ship docked, and we got off. At this stage, it was all still quite good-natured.
We went through customs, then split up into small groups and just went for a bit*

*of a look around the place, even though we'd been warned by a few guys inside the ferry terminal – you know, Dutch blokes – that Rotterdam was a bit of a ****hole and that we should stay out of the red-light area, because it was well moody. Fat chance.*

*It was when these small groups met up that it started to get a bit naughty. We were walking around, chanting and singing, and every now and then some Dutch bloke had said something – probably quite innocent, maybe just having a laugh or whatever. But because so many of us were p***** up, and you couldn't understand what they were saying it's like one plus one equals three, he must be taking the p***. So it kicked off.*

I tell you, it was mental. There were blokes – well, little more than kids, really – going up to these Dutch geezers and giving them a slap. At this stage, of course, it was a couple of hours before kick-off and most of the Dutch fans were probably indoors having their dinner or whatever.

A few got nicked but, to be honest, the Dutch police had enough problems of their own, what with the crime and all that, so they largely just left us alone.

We get to the stadium, and right outside there were about two to three hundred Feyenoord fans giving it large, goading us, so it went from there. Their Old Bill split it up, and then we all started going inside the stadium. Things quietened down for a while. The match started, and most of us – me included – just settled down to watch the game, even though we were still getting pelted and gobbed at by the Feyenoord mob who were right next to us.

*Then Feyenoord scored, and that was it. We sort of all knew that the game was up, because they had two away goals from the first leg, and to be fair they did look a useful side. So it went mad. We ran at them, and they s*** a brick and legged it – five minutes before they'd been giving it the big 'un, and now they're having it on their toes. I honestly believe that wound the Spurs boys up all the more.*

*Well, half-time comes, and even though the Dutch police had moved in to try and stop it, there was mayhem, because their mob had sort of formed up behind the Old Bill, who were laying into us big time – riot batons and everything. Then the second half gets underway, and we tried to watch the game again, but it was f****** pointless, mainly because we were second best to Feyenoord but also because there were bits of stadium flying past your ear and you just didn't know when a piece had your name on it. It stayed that way for most of the second-half.*

Come the final whistle, none of us were interested any more. While we were waiting for the Police to let us out – they kept us back for quite a time – some bloke said to me – and I swear this: "Did you hear Bill Nick at half-time, speaking on a loudspeaker?" I said: "Yeah, of course – didn't you?" He just shrugged his shoulders and said: "He was saying something about calming down, that's how it sounded to me. Easy for him to say, he wasn't getting spat at.".

*And the sad thing is, that's genuinely how some of us felt at the time . . . like Bill didn't have any idea what was going on up there – and in a way, he didn't. Of course, the reason Bill didn't know what was going on was because we were acting like a bunch of a***holes, and the whole world knows that he's a nice bloke. It was totally alien to him.*

We got back to the UK, where the Press were asking people if they'd seen any trouble, which under the circumstances was just about as stupid a question as I've ever heard. You'd need to have been Ray Charles not to have seen it. What they really meant was 'were you involved?' Some silly b******* started laughing and saying yes, we were doing it, but I just kept my mouth shut.

On the train home, I just sat staring out of the window, and all of a sudden it hit me, you know, what we'd done out there. All the press were talking about was the fighting, and it's as if the final itself, and the achievement of getting there, was a side issue, and that's when I began feeling pig sick.

The thought occurred to me that we had in some way caused the team to lose the final – it could have been true, but who knows. Then the following day I read in the papers that Bill hadn't been able to give a half-time team talk because he'd been too busy trying to stop the aggro, and he'd been quoted as saying that the way we were acting made him ashamed to be British, and so I just felt even worse.

Bill Nick resigned not long after that, and although few of us knew it at the time, that business in Rotterdam sort of made his mind up for him. To this day I haven't been involved in anything else like it – even though at times opposing fans can really p*** you off with some of the things they say. I just shout back and leave it at that.

I'm married now with three kids, a good job and I still go regularly to Tottenham. Do I regret what went on out there that night? Bloody hell, yes, of course I do. I don't know if Bill would still have resigned – the team wasn't the same any more – but the idea that I could in some way be partly responsible for us losing our greatest ever manager . . . I hate the idea of that. Now I try and tell young lads around me at games to wind their necks in, you know, calm it down a bit. It's not enough, but it's sort of my way of trying to set the record straight.

I hope Bill would approve.

Phil, Spurs fan from Welwyn Garden City, Hertfordshire

Spurs Road to the UEFA Cup Final, 1973-74

Date	Round	Att	H/A	Opposition	Result	Scorers
19-Sep-73	1 1L	11,000	A	Grasshoppers	W 5-1	Chivers (2), Evans, Gilzean (2)
3-Oct-73	1 2L	18,105	H	Grasshoppers	W 4-1	Peters (2), England, Lader og
24-Oct-73	2 1L	30,000	A	Aberdeen	D 1-1	Coates
7-Nov-73	2 2L	21,785	H	Aberdeen	W 4-1	Peters, Neighbour, McGrath (2)
28-Nov-73	3 1L	42,000	A	Dinamo Tbilsi	D 1-1	Coates
12-Dec-73	3 2L	18,602	H	Dinamo Tbilsi	W 5-1	McGrath, Chivers (2), Peters (2)
6-Mar-74	4 1L	28,000	A	FC Cologne	W 2-1	McGrath, Peters
20-Mar-74	4 2L	40,968	H	FC Cologne	W 3-0	Chivers, Coates, Peters
10-Apr-74	SF 1L	74,000	A	Locomotiv Leipzig	W 2-1	Peters, McGrath
24-Apr-74	SF 2L	41,280	H	Locomotiv Leipzig	W 2-0	McGrath, Chivers
21-May-74	Final 1L	46,281	H	Feyenoord	D 2-2	England, Van Daele og
29-May-74	Final 2L	68,000	A	Feyenoord	L 0-2	

BILL NICHOLSON

So the adventure which began in a cold mining town in Poland in 1961 ended 13 years later in shambolic scenes of chaos in Rotterdam – ironically the scene of Bill's and Tottenham's finest moment. But when people look back at the achievements of Bill Nicholson and Spurs in Europe, the stunning, nerve-shredding nights of glory will long outshine the memory of one night of madness.

Over the course of seven seasons spanning 13 glorious and memorable years, they had been superb ambassadors for their country, and had pitted themselves against the best sides in Europe. On each of the occasions where they had failed in their efforts, it was never by more than one goal on aggregate.

One only has to look at the way Spurs teams down the years transformed themselves once they took to the field in all-white under floodlights to know that European competition is the lifeblood of Tottenham Hotspur Football Club.

They will return.

It's magnificent to be in Europe, and this club – a club like Tottenham Hotspur – if we're not in Europe, we're nothing.
Bill Nicholson

Special thanks must go to the two magnificent publications, 'The Glory Glory Nights' by Cockerel Press, and 'Spurs Go Marching On' by Ralph L Finn, for their unwitting but invaluable help in this chapter.

Chapter 6
Rebuilding

"I have nothing but admiration for Bill Nicholson and the whole Tottenham set-up. They have been the most courageous club in England since the war. Spurs have never been afraid to spend big, experiment, or persevere with attractive, attacking football. Spurs are a great club, with a great manager."
Bill Shankly

The latter part of the 60s saw the emergence of English football in a whole new form. Gone were the days of flair, style and risk taking – at least (with the notable exception of Manchester United) they were if you had delusions of winning the league title. The accent shifted from open, short-passing and free-flowing football that was easy on the eye to a game where retaining possession of the ball and denying the opposition room to play were paramount. Meanwhile, Bill Nicholson had a job to do replacing his ageing stars from the glory years.

Replacing the mighty Bobby Smith
It was in 1964 when Bill said to me: "Bobby, I've decided that I'm going to get somebody younger in. I've got this young centre-forward to play in your place – Laurie Brown from Arsenal, because I think you're going a bit stale."

When he told me who it was, I said to him: "What? Laurie Brown? He's a centre-half! Call yourself a manager?" and I walked out of the office. I thought to myself: 'He's got to be joking.'

Later on, we talked again. "Bill," I said. "Thinking about what you said to me, and what I said to you, it's about time we parted company." And that was about it. A few days later I signed for Brighton.
Bobby Smith

As for his image of being grizzly and tough, just let me say that I cannot recall one player being disciplined by Bill while I was at the club.

The nearest he came to blowing his top was over Bobby Smith who went into print with some strong criticisms of Tottenham in general and Bill in particular. To this day I am convinced Bill was hurt more by the slating of the club than of himself. He had every reason to hit out at Smithy, who used to give Bill some right old headaches.

I particularly remember Smithy's betting bug and how it got him into trouble once over a telephone bill. Even when we used to travel abroad, Bobby would insist on having his bet. I used to room with Smithy. He was good company, a generous bloke when he had cash to spare, and a loyal pal.

BILL NICHOLSON

I would be lying on the bed having an afternoon nap, before a big European tie, and suddenly I would hear Smithy shouting down the phone to a bookie in London. "Is that you, Izzy? Put me a tenner on the favourites in the 2.30 and 3.30." Then he would phone back and get the results. As I recall, he would lose a lot more that he would win. One day Bill Nick called us all together and said that somebody was making telephone calls to London and putting pounds on the Tottenham bill. Before he could say any more, big Smithy stood up and shouted: "All right, keep your shirt on. I'll pay it back when we get home."

The funny thing was that Bill had no idea who was making the calls until Smithy's outburst.

I think it is a sign of how Bill looks after his players that few ever want to leave Tottenham. To be honest, I did not want to go at the death but I just knew I had become an embarrassment to him. Dave Mackay would have preferred to stay on, too. It's that sort of club where you really feel as though you belong.

Smithy is about the only one who was not sorry to get away and in the end Bill Nick played very fair with him by letting him go at a giveaway fee.
Jimmy Greaves

A Man of Principles

Bill was a tough nut when it suited him – you would only need to ask any forward who had tried to get past him during his playing days. But one afternoon, I found another side to the man.

In his quest for a new striker, Bill had noticed that George Eastham had scored 24 goals for Newcastle the previous season. Not that Bill's interest was common knowledge, of course. It was not like it is today, where you only need to mention something, half in joke, to your tea lady, and 10 minutes later it's all over the front pages.

I telephoned Bill one day and said that I had something he might like to hear. He seemed intrigued, so I came over. "Bill," I said. "You know that George is one of the players on strike?" At the time, there was a movement among many professional players to gain a minimum wage, and several of them were refusing to play. One of them was George Eastham. Bill nodded.

"Well, what if I were to tell you that he is staying down at Ernie Clay's place with Harry?" It turned out that Eastham was being 'employed' at 20 pounds a week by Ernie Clay, later to become chairman of Fulham, and was at the house at that very moment. Bill's eyes lit up.

"Do you think he'd be interested in coming here?" he asked me.

"Well," I replied. "He's only on the other end of the phone. Why don't you give him a call?"

But Bill just couldn't bring himself to do it. Eastham was still under contract to Newcastle, and making an illegal approach for a player was something that Bill Nicholson wouldn't even contemplate. As much as he would have loved to sign Eastham, Bill would make sure that it would never happen in a way that would potentially reflect badly on Tottenham Hotspur.
Ken Jones (Ex-professional footballer with Swansea City, Ken went on to be

Bill addresses his players pre-season in 1962. Left to right: Cliff Jones, Terry Medwin, Peter Baker, John White, Jimmy Greaves, Danny Blanchflower and Bobby Smith.

Chief Football Writer with the Daily Mirror for more than 20 years. He is also the cousin of Cliff Jones)

Danny B and the minimum wage

Following the strenuous efforts of the PFA, the maximum wage had finally fallen in 1961 and the players were now in a position to negotiate their own contracts. Of course, when the clubs giveth, they also taketh, so although the players could now earn as much as their clubs were willing to pay them, the clubs demanded their pound of flesh in return, inserting a clause into players contracts that restricted their right to freedom of speech. "Spurs offered me a wage of £3,000 a year instead of the £20 a week I had received the season before," *wrote Danny.* "It was a fair rise but not such a big deal considering we had just won both the League and the FA Cup in one season and Johnny Haynes had been offered £5,000 a year...I did not disagree the money terms but refused to sign the contract because of the restriction of speech clause."

'It's not my idea,' Bill Nicholson pleaded. 'It's not mine either,' I argued. 'Why should I sign an agreement with you to please someone else?'

'Bill and I were on very good terms. We trusted and respected one another. Perhaps he sought legal advice on the matter because some days later I was given written permission (to speak freely). That was not the end of the matter. Pressures were brought to bear on me. 'What would you think if I fined you £5,' Bill said to me one day. 'Not much. I don't know what it is I've done but if you're going to fine me, then let's make it worthwhile – how about £500?' He had learned to be patient with my direct approach to delicate matters.

'Forget it,' he said. 'It's just that we're having a bit of pressure from the league.'

At Spurs, Danny was informed that he'd been known as a troublemaker when he was at Villa. Danny's answer was characteristic. 'Still am, it's just that the results are better now.'

Dave Bowler, from 'Danny Blanchflower – a biography of a visionary'

Dave Mackay – two broken legs won't stop him...

I had been used to using weights at Hearts but once I joined Spurs things stepped up a gear as far as training went. One of our training people was Bill Watson, who had been an Olympic weight lifter for Britain during the 1948 games. They would spend hours doing muscle-strengthening exercises, leg work, that sort of thing, but Bill would be as involved as anybody. He had been the team's coach under Jimmy Anderson, but now he was the manager he was just as keen to stay involved in that side of things.

So when I broke my leg before the Cup Winners' Cup Final in '63, there was never any thought in my mind about giving up. I'm not made that way. I knew that I would have plenty of help from the Tottenham backroom boys, and even though I sat out the final – they won 5-1, so they obviously missed me – I knew I'd be back.

Then, of course, I got another injury a couple of years later to the same leg, and yet again it was a bad one. But, as before, there was no chance of me calling it a day, and Bill never even brought up the subject. I guess he knew me as well as I did.

Dave Mackay

A raw youngster from Ulster

At Watford I met Bill Nicholson for the very first time. I'd only ever seen him on television, but he was exactly as I'd imagined. He turned up carrying a little brief case containing the transfer forms. He told my why Spurs wanted me, made it clear there was a first team place waiting if I came up to expectation and offered me wages of around £38 a week. I said I was both flattered and delighted and that there was no other club I would sooner join, but I pointed out I was earning almost as much at Watford as he was offering, and I surely rated something – from somebody.

It was deadlock. Nicholson was polite, but firm; there was nothing he could offer and he was disappointed because he had never been turned down before by any player he had tried to sign. We shook hands and I flew back to Ireland under the impression it was the end of the matter.

I didn't anticipate hearing from Nicholson again, assuming he would look elsewhere for a goalkeeper. So I was surprised when I got another message from McGarry asking me to contact him. When I telephoned Watford it was to be told that Spurs were still keen and another meeting had been fixed. "No thanks," I replied. "As far as I'm concerned there's nothing left to discuss. I'm having my close-season break – if you want to see me it will have to be in Ireland."

It was a bit of a cheek, you don't have to tell me that, but the message must have got across. McGarry and Nicholson flew over and agreed to meet me at the Grand Central Hotel – now, unhappily, closed to the public – in the middle of Belfast.

I came to the conclusion that there was little point in staying where I wasn't *wanted – and anyway, the longer I spent in Nicholson's company the more impressed I became. So I signed for Spurs at an increased offer of £40 a week plus £5 for each first team game.*

My father had accompanied me to the Grand Central and I could sense he was amazed I even hesitated. He was earning about £11 a week and the money being discussed seemed a small fortune. But he urged me to ask for a 10-year contract. That added up to security, which was more important in his eyes. I didn't, of course, and if I had, I'm under no illusions what Nicholson would have said. Neither of us could have foreseen that I would remain at White Hart Lane for the next 13 years.

Sometimes I wonder what would have happened to my career if Bill Nicholson had not been so persistent in pursuit of a raw kid. I'm only glad he was. I would not like to have missed my time at Tottenham or the chance to play under such a great, and straight, manager.

Pat Jennings

The day Bill lost one of his own

The date of July 21, 1964 will go down in the history of Tottenham Hotspur as the day that the marvellous John White was lost to us forever. Bill had received a phone call from Tottenham police stating that John had been killed. His first instinct was annoyance – he had, after all, received several malicious crank calls during the previous week stating that Jimmy Greaves had been killed in a car crash. Then, after Bill verified the facts by calling the police station, the awful truth dawned . . .

The early 60s were thrilling times to be assigned to Spurs in Europe, even though their manager Bill Nicholson never found it easy to make time for, or small talk among, the following media circus. Yet he is a man whose straight-dealing and brusque Yorkshire honesty I came to admire and, as seasons passed, we became friends.

I was at Bill's house, within a goal-kick of White Hart Lane – it was as though he dare not be too far from his beloved Spurs – on the sad day in 1964 when poor John White was killed by lightning as he sheltered beneath a tree during a round of golf at Crews Hill, Middlesex.

John was known as 'The Ghost of White Hart Lane' – he drifted almost unseen into positions to pull defences apart with his precise passes. The man from Falkirk looked so frail but his talent as a playmaker was of the highest class; he won 22 caps for Scotland and, at 26 years of age, was at his absolute peak. He was the hidden ace in the midfield trio (along with Blanchflower and Mackay) that made the great Tottenham Double team perform. His tragic death came at a time when, both in life and in his sport, he would have been reaching the golden age.

I had gone to Bill Nick's home with my little BBC tape recorder to get an obituary for broadcasting the following day. He and his ever-welcoming wife, Darkie, invited me to stay for dinner. It was as though Bill needed somebody to talk to, to help him over his grief at the death of one of his players. In spite of his bluff manner and tough discipline, Bill always looked on his players as one of the family and this was a hugely painful night for him.

Looking back, I'm always astonished that nobody from Tottenham was on hand to offer him support and comfort; and even more surprised that I was the only journalist who came knocking on his door. Today, the little street where Bill and Darkie continued to live would be blocked by television vans and nobody would be able to move for camera crews.
Brian Moore, former broadcaster

Oddly enough, the one time I saw Bill cry was on my first official duty for the club. It happened before the funeral of the great John White, who had been killed by lightning on a golf course on the day I was travelling from Ireland to report for Tottenham for the first time, for pre-season training.

We all gathered at White Hart Lane before going on to the crematorium. Bill started to talk to us about John, who was only 26 when he died. He had been speaking for only a couple of minutes when he was so overcome that he excused himself and disappeared into a washroom to hide his tears. The players all said they had never seen Bill so distraught.
Pat Jennings

Bill knew that there was always a bit of leg-pulling going on at Spurs – I think, despite his image he showed to the world, he enjoyed it a bit. On this one occasion – it was pre-season 1964 – after I had broken my leg a few months before, I was having difficulty getting my fitness back – my breathing was quite heavy. Bill devised this idea where he gave John White and me a tennis racket each, and told us to play a bit to get my stamina levels up. Well, while this was going on, Cliff Jones swiped John's clothes and hid them. It was typical of the kind of stunts we pulled on each other all the time.

So when John had finished, he couldn't find his clothes. After asking everybody where his togs were, and getting absolutely no sense from any of us, he decided that he'd drive home in his training kit, get changed there, and go straight on to golf.

That, of course, was the last time we saw him alive. John was killed up on the golf course, doing what he probably knew was daft – hiding under a tree during a storm. But I suppose it's one of those things that you always imagine will happen to everyone else, not to you. The news hit us all like a slap in the face. John was one of the Spurs family – and in fact, he was actually the son-in-law of former assistant manager, Harry Evans.
Terry Medwin

The strangest thing happened after John White got killed. John was supposed to have been playing with Jimmy Robertson at the golf course, but then Jimmy got delayed for some reason and, of course, there were no mobile phones in those days, so John's obviously thought 'sod it' and played on a later slot. The rest, as they say, is history – poor John was killed outright. A few of the players – and Bill

– had used that golf course a lot in those days.

But a year to the day later – and here's the weird part – almost at the same time of day, there was a storm going on, and there was this almighty 'crash'. My wife and I both looked at each other in amazement. You can draw your own conclusions from that, I guess!
Peter Baker

A young cockney Irishman with the world at his feet

When I got to 18, Eddie Baily and Bill Nick called me in and said they thought I had a future. They were offering me a two-year contract as a professional.

I said I'd have to think about it. I'd done three years as an apprentice printer and was now on £6 a week. I had a secure future. What security had I as a footballer? Spurs were a very big club. After two years I could be chucked out and never make it. I asked them what chance they thought I had. Bill said he could promise nothing, but I had a realistic chance, if I continued to progress at the same rate.

I went home and told my mum. She said go for it. It's what I'd always wanted to do, hadn't I...?
Joe Kinnear

A debut to forget – and lessons to remember

In The West Ham team was John Sissons on the left-wing and Harry Redknapp on the right. Brian Dear was the centre-forward. He got a hat trick. West Ham stuffed us 4-1. Despite that, I kept my place and was in for the next seven games, till the end of the season.

Bill holding court at Cheshunt. Frank Saul, Joe Kinnear, Terry Venables and Pat Jennings listen and learn.

BILL NICHOLSON

I felt by then I'd made it, that I was going to become a first-team player but you never knew with Bill Nick. He liked to keep you on your toes, fighting for your place. Bill was a perfectionist, and his Double-winning team had been near perfect. We felt a bit inferior to them, and he probably made us feel that way. Bill would stop a training game, just to make you do something properly, or to do it again until you got it right. He'd rant and rave if you did things badly. During a practice game, he'd run beside you and tell you to 'caress the ball' – words you never hear today.

It was still the era of the old-fashioned leather ball, which was like a lead weight. Bill had been brought up to trap the ball under your foot, under your studs. That was what he insisted on, the correct way. But times were changing and new methods were coming in from the continent, and also newer, lighter balls. All the same, he still made us trap the ball his way. He'd stop us bringing it down on our instep. He maintained that if you made a mistake, and the ball bounced off you, you gave it away. By trapping it under your foot, you kept control. That was the theory, the standard practice at the time – trap the ball, push it and run. I would have taught the same way, I suppose, if I'd been a coach at the time.

He also had his own theories about heading. I can still hear him shouting 'throw your eyes at the ball'. He had no need of course to teach heading to someone like Gilly (Alan Gilzean). We practised crossing to Gilly for hours, and he'd score every time. He was the best header of a ball I have ever met.
Joe Kinnear

A world away from St Mirren

Bill and Spurs were well-known in Scotland. Quite apart from the European success, in which they had beaten the mighty Rangers quite convincingly at Ibrox and at Spurs, a couple of Bill's best players were Scots. Bill Brown, John White and the legendary Dave Mackay.

Bill had had me watched at St Mirren several times, so I knew he was interested in me, and when the offer came in for me, I jumped at it. Scotland produced some great players in those days, and many of them were wingers and many of them earned their corn in England. I was hoping to be one of them.

I signed for Spurs in March 1964, just as Bill's greatest side was breaking up. You couldn't help but be impressed by the professionalism of the man. Sure, he was blunt – but coming from Scotland, I could handle that. He commanded respect, and that was from everyone.

Bill was the kind of guy who should have been a boy scout – 'Be Prepared' should have been his motto. That particularly went for pre-season training. It's fair to say that Bill was very innovative in some of his fitness ideas, and his tactical and technique theories were quite revolutionary even by today's standards, But it was pre-season that really stood out for me.

He was determined to set you up for the season ahead, and one of my more telling memories of Bill is the 'cross-country walk'. Doesn't sound too bad, does it? But Bill used to take the lead, striding away like a Guardsman, making sure that everybody was right up with him. And don't forget, the man was in his late

40s by this time!

It's a natural tendency for anybody to want to break into a trot, but God help anybody who did. It was absolutely punishing, because Bill just wouldn't let you slow down.
Jimmy Robertson

Venables – the next big thing

Chelsea had accepted offers from both Spurs and West Ham, but left the decision up to me, and for the second time in my career, I decided against West Ham. Spurs manager Bill Nicholson, one of my idols, had been on the phone to me just before Ron Greenwood had called up to ask me to go to West Ham, but even if Ron had got in first, my decision would have been the same. Bobby Moore almost went to Tottenham at the same time, and was excited about joining Spurs, but his move fell through and eventually Tottenham bought Mike England instead.

If I was sad to be leaving Stamford Bridge, I was elated that the move was to be to White Hart Lane. Tottenham was close to home, my favourite team, and Dave Mackay was another of my heroes, so I thought to myself, that's it. That will do nicely.

Bill helped enforce that feeling of formality – seeming to be a dour, stiff and unbending personality – but his wife Darkie, who we would always see pedalling her bike around Tottenham, doing the shopping, was such a contrast, always laughing and joking, that I realised there must be another side to Bill. When I got to know him better, I found that Bill was a very warm, but shy man, who used his gruff exterior as self-protection, but in my early days at White Hart Lane, he seemed a forbidding figure.
Terry Venables

And another from the West...

I was phoned up one Friday night by Fulham's then general manager, Frank Osborne, and asked to go to his house. After I arrived he started reminiscing about my time as a junior at the club, when I used to clean his car, sweep the terraces and kill the rats, so I said: "Look, it's 9pm, we've got a game against Liverpool tomorrow, so what's the problem?" He said Tottenham wanted to buy me.

I didn't really want to go. I was very happy at Fulham but Tommy Trinder, the chairman, said I had to go because they needed the money. So that was that. I played the match against Liverpool and Bill Nicholson signed me on the Saturday night for £72,500.
Alan Mullery

Tempting the mighty 'Mooro'

Bobby Moore refused to sign a contract in the months before the World Cup. He wanted richer pastures and I know Spurs would have liked him. But Bill Nicholson, a straight and genuine man, never approached me and, in any case, we had no intention of letting Moore go, either before or after the World Cup.
Ron Greenwood

BILL NICHOLSON

Up for the Cup again

Training at Tottenham was very different to that at Chelsea. We had a lot of young players at Stamford Bridge and we were worked really hard – and we found that we used to start the season off with a bang. By the time we got to the end of the season, though, we were very tired. We found out that we weren't at our best when we got to the semi-finals of two FA Cups.

Then, when I went to Tottenham, I found training under Bill not as hard as I expected it to be. It was the exact reverse, in fact – we started rather sluggish, and ended up very strong. It's all about trying to get that balance of the two.

That's what I tried to get when I started coaching at Crystal Palace – to lose that dip in the middle of the season. I thought Bill ran a tight ship at Spurs, without being over pushy. In a way, I thought he was quite lax at times, but he was a good coach and he knew exactly what he wanted. It was Eddie Baily who would do most of the day-to-day training.

Tactically, Bill certainly wasn't behind anyone else, but then nobody put much emphasis on tactics in those days the way we do today. He was, however, a very thorough man who thought about the game, and he would change things around now and again when the situation called for it. He'd usually use the same players, but he'd often change the way they played. He was a good manager and I never thought he was going to get 'out-done' tactically. And he was a very likeable guy.

Bill didn't need any inside information from me before the Chelsea final in '67. He had them watched time and time again, and he knew exactly what to expect.
Terry Venables

Spurs' Road to Wembley, 1967

Third Round Replay, White Hart Lane
February 1, 1967
Tottenham Hotspur 1 Millwall 0
Having survived a tricky trip to The Den, Spurs must have thought that the replay, against second division opposition, would be something of a formality. In the end, it took a solitary Alan Gilzean goal to see off the South Londoners.
Scorer: Alan Gilzean

Fourth Round, White Hart Lane
February 18, 1967
Tottenham Hotspur 3 Portsmouth 1
Even the famous 'Pompey Chimes', sung by their ardent followers, were not enough to prevent Spurs notching up a 3-1 victory in a fairly forgettable game.
Scorers: Jimmy Greaves, Alan Gilzean (2)

Fifth Round, White Hart Lane
March 11, 1967
Tottenham Hotspur 2 Bristol City 0

The phrase 'your name's on the Cup' is often ridiculed by many, but after City had held on doggedly for a draw, they were awarded a penalty. Big Pat saved it, but was adjudged to have moved. The resulting re-taken penalty was missed, and Spurs scored twice, with a penalty of their own, to take them into the sixth round.
Scorer: Jimmy Greaves (2)

Sixth Round Replay, White Hart Lane
April 12, 1967
Tottenham Hotspur 6 Birmingham City 0
As with Crewe Alexandra many years before, the Blues were to rue not taking their chance to see off Tottenham in the first game, as Bill masterminded a six-goal destruction of the Midlanders.
Scorers: Jimmy Greaves (2) Terry Venables (2) Alan Gilzean, Frank Saul

Semi-Final, Hillsborough
April 29, 1967
Tottenham Hotspur 2 Nottingham Forest 1
A closely-contested match against a side challenging for the league saw Spurs take a two goal lead, with unsung hero Frank Saul again getting on the scoresheet. A late Forest goal was not enough, and the Spurs were back at Wembley.
Scorers: Jimmy Greaves, Frank Saul.

FA Cup Final
Wembley Stadium
May 20, 1967
Tottenham Hotspur 2 Chelsea 1
Spurs: Pat Jennings, Joe Kinnear, Cyril Knowles, Alan Mullery, Mike England, Dave Mackay, Jimmy Robertson, Jimmy Greaves, Alan Gilzean, Terry Venables, Frank Saul. Sub (not used) Cliff Jones
Scorers: Robertson, Saul

'GLORY GLORY SPURS!'
Headline from Sunday Express, May 21, 1967

I believe Tommy Docherty made a tactical mistake before the 1967 FA Cup Final which made our task easier in the first all-London final. Docherty was then in his hey-day, cracking jokes and constantly appearing in the newspapers as he guided his young side towards Wembley. In previous matches he used Marvin Hinton as a sweeper and took three out of four points off us in league matches. Our 3-0 defeat at Stamford Bridge was our heaviest of the season. Alan Gilzean did not like playing against a sweeper and it showed in these matches.

But just before the final, Docherty abandoned the idea and played with an orthodox defensive system. When I heard that, I told my players: 'He's done us a favour.'
Bill Nicholson

Alan Gilzean did indeed relish the idea of not playing against a sweeper. He led the line admirably and, all over the pitch, there were good performances from a Spurs side that did just enough to beat Chelsea without ever really being troubled...

Then, just as referee Ken Dagnall was looking at his watch, John Boyle, Chelsea's chunky defensive winger, stupidly fouled Terry Venables just over the half-way line.

From Dave Mackay's free-kick the mobile Mullery, playing his finest game, picked up the ball and ran irresistibly on Chelsea's packed goal.

Once again Tommy Docherty's blue-vested men waited to soak up a Spurs attack like a sponge before counter-punching in their own hard-running style.

But Mullery kept on coming and suddenly unleashed a thundering shot which struck poor Ron Harris's shin to rebound, as if directed by Lady Luck herself, straight to the unmarked Robertson standing on the edge of the penalty area.

Robertson, transferred from St Mirren in March 1964 for £23,000, thumped home an unbeatable drive on the half-volley past the helpless Bonetti.

Robertson proved that he is 100 per cent competitor when, on the great football occasion of the year, he took his chance with brilliant aplomb.

With Spurs in elegant ascendancy, Chelsea crashed again. Mackay threw a characteristic throw-in deep into the Chelsea defence. Robertson touched the ball on and there was Frank Saul, who had to sit on the touchlines when Spurs won their last two finals in 1961 and 1962.

A goal did not look 'on', but dramatically Saul swivelled and hit a surprise shot which slid into the corner of the net.
Sunday Express, May 21, 1967

So despite a late Bobby Tambling goal, there was to be no Chelsea comeback, and the first of four all-London Cup finals saw Spurs lift the trophy for the fifth time. There was much merriment and partaking of alcohol in the Hale household that night.

*When we had retrieved our medals from under the table where Dave Mackay had knocked them, Bill Nicholson gave a serious speech about winning the Cup final, saying that we had not played that well, putting us all down, which was not necessarily what we wanted to hear at that particular moment, and Dave shouted out: "Sit down, Bill, you're p*****!" It was typical of Bill, that he was unable to relax and unwind, even on the night of the Cup Final, but he was already thinking and worrying about the next season instead. I spoke to him later that evening and asked him if he was pleased, but all he could say was that he thought we should go into the transfer market before the next season. Bill's enjoyment was always the football, and nothing but the football, unlike Dave Mackay, who was enjoying himself hugely."*
Terry Venables, after the 1967 FA Cup win, from his autobiography 'Venables'

Above: Bill and Tommy Docherty lead out their teams prior to the 1967 FA Cup Final . . .
. . . Below: Dave Mackay has his hands on the Cup after winning the all-London battle with Chelsea.

Spurs' post-final banquet was a great night. Bill Nicholson sat at the head of the top table with the FA Cup always within his reach. Bill wasn't often given to wit, but he was that night. It was always the custom on such nights for everyone with a club to say something about winning the FA Cup. Everyone was waiting to see what Bill had to say and he didn't let us down.

"An after-dinner speech is an odd thing," said Bill. "You eat a meal that you don't want so that you can get up and tell a load of stories you can't remember to people who have already heard them. My father gave me the best advice on after-dinner speaking. Be sincere. Be brief. Be seated. That in mind, ladies and gentlemen, I give you the FA Cup!"

He brought the house down.

Jimmy Greaves, after the final victory over Chelsea, from his autobiography 'Greavsie'

'Big Pat' on why Bill was so special

So far as I'm concerned, Bill was something special. He was manager of Spurs during my first 10 years at White Hart Lane and during that time there must have been over a hundred players on the books. Not all of them got on well with Bill – but there wasn't one who didn't have the greatest respect for him.

That, above all, was the quality that he inspired in each of them, from the youngest apprentice to the most experienced first-teamer. Nobody ever cheated on Bill because he was always straight with the players. He was hard, he could even be unintentionally hurtful in his approach, but if he made a promise it was always kept.

In my eyes, and of all the other professionals at the club, Bill Nicholson was Tottenham Hotspur. He kept the directors at a distance from us and seldom allowed them into the dressing room. If there was anything to be said to us, Bill was the man who said it.

He had few friends outside football – football in general, and Spurs in particular, was his life. Whether you called at the ground early in the morning or late at night, Bill was always there. It was the same on a Sunday if you had to report for treatment.

It's said that when his elder daughter was married, Bill confided to somebody at the wedding reception that the realisation had suddenly dawned on him during the ceremony that he had not really seen his children grow up. I think that's rather sad, yet I'm sure it's true. Bill was married to Spurs as well as to his patient and always cheerful wife Darkie.

Bill kept the players on their toes, and when he entered the dressing room in the morning – in those days he and his assistant Eddie Baily used to change with the rest of us before training – there was a general hush. Nobody clowned around when Bill was about, not even a joker like Jimmy Greaves. Nobody took liberties.

Bill was always the boss, yet, unlike most managers, he never insisted on being called that by the players. On the contrary, the first time I met him – when he was negotiating my transfer from Watford – I naturally called him Mr Nicholson. "You can forget the Mr, my name is Bill," he promptly told me.

I was quite surprised. I was only a kid starting in the game and here was this legendary figure, who had achieved so much, treating me as an equal. I warmed to him on the spot.

Later I found he wasn't an easy man to know, and he took pains to avoid any of the players catching him with his defences down. Yet after an away game, if we were waiting at a railway station or an airport, Bill would often slip skipper Dave Mackay a tenner and tell him to buy the lads a drink. The money came out of his own pocket, but Bill never made a fuss about it. He rarely even joined us at the bar.

There were occasions too, when I would take one of my daughters to the club if I was calling for a brief spot of treatment on a day off. Looking around to collect her, I would find her sitting in Bill's office loaded with crisps and apples. Bill always had time to chat with any of the players' children.

But Bill didn't often mess about – a bad game and you were out. And if your name wasn't on the team-sheet when it was pinned up on Friday, you knew it was up to you to do the business in the reserve side to try to earn a recall. It never occurred to you to knock on the manager's door and complain.

His dream was always to create another fabulous team, and perhaps he became frustrated by failure to hit the jackpot again. When I look back at photographs which span my Tottenham career, there's no doubt we had a succession of talented players on the books at different times. Somewhere along the line we ought to have won the first division, but we were continually haunted by the spectre of the Double side.

He was seldom satisfied, and even after a 4-0 victory he would find fault. The longer-serving players used to tell how Bill had given the team a rollicking after winning 6-1 at West Ham. He wasn't kidding, either. Although it was, by all accounts, a boiling hot afternoon in August, he was furious that Spurs had eased up after taking a 6-0 lead and allowed West Ham to score.

Pat Jennings, from 'Pat Jennings – an autobiography'

Greavsie on 'The Guvnor'

People often go on about Bill being this great disciplinarian, but he and I never really got into that side of it. I often thought that Bill had bought me, and he knew exactly what he wanted from me. As long as I produced it week in week out, he would have made no bones about it. In that respect, we had an understanding – we were both successful at what we did. We both wanted to win football matches.

I probably sounded a bit cocky when I said it, but on one occasion Bill was talking this and that, about how you do this and how you don't, when I chimed up and said: 'Bill, this is all very well, but the simple truth of the matter is either you can play the game or you can't.' It's a fact of life that I was able to talk to Bill like that without him getting p***** off with me. I've no idea why I could, but I don't know many other people at the club who would – or could – have tried it.

We weren't exactly what you would call close, unlike some of the others who were up his a*** most of the time. I mean, I had nine years as a player under him,

and we were good friends, but it would be just to the extent of stopping and saying: "Hello, Bill, how are things?" and such like. We never really got in each other's way.
Jimmy Greaves

The Tottenham Way, or the easy way?

By the mid-60s, the functionalists were becoming more successful, and it seemed that everywhere you looked, teams were sticking to the ethos that to win was more important than to entertain. It must have been very tempting for any manager to cast off the shackles of keeping the fans happy in favour of challenging for honours every year. But not everyone in the football hierarchy felt the same way. Spurs had friends in high places . . .

When I hear players or managers describing their game plans by saying 'we set out to silence the crowd', I cringe. Winning is of course important in football, but winning in an entertaining way is important. Look at some of the great teams. Hungary of 1953, Real Madrid 1956-60, Brazil of 1970 and Holland, or for that matter Ajax of the Cruyff era, in the early to mid 70s. Did they or any team managed by Matt Busby, Bill Nicholson or Jock Stein ever take the pitch with the intention of silencing the crowd? Never.

They were successful and they achieved their success through entertaining football. That is why such teams are all-time greats and remain a benchmark for what can be achieved in football if you go about it in the right and proper way – with style, flair, grace and a desire to be stunning in every sense of the word.
Sir Stanley Matthews, from his autobiography 'The Way it Was'

All teams get old, and even great sides like ours of the early 60s have to break up eventually. Losing John (White) was a terrible blow, but Danny Blanchflower was getting old, along with the likes of Maurice Norman and Bobby Smith. So when the time came to shuffle the pack, Bill knew that the good of Tottenham Hotspur came in front of any personal feelings he may have had for individuals.

Other great players came in, like Terry Venables, Mullers and Jimmy Robertson, and they should have been good enough. But maybe football was changing faster than Spurs were. We liked to play with wingers, but the success of the England team in winning the World Cup in 1966 without recognised wingers encouraged other teams and managers to do the same, and soon it was becoming obvious that the 4-3-3 that won England the World Cup was the way that many of the more successful teams were preferring to play.

That, of course, didn't fit in with the traditional 'Tottenham way' of playing, where the crowd had to be entertained, and it may go some way to explaining why we never quite got close enough to landing the title again. Spurs could have adapted to the new, more negative way of playing, but the Tottenham fans wouldn't have taken to that style and there was no guarantee that it would have been successful.
Cliff Jones

It always seems that whenever some people talk about Bill, they talk about his 'two great teams' – those of the early 60s and the early 70s. But what a lot of people overlook is the fact that the side that won the Cup in 1967 almost got another Double. They ended the season with 56 points, which was more than any Spurs side since 1961.

It may be because they were largely a mixture of the early 60s side and the early 70s side. From the Rotterdam days there was Mackay, Jones, Greaves, and Saul, while from the next team there was myself, Mullers, Cyril Knowles, Joe Kinnear, Pat Jennings, Phil Beal and Gilly. Only Terry Venables and Jimmy Robertson were unique to that side alone.
Mike England

I've always said that it was a crying shame that the side that won the Cup in '67 didn't get more recognition. In spite of the fact that we had a bad run with injuries to key players at vital times, we were unbeaten in our last 16 league games, and if we'd shown that kind of form at the start of the season we could have had another double. Then maybe Bill would have kept going on at future teams about US for a change!
Pat Jennings

Bill Nicholson is a reserved type – but no soft mark. He brought tremendous success to Tottenham and his teams played great football. Bill can be dour. He doesn't say much, but I always got on well with him, and I respect him.
Bill Shankly, from his autobiography 'Shankly'

Youngsters in, veterans out

I was a Spurs fan as a kid growing up in Chingford. My first memories of Bill had come at a very early age, when I used to watch the Double team on the terraces with my father. I was in awe of him, because he was a big name, having just won the Double, and then the FA Cup the next year, and of course the European nights at The Lane, which were so special.

So, to be honest, there was only one club I was interested in joining, and luckily I did when I left school in 1966. I had the choice of five other clubs but my mind was made up. You go to a club like Spurs and just hope to make an impression.

The following year was my apprenticeship year – 1967, the year we won the Cup again – and Bill was like a God to us younger lads. Whenever he would walk into a room, we'd all nudge each other and look his way.

He was a great coach. He liked his teams to be disciplined, but he never had to enforce it, because the players just had so much respect for him. Bill was always immaculately turned out – he never seemed to have a hair out of place, and when he was formally dressed, everything, from his shoes to his hair, was spotless. He and Eddie Baily were such great coaches – and such different characters. Bill, the stubborn, but thorough Yorkshireman, Eddie, the brash and fiery cockney. They were such a great team.
Jimmy Neighbour

I joined Spurs straight from school, and soon found out it wasn't going to be a cakewalk. The kind of things we had to do as apprentices in those days . . . well, lads today just wouldn't put up with it. Bill, however was big on self-discipline and he believed – rightly, in my opinion – that the way to learn respect for your club is to see it from bottom to top. They would have us not just cleaning the boots of the senior pro's, but preparing the dressing rooms on match days, getting the bath area ready for the team and so on. All the kinds of things that Bill himself used to do.

As a youth player at Spurs, Bill had concerns about my physique. Although he knew I had ability, I think he was of the opinion that I was a bit small for a defender. Bill would watch me and the rest of the youngsters to see how we were coming along, and he must have thought I was worth the risk, because they had me on a special diet to get me 'beefed up' a bit. I would do loads of weights work as well, on my own and after everybody else had finished, and eventually it paid off.

There were loads of teams at Spurs, from schoolboy level right up to the first team, and Bill would make it his business to get along to as many games with the youth players as he could. It was nothing out of the ordinary to see him at midweek games on frozen pitches, watching players who may not even make it to the first team. But he would stay out of the way – there was never any question of him going up to the youth team coach and questioning any of his decisions. He just wanted to keep an eye on what was coming through the ranks – I guess in much the same way the Frank Arnesen does today. That way, when they did get to the first team, Bill already knew a fair bit about them.
Phil Beal

It was just six weeks after I'd scored the winning goal in the FA Cup Final that Bill called me into his office. That's never usually a good sign. He told me that he'd had an offer from Southampton for me, and that he was keen on a young lad there by the name of Martin Chivers. That suggested a player-plus cash arrangement. He made it quite clear that the decision would be entirely mine – there was no pressure on me to go.

I gave the matter some thought. I'd been at Spurs for many years, seen some great times, but the truth is that I always felt that I was going to be knocking on the door of the first team without actually establishing myself. At Saints, I would have a half-decent chance of regular football, so I agreed to go. The trouble is, of course, that once you'd been at a club like Tottenham, almost any move you made after that would be down.
Frank Saul

The England-Scotland fixture provoked some tribal passions in first division dressing rooms. Some clubs had almost as many Scottish players as English ones. Tottenham's Bill Nicholson, one of the most successful club managers of the 60s, insisted that at least two Scottish players were essential components in all of his teams. During his time at White Hart Lane he had some of the great Scotsmen of that era – Bill Brown, Dave Mackay, Alan Gilzean and John White.

It was Bill who first recognised the potential in an Edinburgh lad called Graeme Souness.

Sir Geoff Hurst, from his autobiography '1966 and All That'

There had always been a close bond, a sort of friendly rivalry, between Spurs and Burnley ever since our close tussles at the start of the 60s. They really were some classic games, and Bill had remained friends with the Burnley manager Harry Potts ever since. So when it was becoming clear that I was in demand at White Hart Lane, Burnley allowed Spurs to talk to me. I really didn't want to leave Turf Moor – I had a close bond with the fans there – but if I had to go anywhere, it would have been to Spurs.

I had previous experience of working with Bill Nick ever since he took the England Under-23 side on tour in the late 60s. I knew him as a straight-talking, no-nonsense man who you could stake your life on, and there was absolutely no question that I would not come to London. The really amazing thing is that, by today's standards, the whole transfer went through like lightning. Bill and Harry actually did the deal, after a bit of horse-trading, on a handshake. No bits of paper, no agents lurking on their shoulders – it was all so gentlemanly. It sums up both men perfectly, as far as I'm concerned. You just couldn't imagine that happening today.

Ralph Coates

When I was a kid, nine out of 10 boys wanted to become footballers. To sign for Spurs, and in particular Bill Nicholson, was the icing on the cake, because it's only once you'd worked with him that you realised just how good he was. Even more so after he left, because then some of the things he'd told you make even more sense than before.

I was a bit of a rarity with most of the Spurs boys at the time, in that I'd been working down the meat markets for three years since I was 15, getting up at four o'clock in the morning. I got a trial for Tottenham through a guy called Fred Rye, who was an ex-boxer and a staunch Spurs supporter. I was at Millwall at the time, on apprentice terms. Fred actually knew Bill – he used to travel all over the place with the club, and although in those days, Bill didn't have much contact with supporters, he knew Fred well enough to listen when he said I was worth a trial.

A few weeks before that, Millwall boys had played Spurs, and I'd said to myself at the time: 'I reckon I might have a chance here, playing for this lot.' So Fred organised the trial, and I can remember him saying to me: "Terry – I've stuck my neck out here, mate – don't you let me down."

I got in, and was initially training two nights a week as an amateur. In fact, on Saturdays I was playing for Spurs in the morning and Edmonton (Southern League) in the afternoon. I worked my way up, and at one stage was captain of the youth team when there were eight apprentices in it.

Then one day I was at home in Barnsbury Road when I got a telegram saying that I was playing in the reserves at Crystal Palace, and that Bill wanted to go along and watch me. It was also to be Ray Evans' debut as well. We won 3-1, and Bill had a chat with me after the game. Then in the week, Bill called me into the office and he signed me as a full pro.

That was it – it didn't matter if a car ran over me after that, because my ambition had been fulfilled. I had signed not only for a big club, but also for Bill Nicholson.
Terry Naylor

When my Spurs contract was coming up in 1968, I decided to ask for a lot more, as we'd won the Cup by then. It was the first time I'd ever thought of doing so. But I wasn't really brave enough to face Bill Nick on my own, so I decided to go in and see him with Jimmy Robertson. We discussed beforehand what we were going to say, what we would demand.

When we got into Bill's office, we sat there side by side, in front of his desk. He was reading some documents, which made us both very nervous. He eventually says yes, he's going to offer us both a new two-year contract. He hands us both a sheet each, inside a folder, which we both look at and try to understand. There were no agents in those days, no lawyers to help you. A player was on his own, trying to work out what the language meant. And no player I knew ever thought of asking them to throw in extra perks, a clothes allowance, new carpets, a travel allowance, a car, an extra car for the wife, none of the ludicrous perks that agents get written into players' contracts today.

So we sat looking at our sheets, puzzling out the words. Bill says "Yes, any problems?" We both froze. Neither knew what to say, despite all the things we'd agreed to demand. In turn we said: "Yeah, that sounds all right by me," and then we stood up and walked out. A complete couple of chickens. Once we got outside, we asked each other what we'd got. We got exactly the same, in the same words. I think there was a small rise, taking us up to about £40 a week.

Bill himself earned very little. He was always telling us what a wonderful life we had; just think of the people struggling down the pits. He said we were lucky – and we believed him.
Joe Kinnear

There had been a bit of contract haggling with one or two of us, and I suppose you could say it had caused a bit of tension. It was no secret that Bill didn't really have a lot of time for that side of things – he just seemed to see it as a necessary evil. It really didn't have any effect on my performances, at least I thought it didn't, but Bill might have held a different opinion.

The club was in transition at the time, in between the side that had landed the cup in '67 and the side that Bill was hoping would lead us into the 70s. People like Jimmy Greaves and Dave Mackay were not the force they once were, and I think Bill was looking for some new blood. Then an offer came in for me from Arsenal, and Bill sort of just said: "Jimmy, it's your choice." Bertie Mee was known to be quite keen on me, and was prepared to offer David Jenkins as a straight swap.

I thought it over, and decided that it was for the best. I never quite got to the

heights with Arsenal that I did with Spurs, but sometimes you just have to do what
you think is right.
Jimmy Robertson

It's said that in life, everybody's entitled to one mistake – or in Bill's case, two
– and they were called Laurie Brown and David Jenkins. Strange, but they both
came from Arsenal . . .
Spurs fan Doug Fraser

"Get Mackay? You must be bloody joking."
Derby County manager Brian Clough, speaking to his No.2, Peter Taylor

If there was a single moment of inspiration that transformed Derby from a
humdrum, dilapidated down-in-the-dumps club, it was when Taylor took me on
one side, scanned the young names in the team like McFarland, John Robson,
O'Hare and Hector, and said, in an extremely serious tone of voice: 'We must get
some experience into this side. Go out and try to sign Mackay.'
"Get Mackay?" I said to Taylor. "You must be bloody joking.''
To me, like most people throughout the country, Dave Mackay was the famous
Tottenham Hotspur wing-half, a very big name, someone we used to read about in
the newspapers.
But he remained adamant – Taylor at his far-seeing, selective, inspirational best.
"Go and try," he repeated. "You've pulled off bigger things than this." Even
though he didn't offer an example, I jumped in my car and drove to London.
I was nervous as hell. Arriving at White Hart Lane from the Baseball Ground
was like turning up at Buckingham Palace having just left a Wimpy bar. I took a
deep breath and just bowled in. I can't remember how it happened – whether he
had just wandered into the entrance or somebody had marked his card – but Bill
Nicholson suddenly appeared before me. Nicholson: one of the great managers,
whose team had not only won major trophies but had done it with a style and flair
and honesty that I hoped my teams might emulate. I felt like a bit of an impostor –
a beginner in his field, about to try and take away one of his most influential and
famous players.
I was in awe of Bill Nick at that moment, but I kept hearing the words of Taylor,
repeated over and over in my head: 'Go on – you've pulled off bigger things than
this'. Like Hell I had! But I was brash and cocky in those days. I dismissed my
uncertainty long enough to blurt out: 'I've come to sign Dave Mackay.'
I'm sure dear old Bill smiled a little in a fatherly kind of way while he resisted
telling me to turn round and get back in my car. Instead he told me: 'Well, as far
as I know, he's off to Scotland tomorrow to become assistant manager of Hearts.'
I persisted. 'But can I have a word with him?' I never got an answer, because at
that moment Nicholson's phone rang and he disappeared, saying only that
Mackay was out training. I went and sat on a chair in a passageway for what
seemed like an entire day.
Eventually Dave Mackay, he of the barrel-chest, the League and Cup Double

and 20-odd Scottish caps, came striding in, as only he could. Still in his training gear, he came towards me, hand outstretched. I was only three or four years younger than him, but I remember thinking, 'Christ, he looks 10 years older than me.' No shuffling of feet or uneasy, embarrassing loss of words – I came straight out with it: 'I've come to have a word about you joining Derby.'

"There's no chance," he said. "I'm going back to Hearts tomorrow, to be assistant manager. That's it."

"Tell you what," I said. "Go and get in a nice bath and then we'll have a chat. You never know your luck."

Brian Clough, from 'Clough – the autobiography'

After much horse-trading between himself and Brian Clough, Dave Mackay signed for Derby County 24 hours later. At the end of his first season at the Baseball Ground, Mackay led the Rams to the second division championship – and provided the platform for Derby to go on to win the first division title just three years later. In Derby, many observers still believe Mackay was Clough's best-ever signing.

The Scottish international had been at Spurs for an amazing and unforgettable 12 years, in which arguably Bill's greatest-ever signing won a League and three FA Cup winners' medals and cruelly missed out on a European Cup Winners Cup medal in Rotterdam.

He was such an inspiration, the Governor, on and off the pitch. Bill Nick later told me that he could never find another player to replace Mackay.

Joe Kinnear

It was always going to be a wrench leaving QPR, having spent seven very happy years there, but at the time they needed the money and there were some big name clubs supposedly interested in me, including Newcastle, Chelsea and, of course, Tottenham. It was purely and simply a career move for me, and with Spurs being one of the top sides in the country, it made sense to pick them.

Things had been very different at Rangers. They were a west London club, and that area at the time was really part of the whole 'Kings Road' scene. So Bill signs me, 22-years-old and quite full of myself, and I turn up at my new club in a working-class area of North London in my MGB, with shoulder-length hair, flairs and a kipper tie.

There wasn't just a generation gap between Bill and me, but also a culture gap, and I think from day one Bill and I were destined to give each other grief. He came from a different world – short, immaculately groomed hair, perfect creases in his trousers, and he even had those elasticated metal armbands for keeping your sleeves rolled up.

I knew almost from the off that he didn't approve of the way I looked, but that was the fashion at the time, and we were both strong characters. I guess things got worse when a few of the other Spurs lads followed suit and started wearing their hair a bit longer as well! What had I started?

The training, though, was incredible. I had just joined a top Division One club, and the way things were set out was unbelievable. I had worked with some damn good coaches and managers at Loftus Road – Terry Venables, Tommy Docherty, Alex Stock to name but three – but Bill was right up there. His tactical knowledge, and the understanding that he and Eddie Baily had about what his players could and couldn't do, was something to see.

This club had won just about everything. It was as if the walls of the place were echoing to the sound of push-and-run. There was a definite difference at Spurs to QPR. When I had been at Rangers, I don't remember ever having a bad game, but with the array of talent I was surrounded by at Tottenham, I guess the standards they demanded were that much higher.

For all our differences, though, I had the utmost respect for Bill Nicholson. How could you not have? His knowledge of the game was top class, and not for one second do I regret going to Tottenham. It was just a personality thing between Bill and me – if I'd gone there at another time in my life, perhaps when fashions weren't quite so extreme, things might have been different.
Roger Morgan

The Unthinkable – Spurs without Greaves

By 1970, the last remnants of the great Spurs side of the early 60s were fading away. Dave Mackay had gone to Derby County – only Jimmy Greaves remained.

I took the rally driving so seriously that Bill Nicholson took it as a sign that I was losing my appetite for football and had resigned myself to winding down my career and concentrating on my business interests. I was becoming something of a millstone to Bill. It was none of my doing really, but as Spurs were having a hard time of it, every time he announced a team without my name on it, the press picked him up on it. Eventually I got fed up kicking my heels in the reserves and I asked Bill about my future.

The memories of that conversation are a bit woolly. I think both of us believed that the best thing would be for me to move on, but we were reluctant to commit ourselves to the break. As with marriages and long-term relationships, the decision to split is often easier than the actual mechanics of breaking up. So it was with Bill and myself. Our meeting ended with Bill deciding we both needed thinking time in which to mull over the situation.

Bill talked to the Tottenham board 'in confidence' about my future. In football, six people can keep a secret as long as five of them are dead.

On transfer deadline day, March 16, 1970, Irene and I were moving house once again. Little did I realise that moving house was not the only move I would be making that day.

The telephone rang. It was Bill Nicholson. Bill informed me that he was at the club and that he had Martin Peters with him, who had agreed to join Spurs from West Ham United. Bill went on to say that he was selling me to West Ham as a makeweight in the deal for Martin.

I was taken aback and angry. I was so annoyed with Bill for wanting to bring my

BILL NICHOLSON

Spurs career to an end and I simply said: "Okay. If you don't want me at Spurs, I'll go." I didn't have to go, not if I didn't want to. I still had 18 months on my contract to run. I could have told Bill I was staying at Spurs and there was little he could have done about it. But I was so peeved that he appeared so willing to get rid of me, I went along with it. What's the point of staying at a club that doesn't want you?

Looking back at that day, I wish I had told Bill I wasn't interested in moving. He could have still signed Martin Peters because, as the makeweight, I had been valued at £90,000 in a deal worth £220,000 to West Ham. Spurs could have paid the full fee for Martin and kept me.

Jimmy Greaves, from his autobiography 'Greavsie'

We couldn't believe Bill had done it. We were gobsmacked. Jimmy was still a great player.

Alan Mullery, from the 'Little Book of Spurs'.

A tough act to follow . . .

I had let Martin Peters go to Tottenham in exchange for Jimmy Greaves, because he felt he was the 'third man'. He believed the other two were getting all the credit and limelight. He saw himself as a sort of quiz question 'Who scored England's other goal in the World Cup final?' – with most people getting the answer wrong. Martin was a very likeable person but he became fed up and eventually sure in his own mind that things would be different elsewhere. He began to ask for a move regularly but I did not agree immediately because once again I felt it important he should go to the right kind of club. He needed a manager who understood what his game was all about.

Tottenham, I felt, would be best of all, so I rang Bill Nicholson and said I wanted a chat with him. We agreed to meet outside Chingford greyhound stadium (author's note – Walthamstow Stadium) a convenient halfway point, and we arrived there almost together. I got into Bill's car and at this point he still didn't know why I wanted to see him.

"Martin wants away. What do you think?" I said. Bill's face lit up. We talked about values but I had a deal already in mind. "What about a straight swap for Greavsie?" I asked him. Agreement was immediate. Bill was getting rather the better of the bargain because Jimmy wasn't doing much at Tottenham at the time, but I knew a change could sometimes work wonders. I fancied a go.

The two players were happy and Jimmy even said to me: "Just give me a blank contract and I'll sign it." I felt Jim would give us a new kind of target to play up to and would score those few extra goals which can make such a difference over a season.

In his first outing for us, he scored twice against Manchester City. He was so pleased he asked me if he could wear his number 10 shirt home.

I think everyone believed he would go on scoring like that, but he enjoyed a drink or three, this chap, and his interest in football was cooling fast. He was at the crossroads of his career when he joined West Ham. It was a worthwhile gamble

but it didn't quite pay off.
Ron Greenwood

I was very happy to speak to Bill Nicholson, and Bill obviously took a chance in letting Jimmy go because he was the greatest goalscorer England ever had. But maybe Spurs needed new players because the last time they had won something was 1967. Bill was trying to strengthen the side with a view to winning more trophies.
Martin Peters

So Jimmy Greaves, the mercurial goal machine of Tottenham, was gone, and so was the last member of the great side of the early 60s. A new generation of Spurs fans would soon be watching another of Bill's marvellous teams – and they would have new heroes and new memories. Where Bill Nicholson had brought great success to North London at the early part of the previous decade, so he would again in the next.

Martin Peters – another shrewd signing who made his mark in the early 70s.

Chapter 7
The Class of '71

"The golden age was never the present age."
Benjamin Franklin

The 70s dawned with the realisation that football had changed irreversibly from its golden age, when Bill had led Spurs to such memorable heights a decade earlier. Some would argue that there was a cynicism creeping into the national sport, and that money was not the only double-headed dragon rearing its ugly head: the need for clubs to win a trophy had gone from something the supporters had once simply wished for, to something they expected. Failure was met with scorn rather than sympathy.

Bill knew that the fans of his beloved Tottenham were used to their club being at the forefront of football's annual tussle. But he also knew that, from now on, players would often go where the trophies and the headlines would seek them out, and that loyalty, while still something that was dear to Tottenham Hotspur, was not a quality that was destined to flourish in the game for much longer.

It was time to deliver.

Bill was a very 'correct' man in the way he went about things, from transfers and contracts, to coaching and how he expected his players to behave. I see players nowadays doing things that Bill would never have stood for in a million years. He would always tell us 'never get so close to an attacker that you cannot see the ball – that way, he can't turn you. Leave at least a yard.' Sounds obvious, really, but it was little things like that – teaching his players good habits – than made playing under him so special.
Phil Beal

Bill Nick was a great manager. I admired him greatly and had some great years with him. I played for him in four cup finals – and we won them all. Shows he was doing something right. If he had a fault, it was often that he made out the opposition to be better than they were. Now and again he would frighten the life out of us, making their defenders sound 10 feet tall and their attackers seem better than Pele. I know he was just trying to stop us becoming complacent but I think at times he overdid it.

We also had the Double team hanging over us. He was always on about them, and made us feel a bit inferior, that we would never be up to their level. You rarely got praise out of Bill. Being picked – that was the most praise you ever got. But his record as a manager was remarkable. He was a perfectionist, who ate, slept

and lived for Spurs.
Joe Kinnear

Bill loved to create sides that were great entertainment, but he told me that I used to give him palpitations at times. As a central defender, you often have to make a snap decision on what to do, and if you are in any doubt, you try and hit the guy in row 16.

There were many times when a ball would come across, and rather than just whack it away, I'd either chest it down and play it, or I'd head it back to Pat. Bill once said to me: "Mike, that's okay as long as you're absolutely sure. If you are convinced of what you're doing, that's fine – but central defenders don't usually get a second chance when they balls things up. A midfielder or a forward can lose the ball, and there's usually somebody who will spare his blushes. But whereas I tell Jimmy (Greaves) to take people on, and I know that if he loses the ball it won't hurt us, in your case I leave it up to you.

"Just remember that when it works, it's brilliant. When it doesn't, and it costs us dear, you'll hear all about it."
Mike England

I'd known nothing like the training at Spurs. Bill's ideas were fantastic, and you watched what he did and everything seemed to make perfect sense. He was five minutes in front of most other managers. Plus, you were in awe of some of the big name players around you – and when you see them taking it all on board, you can't help but do the same.

Someone once said to me that if somebody spoke to you for two hours, and only one thing registered, it was worth the chat. Well, with Bill, I'd say that 90 per cent of it registered. Whether you were good enough to do it – well, that's another thing. That's what Bill was there for – to coach you.

With Bill, if you won your games, you could get away with a bit. Especially on tour, he'd think nothing of letting players go out late. If you got back at three in the morning, fine – as long as it didn't affect your performance at training the next morning, and as long as you kept yourself away from trouble, unlike some of the lads you read about today.

Bill wasn't an easy bloke to get to know, but I reckon he preferred it that way. You had to have that bit of distance, and that's why I think he had that air of authority about him.

Bill knew that everybody in his teams was there to do a job. As much as he liked to have the players who could turn on the magic, he also expected them to know that they'd be lost without the 'hard men'. And don't forget – there was a standard in Bill's teams that all his players – and I mean ALL his players - had to keep up to. So just as he expected the ball-players to dig in a bit when things got tough, so the rest of us had to know what to do with the ball. If anybody didn't do their jobs, he'd soon let them know. Everybody had a role to do, and we all knew that.

Bill would have so much knowledge on his opponents, you wouldn't believe it. He'd go through all their players like a scientist – 'This guy doesn't like you running at him, the keeper doesn't like crosses – so you went at their weaknesses. At the same time, he knew his own players like they were his sons, so when he looked at the opposition players, he would look at their strengths and see straight away where they would cause us problems in certain positions.

He and Eddie would then go about telling us how we could counter those threats – but quite often, he could only do so much, because if a player was that good, and occasionally some of them were, there wasn't much you could do about it anyway.
Terry Naylor

Training under Bill could be tough, but he had a lighter side. Bill would enjoy a laugh and a bit of a giggle with players, but you knew that there was a time for it and a time not for it. He didn't get too many egos, mainly due to who he was. Some egos may have come out with other managers, but not Bill. He didn't take nonsense.

I learnt a hell of a lot from Bill, and not just football wise. He taught us that you have got to have a bit of self-respect. There are plenty of little skills he used to teach us that we still pass on to the youngsters at Spurs today. All right, the game's got a lot quicker nowadays and a lot more physical, but it's still football, it's still 11 against 11, and you've still got to score in those little white posts, and that will never change.
Jimmy Neighbour, under-16s coach at Spurs

Bill used to insist that we treated friendlies as proper games. No matter who we were playing or whatever for, he did not want a Tottenham Hotspur side to lose.

The club would run two kinds of tours. There were those that were held in places like the USA and Japan, which were basically money-making exercises for the club. Then there were the ones that were largely for the lads to have a bit of a sun-bathe, let off some steam and so on. But no matter what the tour, Bill insisted that we didn't let the club down.

It's quite well known that Bill treated his players like adults, and he would never frown on them having a good old drink after a game. But you could just see his face if we were out hitting the town and making merry if we'd lost, or God help us if we'd played badly and still thought we deserved to live it up. He would not be amused.
Phil Beal

Bill was hard to please, I think it's fair to say. We'd just beaten Blackpool, who at the time were a good side. I'd had possibly my best game and was feeling really good about myself.

In the changing room after, Bill was going around the players, doing what Bill would do, and I was waiting for him to tell me how well I'd played. I'd been up against Jimmy Armfield, who was an ex-England full-back, and as experienced a defender you could find. I'd given him a right torrid time. I waited, but the expected praise never came, so I thought I'd ask him.

"Bill," I said, pleased as punch with myself. "What do you reckon on me today?

I had Jimmy Armfield in my pocket."

"I should bloody well hope you would," he replied. "Jimmy's an old man."
Roger Morgan

It wasn't the same at Spurs as it had been at Burnley – there were so many quality players that you knew that one bad performance and you were in the reserves. I'm not talking about mistakes – they happen, I guess – but rather just a lack of concentration or effort. Bill would not tolerate that under any circumstances.

I can't remember which game it was, but we were 2-0 up and both goals had come from my crosses. I came in feeling pretty pleased with myself, and all of a sudden Bill says to me: "Coatsie, what were you thinking of with that cross? If you had connected properly, players were unmarked." He was referring to the fact that I had put in a cross and, instead of reaching a white shirt, the ball had hit the post and gone out.

I brought it to Bill's attention that I had supplied two very good crosses for our goals, but he just laid into me all the more, saying: "I'm not interested in all that, listen to what I'm telling you." I was slightly miffed, but we just got used to it with Bill.

He wasn't an ogre, or course. You hear of managers imposing curfews and the like, but Bill knew we were grown men and he treated us that way. He would allow us to go out and have a good time – and there were quite a few at the club who knew how to do that all right – but come the next morning at training, God help anybody who wasn't up for it. Bill and Eddie would make his life hell if they thought any player was selling them or the club short because they had overdone it the night before.
Ralph Coates

Bill shows the way in training before the 1971 League Cup Final.

BILL NICHOLSON

Football League Cup

Spurs' Road To Wembley

Second Round, White Hart Lane
September 9, 1970
Tottenham Hotspur 3 Swansea City 0
Spurs made heavy going in this match against third division opposition, who never looked like bringing off a shock, but seemed intent on making their first division aristocratic opponents work for the win.
Scorers: Martin Peters, Roger Morgan, Steve Perryman

Third Round, White Hart Lane
October 7, 1970
Tottenham Hotspur 2 Sheffield United 1
Another side renowned for 'digging in', the Blades did just that in another battle at The Lane. Jimmy Pearce came on for the injured Roger Morgan, missed two half-chances then scored, having received some grief from the crowd in the process.
Scorers: Jimmy Pearce, Martin Chivers

Fourth Round, White Hart Lane
October 28, 1970
Tottenham Hotspur 5 West Bromwich Albion 0
Traditional cup specialists West Brom produced another gritty performance by a lowly team against Spurs. But they had no answer to the guile and craft of Gilzean, who scored two, and Peters, who notched his first hat-trick in a Spurs shirt.
Scorers: Martin Peters 3, Alan Gilzean 2

Fifth Round, White Hart Lane
November 18, 1970
Tottenham Hotspur 4 Coventry City 1
Another tough, fiercely contested battle against an emergent Coventry side, who had the audacity to take an early lead. Spurs then asserted themselves, led 2-1, but faced a spirited resistance from the Sky Blues until the last few minutes, when two late goals put Spurs into the semi-finals, courtesy of a Chivers hat-trick.
Scorers: Martin Chivers (3), Alan Gilzean

Semi-final, first leg, Ashton Gate
December 16, 1970
Bristol City 1 Tottenham Hotspur 1
After a gruelling, hard-fought goal-less first half, second division City took the lead after a mix up in the Spurs penalty area. This led to a sustained period of pressure from the West Country outfit, until Gilly headed home an equaliser. Then

118

it was City's turn to hang on until the final whistle.
Scorer: Alan Gilzean

Semi-Final, second leg, White Hart Lane
December 23, 1970
Tottenham Hotspur 2 Bristol City 0 (AET)
Spurs won 3-1 on agg.
Bill had devised a plan to avoid the same dogged resistance that City had offered
in the first leg, but his opponents served up a repeat performance to take the game,
goalless, into extra time. Class told in the end, with two late goals putting Spurs
back at Wembley for the first time in four years.
Scorers: Martin Chivers, Jimmy Pearce

League Cup Final
Wembley Stadium
February 27, 1971
Tottenham Hotspur 2 Aston Villa 0

Spurs: Pat Jennings, Joe Kinnear, Cyril Knowles, Alan Mullery, Mike England,
Phil Beal, Alan Gilzean, Steve Perryman, Martin Chivers, Martin Peters, Jimmy
Neighbour. Sub: Jimmy Pearce
Scorer: Chivers (2)

Bill with two-goal Martin Chivers and Alan Mullery after beating Aston Villa in the 1971 League Cup Final at Wembley – the club's first success in this competition.

119

Bill wasn't afraid to do something if he thought it was right, and he gave me my full debut against Bristol City in the second leg of the semi-final of the League Cup. I was 19! I had no idea that, four games later, I would be playing at Wembley in the final.

Then suddenly, there I was – I had made it. It seemed like one minute I was an overwhelmed kid looking around me at all these guys with medals to their name – don't forget, when I came to Spurs, the likes of Cliff Jones, Dave Mackay and Jimmy Greaves were still there – and the next, I was standing on the pitch at Wembley holding a winners' medal.
Jimmy Neighbour

There was no way that we were going to be complacent about playing a third division side in the League Cup final. A couple of years before, Arsenal had been beaten at Wembley by Swindon Town, and Aston Villa were a good side. They had big Andy Lockhead up front, and he was a real handful. Bill, of course, would make sure that we knew everything about all their players, and he was doing his thing, running through them one by one, telling us what each one was good at.

One or two of the lads suggested the idea – not out loud, of course – that if Villa were that good, why were they in the third division? Bill's answer, I think, would have been something like: 'If they weren't that good, how could they get to the final?'
Pat Jennings

'PAIN AT THE LANE'
Tottenham Hotspur 0 Arsenal 1
Football League Division One
May 3, 1971

As a Spurs fan of many years, this is without doubt the hardest and least satisfying piece I have ever had to write. But football is about ups and downs, about struggle and joy, and it also reveals that players, managers and supporters have to deal with the highs and lows of the beautiful game. How they deal with the lows says as much about them as how they enjoy the highs.

Ours is a game of extremes. Just as it can lift you into the clouds, it can put you in the gutter just as quickly. With the 1970-71 season drawing to a close, there could be no more dramatic ending if some master dramatist had planned it.

Spurs, having already landed silverware in the shape of the League Cup, simply had to stop their arch-rivals winning on our hallowed ground to prevent them from landing the league title.

Bill could only stand and watch. It was the classic battle of the master swordsman against the ugly giant armed with a hammer, played on a beach that passed for a pitch. With even more than local pride at stake, neither dared lose...

We were queuing round the ground the night of that game. I can still remember a very strange fact – that in those queues, you could see blue and white scarves

mixed in with red and white ones. You would think, with what was at stake, it wouldn't have happened. You'd never see it today. I just wish Bill and Spurs had had a bit of the rub of the green that night – because Arsenal's win proved beyond any shadow of a doubt that the day of the artists was over.
Tom Hennessey, supporter

As a man who cared passionately about Tottenham's fans, Bill was absolutely adamant that we shouldn't concede the league title to Arsenal on our own ground. None of us, of course, needed reminding that they were already in the Cup Final, and that Spurs sort of had ownership of the Double. Now that was under threat, and Bill Nick did not want to see it given up lightly.

It wasn't a spectacular match – there was too much riding on it, and it was an end-of-season game on a pudding of a White Hart Lane pitch, which was more sand than grass in those days. It was a real blood-and thunder sort of game, but to lose it so late, even though we nearly got back at them at the finish, was a sickener.

Fortunately, we got off the pitch before the Arsenal crowd swarmed on – it must have been hell for our fans to have to watch it. (Author's note – it was).

Back in the dressing room, we were all quite down. Bill, you could see by the look on his face, was devastated. He was Tottenham through and through, he'd been the manager that had landed the Double, and here it was almost in the hands of our biggest rivals. But he was also friendly with Bertie Mee, and he had the nobility to walk into their dressing room and congratulate them. However much it hurt him, I believe he meant it.
Mike England

Spurs' Road to Wembley, 1973

Second Round, White Hart Lane
September 6, 1972
Tottenham Hotspur 2 Huddersfield Town 1
A scoreline that gives a misleading impression that this was a close game, when in fact Spurs were never in much danger of throwing this one away, but doing just enough to get the job done. It would be interesting to have heard Bill's thoughts on that.
Scorers: Alan Gilzean, Martin Chivers

Third Round, Second Replay, White Hart Lane
October 30, 1972
Tottenham Hotspur 2 Middlesbrough 1
Having drawn the first game at home, courtesy of a Jimmy Pearce goal, then seen a goal-less draw at Ayresome Park, Spurs won the toss for a home draw, and got through another tough encounter with second division opponents.
Scorers: Martin Peters, Alan Gilzean

BILL NICHOLSON

Fourth Round, White Hart Lane
November 1, 1972
Tottenham Hotspur 2 Millwall 0
A London derby against second division Millwall saw a huge police operation prevent a potentially explosive crowd problem. The game itself was nowhere near as dramatic, with two goals enough to steer Spurs through against the South Londoners.
Scorers: Steve Perryman, Martin Peters

Fifth Round Replay, White Hart Lane
December 6, 1972
Tottenham Hotspur 3 Liverpool 1
After an unlikely draw at Anfield against the league leaders, Spurs hammered three goals past a stunned Liverpool defence in an early blitz at White Hart Lane. Although Liverpool pulled a goal back, it was never going to be enough. Many have said this was once of Tottenham's finest ever games – a glowing testimony to all who were involved. Scorers: John Pratt, Martin Chivers (2)

Semi Final, first leg, Molineux
December 20, 1972
Wolverhampton Wanderers 1 Tottenham Hotspur 2
Spurs, as in their successful first leg of the UEFA Cup final the season before, scored two goals at Wolves' Midlands fortress, before a late penalty conceded by Cyril Knowles made it a jittery conclusion to the game.
Scorers: John Pratt, Martin Chivers

Semi-Final, second leg, White Hart Lane
December 30, 1972
Tottenham Hotspur 2 Wolverhampton Wanderers 2
As in the European game the season before, Spurs seemed to overlook the fact that Wolves can bite when they are wounded. After falling behind, Spurs equalised, but then sat back. A late Wolves goal took the game into extra time – but the drama was not over yet, because Chiv displayed his penchant for the dramatic with a last-gasp goal in extra-time to take Spurs through.
Scorers: Martin Peters, Martin Chivers

League Cup Final
Wembley Stadium
March 3, 1973
Tottenham Hotspur 1 Norwich City 0
Scorer: Coates
Spurs: Pat Jennings, Joe Kinnear, Cyril Knowles, John Pratt, (sub Ralph Coates), Mike England, Phil Beal, Alan Gilzean, Steve Perryman, Martin Chivers, Martin Peters, Jimmy Pearce

We had played well throughout that whole League Cup campaign, and Bill obviously felt that we shouldn't need any motivating to play at Wembley. He had a minimum requirement of the standard he expected from his sides, but that day was difficult. Norwich didn't really come with much ambition other than to defend and hope for a breakaway, and when teams do that it's sometimes difficult to do yourself justice.

After Ralph Coates came on for Pratty, you could see he was like a terrier, chasing everything, and when he scored it was no great surprise. The move was something we had worked at on the training ground, and it's quite satisfying when things like that come off. Ralph hit it as sweet as a nut, and their keeper didn't get close to it.

In the past, Bill would maybe have been a bit disgruntled that it wasn't the exhibition-type football that Spurs fans had become used to; but he also now realised that it was a way back into Europe, and having had a taste of that life, he was delighted to get another shot at it.

Climbing up those 39 steps to receive a trophy at Wembley is a feeling that you can't put into words. I'd done it in 1966 with England, but this time I was captain and that in itself is such a magical feeling.
Martin Peters

Martin Peters lifts the League Cup as skipper after victory against Norwich City in 1973.

I had a slight injury which I don't think Bill wanted to risk in a major Wembley Cup Final. I'd told Bill it was okay, but I think he had a little bit of doubt in his mind so he left me out. It was a little disappointing to start with, but the day ended on a terrific note for me and I will never forget it. I came off the bench to score and it was a terrific feeling.

BILL NICHOLSON

It was a move we had worked on in training. Martin Chivers took a long throw in, Alan Gilzean, who was great in the air, flicked it on and I came running in from outside the box, knowing exactly where the ball would land. I managed to keep my shot low, and it went in the bottom corner past the Norwich keeper. Scoring the winning goal at Wembley is something you always dream about.

If Steve Perryman hadn't caught me and grabbed hold of my shirt, I think I would still be running round Wembley now!

Ralph Coates

Ralph Coates trying not to let his Wembley heroics in 1973 go to his head.

Tottenham Hotspur 0 Middlesbrough 4
League Cup, Second Round
September 11, 1974

I can remember getting home from this game and throwing myself down on the bed in disgust. Middlesbrough, I thought…'bloody Middlesbrough!'. They weren't the kind of team then that was packed with the international quality they have nowadays. They were a workmanlike, well-organised side with a few talented individuals, but that night they had played us off the park like we were a Southern League side. It was a gutless, disorganised shambles of a performance that was as far removed from the ideals of Bill Nicholson as it was possible to get.

All sorts of thoughts ran through my mind – like clearing the squad out. Fielding the reserves. Going into the transfer market like there was no tomorrow. But it's strange, the one thing that never occurred to me for a moment was to get rid of Bill Nick. Many managers have been and gone since, and every time we had a bad sequence of results, the first thing that reared its ugly head was the possibility of a change of regime. But Bill? Never . . .

Bill was coming to the end of his time. His touch was probably failing. He didn't seem in tune with all the new things happening, the new tactics, the new attitudes, the new ways of doing things, on and off the pitch. He'd begun to say to himself lots of times, that he didn't like the way football was going, all the money coming in, all the greed and commercialisation. In his day, as he was always telling us, people played for the love of the game, as he had done.

The 1973-74 season was pretty horrendous. We ended 11th in the first division. The next season began very badly. It was clear Bill would be going soon.

He did discuss with me who I thought should take over. His idea was to hand it on to Johnny Giles and Danny Blanchflower – Johnny as player-manager, Danny as sort of general manager. I thought this was a good idea. I admired both of them, and had played with both of them. Johnny had been player-manager of Ireland for a time.

I discussed with Bill the chances of me joining the staff in some capacity. He said it was a hard job, coaching, trying to keep everyone happy. But he was quite encouraging. Me and Bill used to discuss players a lot, the younger ones coming through, how they were developing, what their chances were. One of them was Glenn Hoddle who became a Spurs apprentice in 1974. Yes, you didn't have to be a genius to recognise his natural talents.

In my mind, I saw myself as being a youth coach, then slowly coming up through the ranks and one day managing Spurs. That was my fantasy.
Joe Kinnear

If Spurs fans thought things couldn't get any worse, they were in for one hell of a shock. Not only had the club just had its name dragged through the gutter after that horrendous night in Rotterdam, but they had also suffered their first defeat in any major final. The signs were there that things were beginning to go awry. But,

BILL NICHOLSON

following a less-than-inspiring start to the 1974-75 season, and after a 4-0 home thumping by Middlesbrough in the League Cup, the unthinkable happened. After 16 glorious years and eight trophies, Bill Nicholson resigned as manager of Tottenham Hotspur.

The public can't be kidded. They know what they want to see, what is good, what is bad and what is just average. At least I believe they do.
Bill Nicholson

PART 3
LIFE GOES ON

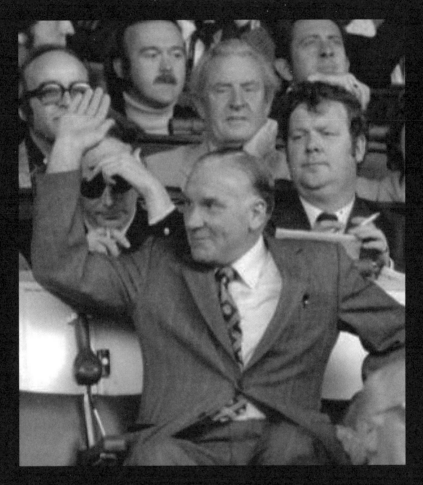

Chapter 8
The End of the Dream

"I despair when I think about the future of coaching in this country.
Where are the experienced players, nearing the ends of their careers,
who have the experience to become the Bill Nicholsons or the
Ron Greenwoods of the 90s?"
Bobby Robson

In the cold light of dawn following Bill Nicholson's decision to resign, Tottenham fans from all walks of life were left to wonder what lay ahead for their club. Many may have been of the opinion that it had been coming for a while. Others felt that he had been too hasty, but perhaps they didn't know what Bill did. Then there were others, like life-long Spurs supporter Lewis Hale, my late father, who were bemused, shocked and more than a little angry at the fact that the man who had been the cornerstone of one of the country's leading football clubs had been allowed to drift off without so much as a word of thanks...

It was such a shock. We all thought that Bill would be at Tottenham forever. It was only when Terry Neill came in that we realised that the great era was over and rebuilding was under way. I remember one morning turning up for training and saying to Steve Perryman: "Heck, we're the only ones left."

Until then, everyone had known Bill and had known that they were wanted. I was only ever on a one-year contract in 16 years at White Hart Lane.

Suddenly we didn't know what sort of players the new manager was looking for and if we were going to be in a job any longer. It was an unsettling time. Then, periods of change always are.
John Pratt

It was no secret that Bill was becoming increasingly disillusioned with a lot of aspects of the modern game. He absolutely hated hooliganism, and the events in Rotterdam were the worst thing he had seen. This was his club being shamed, and after the first few games of the 1974-75 season, it was clear that he didn't really have his heart in it. Players attitudes were a bit different in the 70s, and their expectations were as well, and Bill wasn't about to change the way he felt about the game to suit the times.

After he had resigned, we played a game – it may have been a 2-0 win over Derby – and I went in front of the cameras on Match of the Day to plead, on behalf of the players, for Bill to reconsider his decision and stay; but he had clearly made his mind up, and there could be no going back.

It would, I suppose, have been a very awkward situation for all of us as well as Bill if he had. There was a very unreal feel about that whole period – a lot of uncertainty. The idea of Tottenham without Bill Nicholson was weird...nobody could quite believe it.
Martin Peters

I don't think Bill was pushed, but he might have been given a nudge. He'd bought a few players who hadn't quite worked out, like David Jenkins from Arsenal. That didn't help. But his end was coming, and we all knew that it couldn't go on.

He wasn't, of course, going anywhere else. How could he? He loved Spurs too much, he had given his life to Spurs. He created that Double team of 1960-61, that no-one will ever forget, and went on to win another five major cups. So he just retired. I think they made him Honourary President or something, but it wasn't really handled very well, not very dignified. I felt sorry for Bill, the way he was just allowed to creep out of the club.

Johnny Giles and Danny didn't, of course, get the manager's job. I've spoken to Giles about it recently – and he says that it was a serious offer, at least he thought it was at the time. Bill Nick had spoken to him about it several times. But when Bill suggested it to the club, they said: "P*** off, it's nothing to do with you, who do you think you are . . . we'll pick the next manager."

In those days, a manager who'd had great success, like Bill Shankly at Liverpool, did help to appoint the next manager, or help pick his successor. Bill Nick was only doing what he thought was best for the club, a club he'd worked for all his life, for almost 40 years, since he'd joined them as a boy in 1936. He'd been totally loyal to them. And what did they say? What amounted to 'get lost.' Instead in came Terry Neill – from Arsenal. (Author's note – Hull City)

I'll always be grateful to Bill Nicholson. He took me on, gave me a second chance after the Watford rejection. During my time in his first team, he always stood by me. He could easily have replaced me by buying someone new, but he never did. I was lucky, playing under Bill.
Joe Kinnear

It was surely the ultimate irony for Spurs fans that, with their own once-mighty club facing the prospect of life in the second division, and gearing up for fixtures against the likes of Mansfield Town and Orient, that their former manager should be helping London rivals West Ham seek glory in Europe in a competition made famous in this country by Spurs. West Ham United, having themselves previously won the trophy in 1965, looked to Bill's experience in their new bid.

It proved to be a wise move. With nothing like the amount of resources to call upon as many of their more illustrious opponents, the Hammers still managed to make it all the way to the final before losing out to Belgian champions Anderlecht. Hammers' John Lyall was in no doubt of Bill's contribution to their cause . . .

You are expanding your knowledge in Europe but I was lucky that Bill Nicholson had joined us from Tottenham by then. Bill Nick would go off to watch our

BILL NICHOLSON

European opponents.

Lyall's admiration for Nicholson is barely less than that he reserves for his beloved mentor, Ron Greenwood.

I couldn't fail, could I, with Bill on hand? It was Ron's idea to bring him in after our chief scout, Wally St Pier, retired. Ron and I tried to do Wally's job but we couldn't do it effectively, so I was delighted when he suggested we should bring in Bill. I've always had older people around me and I found it invaluable.

Ronnie Boyce and Mick McGiven were excellent in reporting in detail on the opposition but Bill was forthright, honest and fair in his judgment of players and of our own performances.

We used to share scouting missions in Europe – for instance, Bill and I went to see Eintracht Frankfurt before the semi-final in 1976. I got on famously with him but you couldn't help but like Bill, a very sincere man.

Keith Burkinshaw was clever, because when he took the Tottenham job he pulled Bill back to White Hart Lane, so we only had the benefit of him for just a year. He was ever so sorry to leave us, didn't want to let us down, but he was going back to where he belonged, so we were delighted for him.

John Lyall, former West Ham United manager, speaking to EX magazine

Jimmy Greaves was not the only celebrated ex-Spur we had at Upton Park. Bill Nicholson himself was with us for a year. I felt really upset when Bill dropped out of football after leaving Spurs and I got our board to put him on our payroll. Bill's experience was an enormous help in all kinds of ways, and I liked having him around. When Wally St. Pier left I offered him the job of chief scout. But Bill said he didn't think he could do it, and I said I didn't think I could either. Chief scout is a specialist job. It means a lot of cloak-and-dagger work, endless frustration, dogged persistence and watching football in all kinds of weather. It is hardly a job for a manager who has won everything worth winning. Bill asked for a week to think about it; but in that very week he was asked by Keith Burkinshaw, who had by now taken over at Tottenham, to go back to White Hart Lane. "Get back there quickly because you shouldn't have left in the first place," I told Bill. I was delighted for him.

Ron Greenwood

Irving Scholar on Bill's relationships with managers
From his autobiography 'Behind Closed Doors'

Football is different to any other business, but like all businesses it has successes and failures. Somebody has to pay the price of failure. Since managers of English football teams invariably claim all the glory when their teams are successful, why should they not pay some of the price when their teams fail? Are they somehow immune to the general law of life in business? It certainly appear so, given the way that managers bleat their hardships to the press and the role of those romantic, albeit misguided journalists who play up to their bleatings.

One man who was an exception to this was Bill Nicholson. In 1974, when he felt he could no longer command the support of the players or the board, he resigned.

Bill was pushed, and the real dishonour was that the then Tottenham board allowed him to leave White Hart Lane and work at Upton Park for 18 months. This for a man who was really responsible for the 'glory glory' days at Tottenham, and for making the club great in the 50s and 60s – the greatest manager Spurs ever had. When I took over at Spurs, I was determined we should utilise the expertise and the experience that Bill had.

Yet it was not easy to make the Tottenham managers appreciate Bill Nicholson. Just as one of Howard Wilkinson's first actions in taking over Leeds United was to remove a photograph of Don Revie and his team from the foyer, to banish the ghost of Revie's winning sides from the 60s and 70s, the Tottenham managers that I worked with in the 80s were always trying to pull down Bill Nicholson. They knew they could not hope to match his Double achievement, or to supplant him in the memory of Tottenham fans. They would often niggle and moan about what Bill did.

By the time I arrived at Spurs, Bill was in charge of the scouting system, and nobody was more critical of his scouting abilities than Keith Burkinshaw, the then Tottenham manager. Keith felt that Bill never seemed to like modern players; none of them seemed good enough to be signed for Spurs. Yet, ironically, it was Bill who signed one of the best players Tottenham was to have in the 80s: Gary Mabbutt.

One day Bill received a phone call from Peter Anderson, then manager of Millwall, asking him what he thought of Gary Mabbutt. Bill thought he was worth around £250,000, and that he was an outstanding prospect. Anderson told him that he had just put the phone down to Bobby Gould, then manager of Bristol Rovers, who wanted to sell Mabbutt at around £105,000. Millwall couldn't afford the fee, and Bill urged Keith to sign Mabbutt. Fortunately for Spurs, Keith took the advice, and despite Mabbutt's diabetes, something that had put off other clubs, he became a Spurs player and has become an outstanding talent.

The only Tottenham manager during my time to share my admiration for Bill Nicholson was David Pleat. Like me, David would often sit in Bill's office and ask his opinion on team matters and listen to his views. One of my lasting regrets is that I never managed to give Bill Nicholson the sort of father-figure role that Bob Paisley acquired at Liverpool. Who knows, had David Pleat remained at Spurs, that relationship might have developed, making a lasting bridge between the Tottenham of the 60s and the Tottenham of the modern era.

Mr Scholar's views, however, seem to be at odds with other key figures at White Hart Lane . . .

Keith Burkinshaw – Why I brought Bill back

When I first took over at Tottenham, my assistant manager was Pet Welton, and he was always telling me about Bill and the way he had liked to do things when he was in charge. Then it occurred to me that here was this blue and white-blooded Spurs man, across town earning his corn at West Ham when he could be helping Tottenham. To be honest, the way he liked his team run sounded just the way I wanted to run Spurs, so he would be the ideal man to give me a few hints. So we

Bill with Keith Burkinshaw, the man who brought him back to his spiritual home.

invited him back as Head Scout.

When we sounded him out, he didn't waste much time in coming back – and straight away I knew it was right. Bill had Tottenham in his blood, but I was never for a second worried that he would interfere in team matters. Of course, we would talk football for hours – but we were both Yorkshiremen who didn't mince our words and we were both clear about who did what. Bill would often give opinions about players and such like, and I was only too glad to listen – people with his amount of experience don't come along too often. Sometimes, we would talk about football for so long that what came across eventually contained some useful advice. On the odd occasion I would ask his opinion about events on the pitch, and he would offer it. But only ever when I needed it.

Bill was very specific about the kind of players he thought should play for Tottenham Hotspur. Quite often I got the impression that there just weren't the amount of players out there of the kind of calibre Bill was expecting to sign, but rather than seeing that as a criticism, I suppose that was just Bill the perfectionist coming out. He'd been used to some great players down the years, so I guess he had that standard to aim for.

Terry Venables on Bill Nick back at The Lane

Coming back to Tottenham was great enough for me but having Bill there was even better. I'd seen him off and on down the years, at different games and such. He was really pleased to see me come, and I was equally pleased to be able to catch up with him again, because he'd been away from Tottenham for a while, then he'd worked for West Ham for a while.

He was always there for you, ever helpful. He never pushed himself on you, and he was always happy to chat – he could talk all day about football.

Bill had very high standards in what he wanted in a player. We would look around for players quite a lot, but what people have to remember was that when Bill was manager, Tottenham were one of the clubs that were always in for any top player that became available. I had no problems with Bill in that way at all – he would tick a player as he saw fit, and would recommend whether or not he'd like to see him again, but obviously the manager had the final say.

I can honestly say – and I know Bill would have agreed with me – that we got along like a house on fire.

Ron Atkinson – on Bill Nick, the font of all knowledge

In my managerial career, I have been fortunate to have shared a fair bit of football history with some of the most accomplished men to hold down the job. I was a little late to come on the scene for the likes of Stan Cullis, Sir Matt Busby and, of course, the great Bill Nick, the wise and wonderful Bill Nicholson of Spurs.

At the time, I was forever seeking help and advice from Bill at White Hart Lane. He had this dour, grimly determined image, but Bill was one of the most illuminating advisors you could run to.

As a young hopeful in the management business, I was never too shy to seek out the people who had been there and done it. They were of enormous help, too, when I wanted to pick their brains and unearth all the trade secrets.

Ron Atkinson, from his autobiography 'A Different Ball Game'

An appointment with HRH The Queen Mother

Bill Nicholson's departure from White Hart Lane after so many years was one hell of a wrench. The manner in which he left must have caused him a lot of anguish, but not long afterwards he found that life was not all bad when his years of loyal service to the game, and to his beloved Tottenham Hotspur, was to be recognised by the awarding of an OBE.

It was in the New Year's Honours list of 1975 that Bill discovered that an ordinary working class lad from Yorkshire could rub shoulders with royalty.

Testimonials

Two testimonials? That man could have had 10 testimonials, and it still wouldn't come close to repaying what he'd done for my club.

Doug Fraser, Spurs fan interviewed at Bill's memorial service November 7, 2004

Tottenham Hotspur 1 West Ham United 1
White Hart Lane
August 21, 1983

BILL NICHOLSON

Tottenham Hotspur (from): Ray Clemence, Danny Thomas, Chris Hughton, Graham Roberts, Paul Price, Paul Miller, Gary Mabbutt, Tony Galvin, Glenn Hoddle, Osvaldo Ardiles, Steve Perryman, Mike Hazard, Steve Archibald, Alan Brazil, Garth Crooks, Mark Falco

West Ham United (from): Phil Parkes, Tom McAlister, Ray Stewart, Frank Lampard, Paul Brush, Billy Bonds, Alvin Martin, Neil Orr, Alan Devonshire, Steve Whitton, Paul Goddard, Dave Swindlehurst, Trevor Brooking, Geoff Pike, Paul Allen, Alan Dickens

Scorers: Spurs – Alan Brazil; West Ham United – Dave Swindlehurst

The main match was preceded by an exhibition game of 20 minutes each way, between teams of former players. Blues played Yellows for the honour of gaining Bill Nick's approval, and to their delight (or was it relief?) the Yellows ran out 3-0 winners with goals from Martin Chivers, Eddie Clayton and Phil Holder.

Yellows: Pat Jennings, Joe Kinnear, Cyril Knowles, Dennis Bond, Mike England, Phil Holder, Jimmy Neighbour, Terry Dyson, Martin Chivers, Martin Peters, Eddie Clayton.

Blues: Tony Parks, Terry Naylor, Ron Henry, Jimmy Robertson, John Lacy, Peter Collins, John Pratt, Jimmy Greaves, Alan Gilzean, Johnny Brooks, Cliff Jones.

Danny Blanchflower, writing in the programme on the occasion of Bill Nicholson's first Testimonial match in 1983:

When I arrived at White Hart Lane in December 1954 it was to take over Bill Nicholson's old place at right-half-back. Bill had just been appointed club coach and Arthur Rowe had bought me from Aston Villa to succeed Alf Ramsey as club Captain when the time came.

Bill and I did not have a lot in common at the time. Our wing-half styles were different so we saw such things from different angles. I was nearly 29-years-old – too old a dog to want to learn new tricks. And I had a few of my own I wanted to try out. That is why I had come to Spurs.

But three months after I arrived Arthur Rowe had vanished in the way that managers used to do at White Hart Lane. Jimmy Anderson took over and Alf Ramsey moved out. And I was appointed captain.

Then Jimmy and I had disagreements about the captaincy. I wanted authority to make changes on the field, if we were losing a match where the result was all important, as in a Cup-tie, Jimmy wanted me to leave bad enough alone but I could not go along with that. They shuffled around this business like Smiley's people and I was left in the dark a couple of times. So I threw in the captain's towel to make my absence legitimate.

Meanwhile I played with Ted Ditchburn, Harry Clarke, Len Duquemin, Eddie Baily and Alf Ramsey for a time. I could see the beauty of the old push-and-run team fading away. They were something special and Bill Nick had been part of it. So I had that respect for him.

Then Jimmy Anderson caught the Midnight Express from White Hart Lane – no more manager. And Bill Nicholson was appointed.

BILL NICHOLSON

We beat Everton 10-4 in his first match in charge. "How can we improve on that?" I asked. "We can only get worse."

We did get worse and this time I was dropped. But Nick did it properly. He told me first and said he needed a better defensive balance in the half-back line.

I shrugged my shoulders and hung around without animosity for a month or so. There were other places I could go; but there, I might have had to start all over again.

Then I asked him for a transfer but he refused my request. That meant he did not want me to go. So I hung around some more, biding my time.

Then he surprised me. It was on the 2nd of March 1959. He did not travel up with us to Wolverhampton for a vital match against Wolves. We were on the brink of relegation and they were League champion favourites. I hoped it was not another Midnight Express trip.

He arrived late and hustled us into a private room in the hotel for a team talk. He said he was making me the permanent club captain and told the players to respect my authority.

"We will talk about that later," he said.

We earned a point that night in the Wolves den and thrashed Leicester City 6-0 the following Saturday, at home.

There was no more relegation talk after that. We were on the move again. Nick had decided to build around me. He went out and bought Dave Mackay, Bill Brown and John White, then later, Jimmy Greaves.

Bill and I became partners. Now we had lots in common with the best interests of the club at heart. We had total respect for one another when we learned that our different experiences and angles could blend into better teamwork. When he had doubts I could give him a second opinion. When I was too flippant he would bring me down to earth.

It was not all buttering up. We often disagreed. But we agreed to disagree.

After that, almost all our dreams came true. It was a hell of a time we had together. And every time we meet now that feeling is still there between us.

You could call it satisfaction that would be very hard to beat.

PFA Merit Award 1984

At the annual dinner of the Professional Footballers' Association in 1984, the country's top professionals were unanimous in their choice for their annual Merit award – Bill Nicholson. Bill, by his own admission, was surprised to join the long list of football dignitaries that included Sir Matt Busby, Bill Shankly, Tom Finney, Denis Law, Bob Paisley, Bobby Charlton, Joe Mercer and many others. The fact that Bill should be surprised at being considered on a par with such lofty names should, in itself, be no surprise. Throughout his life, Bill had a habit of understating his own achievements, preferring instead to share the limelight with a team that he alone would have assembled anyway.

Freedom of the Borough

In December 1998, Bill received the Freedom of the Borough from Haringey

Council and the road leading to the club from Tottenham High Road was re-named 'Bill Nicholson Way.' The announcement was made on the evening of Monday, December 14, 1998 at Wood Green Civic Centre after local councillor and avid Spurs fan Peter Jones had nominated Bill for the honour...

Bill Nicholson Way – now it's official

Fans of Tottenham Hotspur had long been calling for a permanent reminder of Bill's wonderful years as head of the Tottenham family. On Saturday, April 24, 1999, they got just that.

In a short ceremony that took place before Spurs' home match with West Ham United, the short stretch of road which leads to the front of the stadium from Tottenham High Road was officially named 'Bill Nicholson Way', in the presence of the Mayor of Haringey, Councillor Sheila Peacock.

Several of Bill's players from yesteryear were there, and Bill himself seemed in good form. Bill could never have believed that when, as a young lad of just 16, he stepped through that very same front gate one day it would bear his name. In fact, the name of the road is now incorporated in the club's official address.

The road to glory...the Great Man himself toasts the official opening of Bill Nicholson Way, the small road leading from Tottenham High Road to the main entrance of the stadium.

BILL NICHOLSON

Bill's second testimonial...

Tottenham Hotspur 3 Fiorentina 0

White Hart Lane

August 8, 2001

Tottenham Hotspur (from): Neil Sullivan, Stephen Carr, Mauricio Tarrico, Steffen Freund, Goran Bunjevcevic, Chris Perry, Darren Anderton, Tim Sherwood, Les Ferdinand, Teddy Sheringham, Sergei Rebrov, Gary Doherty, Gustavo Poyet, Willem Korsten, Steffen Iversen, Oyvind Leonhardsen, Ben Thatcher, Chris Armstrong, Christian Ziege, Stephen Clemence, Ledley King, Steven Ferguson, Matthew Etherington, Simon Davies, Anthony Gardner, Alton Thelwell, Gavin Kelly, Ciaran Toner, John Jackson, Yannick Kanaman, Ian Hillier, John Piercy, Maurizio Consorti

Fiorentina (from): Giuseppi Taglialatela, Mattia Passarini, Mario Cassano, Daniele Adani, Allesandro Pierini, Tomas Repka, Paolo Vanoli, Andrea Tarozzi, Moreno Torricelli, Christian Amoroso, Emiliano Moretti, Allesandro Agostini, Sandro Cois, Fabio Rossitto, Angelo Di Livio, Mirko Benin, Domenico Morfeo, Marco Rossi, Ezequiel Gonzales, Giorgios Vakouftis, Enrico Chiesa, Predrag Mijatovic, Leandro, Nuno Gomes

Italian Cup holders Fiorentina were brushed aside by a slick and confident display from Glenn Hoddle's new-look Tottenham outfit. Bill Nicholson proved the star of the evening but the current Spurs side put on a performance which would have made the great man proud.

The loudest cheer of the night greeted Bill Nicholson's entry onto the pitch before the match kicked off as the Spurs fans saluted his achievements as the most successful and, arguably, the most important person in the history of the club.

David Brawn reporting in Spurs Monthly

Attendance; 35,877 (all standing as one to acknowledge the man who changed the face of British football), a constellation of Spurs legends, and one tearful Spurs fanatic with a lump the size of a golf ball in his throat . . .

Yes, 35,877 idolatry Spurs fans of all ages; standing as one to acknowledge the man deservedly known as Mr Tottenham Hotspur. Compare that with the 12,000 who crept sheepishly into Highbury for Tony Adams 'great' night, and that should tell you something about where the real passion for football lies in North London!

They came in their droves. A reverberating White Hart Lane, bulging to the seams with people eager to pay their respects to a man very much alive, and still revered by managers, trainers, players, fans; and a global football world still learning from the philosophies of the king of panache.

I took my seat in the Park Lane upper, feeling a humbleness that I'd rarely experienced in my life. The man gave me so much. As a small lad, I was brought up in enemy territory. Bill's teams enchanted and mesmerised; enticing me across the river like a moth to a very bright lamp. Greaves, Gilzean (they tripped off the tongue as naturally as coffee and cream or day and night), Blanchflower, Jones, Chivers, Jennings and Knowles. Football people. Spurs people. Great people. People who lived, breathed and ate a Nicholson induced brand of swashbuckling, flamboyant football. Even his first game in charge, which I was lucky enough to attend, ended 10-4!

After experiencing such a great era in my chosen football team's history, then living through the sheer torture of the last dozen or so years, my eyes started to fill up. The famous old words go; 'Mine eyes have seen the glory of the cups at White Hart Lane..." well, for a few moments last night, I couldn't really see a thing. I tried to hold back the tears to no avail. I sprang to my feet as the great man took to the pitch, held upright by the still commanding figure of big Martin Chivers. I knew in my heart how much that would have hurt 'Nick', having to walk out in front of that crowd assisted by a steadying arm. After all, that's exactly what he gave our great club. A steadying arm through an era of 'firsts' that would shake the modern game to its core.

I went to last night's game with a lapsed Crystal Palace fan. "I used to go when they were good," she told me.

"I used to go when they (Spurs) were great," I told her. Encapsulated in my small moment of unbridled gloating dwelt my reasons for supporting Spurs. Bill Nicholson made us great. He gave us pride. He turned a crumbling, poor, yet bustling part of North London into one of the most passionate couple of acres in the world. Without Billy Nick's ideals and values, Spurs may not have been the global attraction that they became over the duration of his leadership. We certainly would never have attracted the players from the various corners of the world who have graced the white shirt with such style.

Bill supported by Martin Chivers at his second Testimonial match in August 2001.

139

BILL NICHOLSON

As I stood, looking up in awe at the man who had affected my childhood even more than my own father, I couldn't help but hope that all his sterling work would not go in vain. We mustn't waste his efforts or what he has built here, I thought to myself. This is Tottenham Hotspur. MY Tottenham Hotspur. A hotbed of passion; a proud, burgeoning history of entertainment and style; a veritable world of fantasy in a universe gone mad.

In many ways, last night was an important pivotal point in the future of our great club.

With Bill Nicholson at the top, and loved by all; with new owners, obviously working tirelessly for our future; with new players, young and younger; and the prodigal welcomed back to the manager's chair. I genuinely feel for the first time in a dozen years that Tottenham Hotspur are on the way back to their rightful place at the head of British football.

Mr Nicholson, I hope I speak for every Spurs fan that ever visited the ground, or listened to, or watched your teams on countless TVs and radio sets around the world. Thank you. Thank you very much for touching each one of our lives.

South London Spur
(Thanks to Harry Hotspur for allowing use of this piece)

Hall of Fame

On March 11, 2004, Bill was the guest of honour at a dinner attended by many of his Double-winning side to celebrate Bill's induction into Tottenham's Hall Of Fame. Nobody could possibly deny that of all Tottenham's illustrious names from its fabled past, Bill should head the list.

I think it is a terrific idea on the part of Tottenham to start a Hall of Fame and there couldn't be a more appropriate first recipient than Bill Nicholson.

I think everybody knows what a fantastic contribution he has made to Spurs over 50 years since coming here as a young player in 1936. Of course, the rest is history.

My father brought me to Tottenham on a number of occasions in the early 60s when Bill was manager and I did see that team play, standing over on The Shelf watching Danny Blanchflower and Dave Mackay.

I remember the joyful football that they played. Looking back on it, it was a completely different football to what we've got today. The game was more open and hadn't become quite as defensive. I think there was more individual skill on the ball, more time for players to express themselves.

Tottenham was the place to come and see the best football – I don't think anybody at the time could have argued that.

The memory of that Tottenham team is of the fantastic football played and, when I talk to fans of many years, one player has been singled out as probably the finest player ever to wear the shirt – Dave Mackay.

When I met Bill as a very young commentator – with him a very experienced manager – he never left a stone unturned, he was so conscientious about his job. It wouldn't surprise me if he was on every train going just to check on players himself.

I don't think he would have let the lack of video evidence affect his judgment. The signings he made, almost without exception, were all ones who made their imprint on Tottenham Hotspur in the period in which they played.
John Motson

A whole raft of Spurs names from the past were present to see the very first inductee into the Spurs Hall of Fame – and nobody who ever supported this fine, old club could argue with the choice. At least, nobody who knows what they're talking about.

It would be very easy for younger Spurs fans whose eyes haven't seen the glory of anything at all to pick some illustrious names out of thin air, based on their limited experience. Jürgen Klinsmann, Osvaldo Ardiles, Glenn Hoddle, Paul Gascoigne, David Ginola . . . all fine players, and during their playing careers all probably gifted with more natural talent than Bill possessed, but in terms of the long-term impact on this club, none of these Spurs icons comes close to Bill Nick. I feel sure that each of them would agree with me.

In the fullness of time, the Hall of Fame's ranks will swell with names that should bring a tear to the eye of many a Spurs supporter; but to those of us who remember Bill Nick, we have a duty to pass on what we remember to those unfortunate enough to have never known his glories.

I am grateful for this marvellous tribute but I am not sure what I have done to deserve it. But I am glad you feel the need to warrant such a reception!

What was achieved at that time was down to the players and staff plus a lot of hard work. This club has been my life and will always remain so.
Bill Nicholson

Chapter 9
Bill's alter ego – Eddie Baily

It's a fact of life that, whenever great people reach a state of high achievement in their lives, there are usually other people who do not receive enough recognition for their part in the success story. Eddie Baily is one such person.

Assistant manager under Bill since 1964, Eddie was with his boss every step of the way. Where Bill could be quiet, even withdrawn at times, Eddie would be fully 'hands-on' with the players. He would be the one doing most of the 'donkey work', the everyday things that could free Bill to work on more noticeable and high-profile club matters.

Not, of course, that Eddie Baily was short of know-how himself. Far from it – many of the tactical appraisals of opposition players that are often accredited to Bill were in fact often the product of hours of painstaking research, carried out by Eddie on Bill's behalf. To this day, they are acclaimed inside the game as some of the most comprehensive and far-sighted 'spying' missions ever undertaken by a coach.

But if the manner of Bill's exit from White Hart Lane was viewed in many quarters as a national scandal, Eddie Baily's was, if anything, even worse. At least Bill Nick had the satisfaction inside his own mind of knowing that he had made the choice to go, albeit for reasons not entirely of his own making. Eddie, on the other hand, while all the time clinging to the belief that he would be groomed for the job that he knew inside out, suddenly found that when it came to the crunch, his years of dedication, experience and sheer hard work counted for next to nothing.

The board of the time looked elsewhere for Bill's successor. And to add insult to considerable injury, they chose to appoint Terry Neill – a man with absolutely no Tottenham connections, and one who actually spent the lion's share of his playing career at the wrong end of Seven Sisters Road.

Bill On Eddie

He is a typical East Ender – amusing, sometimes barbed in his comments, but a loyal friend. He was the man who gee-ed up the players before matches, employing a wide range of similes, most of which were related to his time in the services during the war.

'Fixing bayonets and going over the top to them' was one of his favourites. The same phrases tend to be repeated in football – clichés abound. But Eddie would usually find something original to say and I laughed at what he could come up with.

He had been a very skilful player and even in middle age he could still perform skill practices better than most of the players. He always complained about the failure of certain players to make their tackles count, yet as a player he never tackled anyone!

Bill Nicholson, from his autobiography, 'Glory Glory- my life with Spurs'

Eddie was approached by Bill after Harry Evans (Bill's own assistant manager) passed away. Eddie was at Orient in those days and had built an extremely successful side out of what amounted to next to nothing. Bill was very impressed at this, and despite the fact that Eddie was a boyhood Orient fan (he used to sneak under the fence with his mates), Eddie decided on the spot to leave and join Bill.

Eddie had obviously been a top Spurs player, having been a part of the push-and-run team and played for his country. Assisting Bill did not daunt him, though, and one of his opening lines was to tell the squad that 'anything they could do, he could do better!' This was typical of Eddie, a lively, confident and, by his own words, 'cocky' young man who would not let the big Spurs names get the better of him. Eddie's personal role was more of coach than anything and he was a well-known figure in football in this role for his famous dossiers that his managers loved to receive from him.

Eddie was told right from the start by Bill that he would 'look after him'. This Bill repeated at the time of his departure. Eddie strongly feels that this didn't happen and that while Bill enjoyed two testimonials at White Hart Lane, Eddie had one – at Enfield Town's ground. He was then thrust on to the dole queue and had to wait for old friend Ron Suart (Chelsea) to ask for his help. Eddie's dossiers proved invaluable to Bill, Ron, and both West Ham managers, John Lyall and Ron Greenwood, who Eddie feels treated him very, very well.

My overall impression from Eddie is that he was badly mistreated and overlooked when Bill left, and judging by comments from ex-players, I would tend to agree with him.

Eddie, now 79, has an astute, tactical footballing brain and is still a natural leader. No manager can do the job on his own, and it is abundantly clear that Eddie Baily was a major driving force behind Tottenham Hotspur's successes.

Keith Palmer, author of the forthcoming book 'White Hart Lane Legends'

They were an odd couple, Bill and Eddie. Apart from the fact that they both wanted the best for Tottenham, you couldn't get two people more unalike. Bill was the kind of person who would never get straight into players right after a game – he believed that it was best to calm things down, wait until Monday, then talk things through firmly but sensibly.

Eddie, on the other hand, was your classic 'hair-drier' assistant manager. He was a brash cockney, but one with a brilliant sense of humour who was far more intelligent than he would at first seem. Eddie didn't pull any punches when it came to letting people have it, and if it upset them . . . well, tough. He quite often reminded players that at their age he was fighting a war, and that having to listen to his ear-bashings was nothing by comparison.

BILL NICHOLSON

The irony is that, as management and coaches, they were absolute opposites of how they were as players. Bill was an uncompromising, tough tackler who wasn't known for being showy or adventurous – in short, he didn't take risks. And yet, as a manager, he was the one who always encouraged people to stroke the ball around, make runs into space, and who was always preaching the gospel about entertaining the crowd.

As for Eddie, as a player he was a gifted and exciting midfielder. He had more flair than Bill, and yet as assistant manager he would be the one telling us week in, week out to maintain our shape, keep doing the simple things, don't take unnecessary risks and so on. It's almost as if they were both trying to instil in us the qualities they weren't known for as players themselves.
Mike England

Eddie was part of the furniture at Spurs in my early days. He was a real character – a cockney boy right down to his boots. There were times when he would go into one, and of course, it all depended on the circumstances, but you'd either think: 'hold up, I'd better not push my luck here,' or alternatively, he'd have you in stitches. He could really get on your tits at times, but I suppose if he didn't he wouldn't be doing his job right, would he? Eddie really knew his stuff, and if you wanted to get on in the game you listened to people like Eddie Baily. Bill Nick certainly did.
Terry Naylor

Eddie Baily was clearly as passionate about Tottenham Hotspur as Bill. His unbending stance on players who he felt did not seem to feel the same was never better illustrated than by his comments in Hunter Davies' acclaimed 1972 book, 'The Glory Game' . . .

"The basic things haven't changed that much," he said, pointing to a diagram in a 1934 book. "The skills you have to work on are much the same. Trapping the ball under your foot is as sensible now as it was then. The big difference is speed. The quicker you can do things, the better, because time is space.

"Even top professionals make a mistake in trapping a ball. A great player is the one who makes fewest mistakes. A truthful player comes off the field concerned about the mistakes he's made, not boasting about all the good things he's done. Some players can make the same mistake week after week. There is obviously something wrong. It's got to be corrected in training.

"I know many players resent being told to do something. They often think it's a waste of time. But standing still is the biggest waste of time. Moving is doing something, even if the ball is 40 yards away. It's human nature to have spasms when you don't move enough. I know that. So you've got to keep at them. You use anything to motivate them. Shouting, insulting them, touching their ego. I understand my missus. I know what affects her. A coach has got to understand each player and what has an effect on him.

"When you know it's not the skill that's lacking, you've got to get at them. If they

don't do it voluntarily, the way Steve (Perryman) does it, you've got to make them do it involuntarily, even if they hate you for it.

"I would sack the ones who don't try. There's no good applying skill standing still. You want to be on the London Palladium if you want paying for standing still. I wouldn't have them at the club. And I know which ones I wouldn't have. It all comes down to character. I can tell by a face whether a person has a weak character. I know by looking at people who will be the fighters and who won't. If you've got a fighter, you can improve him all the time. I want them all to do better all the time. I know that Roger Morgan is never going to be able to lift weights like Spud Collins, but all I've wanted him to do is to try harder every time. I know what he's been saying under his breath at me. All I want is for him to be a fighter so people can see what a good player he is."

Eddie Baily was a member of the famous push-and-run side before working so successfully alongside Bill Nick in the Spurs dug-out.

Chapter 10
The Family

It must be hard for most of us to imagine, but Bill Nicholson was, for the most part, an ordinary man with an ordinary family life. To Spurs fans of all ages, he will always be 'The Legend', or 'Bill Nick'; the man who, more than any other, lifted Tottenham Hotspur Football Club onto the shoulders of giants. But to his wife Darkie, daughters Linda and Jean, and grandchildren and others, he was simply the man they all knew and loved with a special fondness.

Few of us could even begin to comprehend how his amazing family could so willingly 'share' the head of their family with a board of directors, a first team squad, reserves, youth players, coaches, ground staff and a host of support workers. Then there are the tens of thousands, or possibly hundreds of thousands of supporters around the world, who all felt a special bond with Bill Nicholson down the years.

In the next chapter of this book, members of the public recount stories of how they came across Bill Nicholson in everyday life. All will tell of the man who treated them as equals; of a man who could consort with Kings and Commoners while feeling comfortable in the company of both.

To go some way towards explaining this, here are the words of Bill's son-in law Steve Bell, read out on the occasion of Bill's funeral and kindly allowed by the Nicholson family to be reproduced here. They wanted the whole world to know how special the man was to those who knew him best . . .

I am so, so privileged to pay this tribute on behalf of the family and to be able to recount just a few of the many warm memories of Bill that we all hold.

The family want everybody to treat today as a celebration of his full and wonderful life – many know of Bill's professional life, it has been well documented and, of course, we are all immensely proud of his achievements and of the way they came about. We'll let Cliff (Jones) elaborate on this. We want to savour a few thoughts of Bill the family man – a dear husband to Darkie, the much loved dad of Linda and Jean, the fantastic grandad to Richard, Colin and Shaun and to all who met him, the fond image of a favourite uncle – Bill.

In this past week, we have kept a sheet of paper pinned to our kitchen wall – although emotions have been delicate for all of us, each time a pertinent thought came into one of our heads, we scribbled it down. The single sheet finished up as many. We have pruned the list down. These words are a brief contribution on behalf of us all . . .

Bill was born in Scarborough, North Yorkshire on 26 January 1919, the second youngest of nine. He was raised in a happy, close and loving family – working

146

class – all in a small terraced house where his beloved mother "ruled the roost". Older brothers and sisters were expected to look after the younger ones – it was the only way to cope. From a young age, he loved to help with mucking out the stables for his father – a hansom cab driver down on the promenade.

Although brought up at the seaside, Bill never properly learned to swim – the sea-water was too cold and rough, and besides – those "hand me down" woolly trunks tended to drag your bottom to the bottom! He spent any free time with his mates kicking about a tin can – or anything else that they could afford – in the alley behind the back yard. The neighbours must have been irritated but the skills learned obviously bore rich harvest.

Photographs of Bill's mum and dad hang in his bedroom to this day – the same back alleys are now clogged with cars.

Bill came down to Tottenham in 1936 at the instigation of a club scout – Ben Ives. The roughly pencilled letter of invitation is still tucked away somewhere. It gave tender reassurance to his mum that the club would look after her 17-year-old. Bill always enjoyed returning to his roots to see the Nicholson family and reacquaint himself with Yorkshire. There was a family holiday to Scarborough every year without fail. He knew the local streets like the back of his hand. The whole family knew the best fish and chip shops, greeted auntie Mary's donkeys by name – just like old friends – and either got stuck into cricket on the beach, built sand castles against the tide, investigated rock pools, or followed our most well-practised pursuit – sheltering from the rain.

Sundays were spent up on the Yorkshire moors with a picnic near Goathland – always in the same spot. Bill tolerated having his picnic food presented on a paper plate on such occasions but we all knew that he would rather have had it sitting at a decent dining table with a knife and fork! Evenings were frequently spent in the family home where his older sister Edie continued to live – playing cards for pennies – which Edie kept from year to year in one of Harold's old tobacco tins. We were creatures of habit. Sadly all of Bill's generation of Nicholsons have now passed away.

When Bill was 20, the war started. He served in the Durham Light Infantry as a Physical Training Instructor. Time was served both in Yorkshire and Italy. Life skills were honed at this time. Bill often gave credit to these years for his management acumen although they severely restricted his great joy of playing football.

Bill married my wonderful mother-in-law, Darkie, in 1942 – 62 years ago. With due respect to some here today, the signing of that register was the best signing he ever made. He moulded many successful teams but the team of 'Bill and Darkie' clearly wins the family accolade.

It became obvious to anybody who met Bill that he enjoyed every aspect of his life. His simple pleasures were to look after his family and to play football. His core values were to do anything and everything to the best of his ability, and to thus be worthy of respect. Fame or fortune, I am sure, never crossed his mind.

His stressful burden of professional management ended in 1974 with his resignation – all well documented. Some people thought that they saw a seed change in his personality at that time – but not the family. He never had been dour or reserved to those who really knew him – he was fun loving but he had just had a lot on his mind. He had never courted publicity for himself and, without fail, told the truth, even if sometimes it was not welcomed.

He picked up his OBE in 1975 – no fuss – it had been offered earlier but he put it off in case it encumbered his role as Tottenham manager. Other honours followed including the naming of "Bill Nicholson Way" and "Freedom of the Borough of Haringey". It made him chuckle.

He retired from salaried employment in 1997 – at the age of 78, although of course, he graciously enjoyed his continuing role of being Club President. His last public engagement was the inaugural dinner to the Hall of Fame at the club in March this year.

I go back to the kitchen list – the man himself – what mental pictures do we hold?

He always took great care with his appearance; immaculate grooming with a constant public smile, hair closely trimmed and Brylcreamed. Inevitably a collar and tie – even when just pottering around the house. Suit trousers neatly pressed and, of course, highly polished shoes.

He enjoyed driving until late on – his old car was always spotless inside and out and it was serviced three times as often as anybody else's.

The lawn at Creighton Road was cherished. Mowed by a tiny old hand-pushed cylinder mower. The family cry would often go up – 'get the nail clippers out, he's going to trim the edges.

He was a 'meat and two veg' man – none of this Chinese or Indian malarkey! But nobody mastered the culinary art of making real Yorkshire Puddings like his old mum used to make! Perhaps a cheeky glass of red wine or two during the week, and a gin and tonic on Saturdays. Although, with his hands becoming a little shaky in later years and with his over-generous nature towards guests – one had to be careful not to get more like a tonic with gin! After meals, he always insisted on doing the washing up – needless to say using gallons of hot water.

Grandson Shaun was brought up and lives in America. He played American football at college in Connecticut. The rules and set-plays of this game bemused Bill at first but he soon picked them up. Not a patch on soccer though!

In the early days before the children, Bill and Darkie enjoyed bike rides in Epping Forest. In later life at our house, Friday nights became fish and chips and a game of pool with the grandsons Richard and Colin on our warped old table. He inevitably won. His hands would stop shaking just long enough to pot the crucial balls. Infuriating!

Saturdays at Creighton Road following a game always showed a mountain of food on the table with drinks for everybody. Bill was always prepared to listen to our totally naïve and prejudiced opinions on the game while only occasionally coming out with his own so clinical observations. He definitely preferred the family banter and relaxed home comforts to being on display in a formal environment. But he succumbed to what was expected of him – just to please people.

His grass root values never faltered. He treated everybody with equal status and with respect, be they chairman or tea lady. He was pleased to meet people and liked to ask about their welfare rather than offer his own. With people more familiar, the men got a handshake or pat on the back; the ladies a little cuddle. I was always envious of how he managed that! People noted his affinity with animals – especially horses – which must have come from his formative years with his dad.

He was a strong believer in teamwork – and to the end, he expressed his gratitude, along with the family, to the doctors and nurses who cared for him, especially at the Potters Bar Community Hospital.

He passed away peacefully at 5.00am on Saturday, October 23, 2004 – no fuss, no bother – and on a match day, inevitably. The family knew his time was close – although we were a little surprised that he didn't keep going until 5.00pm just so that he could check the football results!

In conclusion, the family feel that we all owe something to the memory of this great man. If we are to correctly celebrate the life of William Edward Nicholson – he would want us to do it properly, so please do.

But most of all, do it HIS way . . . with some style!

The essence of Bill's success at Spurs was possibly the stability he knew at home. It is quite difficult to imagine any other line of work other than managing a very special football club where the head of a family could spend so long away from the family home and still have the blessings of his nearest and dearest. It may, perhaps, have had something to do with the fact that Darkie was herself a Tottenham girl (a point she was quite keen on making to those inside the club unfortunate not to be able to make the same claim).

Players who came across her down the years will remember that bike. I'm sure there must have been more than one, but…surely there must be a place for it in the Spurs museum? They will also remember the woman who always had a laugh and a joke, even when the weather was awful and the football wasn't much better, which thankfully in the case of Bill's sides wasn't very often.

But possibly the most telling observation comes from a segment of the speech given by Bill's eldest daughter Linda, on the occasion of the memorial service held for the great man on Sunday, November 7, 2004 . . .

"Of all the places dad visited all over the world he always liked to be with his 'family' best. But he actually had two families, being at home with us and being with his other family, Tottenham Hotspur, where he spent most of his life."

Not that Bill's love affair with Spurs was achieved without some personal cost. Darkie, Linda and Jean will, I hope, forgive me for mentioning the fact that on the occasion of Linda's wedding, it suddenly occurred to Bill that he had missed large swathes of his children's early lives. It is something all too common in people who are focussed on something for much of their lives. And yet the Nicholsons seemed to have accepted that this was just how Bill was, and their love for their remarkable father remained undiminished after all those years.

When I first considered the idea for this chapter, the thought that crossed my mind was that, in spite of all the magnificent players and coaches that have graced the scene at White Hart Lane down the years, perhaps one should consider that every one of Bill's shining silver cups that glisten in the trophy room at Spurs could have the unseen, but present, fingerprints of the Nicholson family on them somewhere.

Bill was Tottenham. And so were his family.

Chapter 11

The Legend in the Blue Cavalier

Bill Nicholson devoted the best part of 60 years to the cause of Tottenham Hotspur before finally becoming a man of leisure. To many of us, that would be the cue to disappear to exotic lands, where the sun is kinder on the bones and the life is gentler. But, of course, that would involve moving away from Tottenham, and to Bill that would be a bitter pill to swallow, having lived within shouting distance of White Hart Lane for the best part of his life. So he stayed put.

Urban myths exist everywhere, but in the case of ordinary people who claim to have struck up a dialogue with Bill down the years, nobody could deny that every case sounds perfectly plausible. He was that kind of man. How else could you explain the fact that he was equally at home being 'gonged' by HRH the Queen Mother as talking to complete strangers at Spurs Lodge?

I had the good fortune to meet Bill whilst he was out in his famed blue Cavalier. Like most people who stumble upon somebody famous, it happened completely by accident. Driving in my car one sunny Saturday morning, I pulled up at a set of lights in Woodford.

Drivers being what they are, it's a natural tendency to look around at the other people on the road, and I just happened to throw a sideways glance at the guy next to me, who on this occasion was Bill Nick. I was gobsmacked. For a second or two, I just wondered if it was actually him, or just a doppelganger. Then the smile

appeared on his face – the kind of smile you see on people who are used to complete strangers gawking at them – and the penny dropped that I was a couple of feet away from one of my heroes. It was then I uttered possibly the most incisive opening gambit any journalist could make.

"Hello, Bill."

He said hello back, and that was my cue. "How's Darkie?"

Bill, without the smile dropping for a second, replied: "Why – do you know her?" Now, if it had been anybody else other than Bill Nicholson, the obvious conclusion to be drawn from his answer would be that he was asking the question to establish who the hell I thought I was, digging into his private life when he had no idea who I was. With Bill, however, it was more likely that I could easily have known Darkie. because the two of them were common sights in and around the North London area.

"No," I replied. "Well, not personally. But everybody sort of knows her, don't they?"

If Bill was of the opinion that this conversation was getting more surreal by the minute, he hid it well. I pressed on.

"Need three points today, Bill," I offered.

"It'd be handy," he replied. At the time, we were under the expert tutelage of Christian Gross, and gaining three points would have been like finding the Holy Grail.

"Tell you what, Bill, I reckon they could do with you in charge there right now," I said – and part of me meant it, irrespective of his age.

Then, in one fell swoop, Bill Nicholson displayed just what it is that made him such a remarkable man. He smiled the inscrutable smile of Confucius and simply said: "The lights have changed."

He headed straight on, presumably back to Tottenham, and I turned right. I pulled over and thought about what had just occurred. Bill Nicholson . . . the man himself. He had the perfect opportunity to bad-mouth a successor of his, or to make unfavourable comparisons between himself and the unfortunate Swiss coach. Instead, he had simply smiled and made it clear that he knew how good a manager he had been, and he knew how bad he may have thought CG was, but it wasn't in Bill's make-up to say either.

There was a lesson in tact and diplomacy born out of old age and humility.

The following accounts give witness to numerous people, some famous and many completely anonymous, who had the privilege of meeting and speaking to Bill in the course of his 64 great years at White Hart Lane . . .

About 20 years ago, when I started getting into collecting Spurs programmes in a big way, I was fortunate enough to contact the old printers, Thomas Knight & Co. As you may know, they printed the Spurs programme and assorted other bits and pieces (tickets, handbook, etc) from 1946 to 1980 or thereabouts. Anyway, I contacted them four years after they had ceased printing for Spurs and managed to reach one of the two brothers who had inherited the company. He told me that they had decided to get out of printing in 1980 when they realised they could actually make more money converting their print factory into smaller units and leasing them out.

Apparently, I was the first person to have contacted them since they had stopped printing for Spurs and they did have some spare programmes and items they thought I might be interested in, so I went over to the old place at Hoddesdon, agreed a deal with them and took numerous boxes back home.

One of the more interesting items was a menu from the 1950 banquet to celebrate the second division championship and promotion to the first division. In fact, it was such a great item I thought I'd try and get it signed by Bill Nicholson. I knew Mike Rollo, the club's commercial manager at the time, and mentioned to him what I had and what I wanted and he said he'd speak to Bill and let me know if he would agree to my request. Three days later a handwritten letter from Bill dropped through my letter box, saying that Mike had mentioned the menu card and that he would be more than happy to sign it. He also said he would send it on to Arthur Rowe for him to sign as well.

You can imagine my shock. I'd only ever wanted Bill's autograph on my menu card, and now I had something even better, a personal letter. I did send in the card, Bill did sign it and also got Arthur Rowe's autograph on it as well. I've still got both items and they mean as much to me now as they did when I first got them."
Graham Betts

It was tough being a Spurs fan as a kid in Hong Kong. All those years back the only way to keep up to date with the games was listening to the BBC World Service late on a Saturday night or the excitement of opening the Sunday paper to see the score. Highlights got to us about four or five days later.

Summer holidays back home in Blighty seemed to coincide with the end of the season and the chance to see Spurs never really materialised as neither of my parents shared my love. I even managed to miss Spurs when they came out to Hong Kong for pre-season.

To make up for this my mum promised to accompany me to White Hart Lane to go to the Spurs shop and maybe to see if it was possible to just have a look at the stadium. I'd never been. It was an exciting day and I remember it seemed like an epic journey up from Kent on the train, then on to the Underground and finally the bus. Just to visit the shop was excellent but the lady at the counter suggested there was no harm in asking at the stadium if it was possible to 'just have a look' as we'd come all the way from Hong Kong.

We walked into the lobby of the stadium and told the lady behind the desk the whole sob story. She said she would see what she could do for me and she got on her walkie-talkie. After a few minutes she said that she had found someone who would show me around. I was ecstatic. An old fella came out and took me around the stadium. Awesome. This chap was amazing as he seemed to know everything about the club. I thought with all my reading I was pretty genned up but this chap knew all the history and all the great players. We went on the pitch and he just smiled away as I just looked around in awe. I thanked the old man and was just leaving the stadium when I saw him drive up in a big old Mercedes. He wound down the window and asked if I had seen his bus? Now I really couldn't believe it! Not only had I seen the ground but the Spurs coach driver – yep, that guy who drove the team to Wembley all those times had shown me around. I was dumbstruck. That was when he laughed and said: "No...my bust, in the lobby."

OH NO! It took me all of a few seconds to realise my mistake. I had just walked past the bronze bust of Bill Nicholson in the club's reception area. Spurs' greatest manager had just shown ME around White Hart Lane. As a kid I had read an old 1972 Sun Soccer Annual and it was the only time I had seen a picture of Bill Nick – and when I looked now it was him who was sat before me. I got his autograph, offered 1,000 apologies and that was that.

So apart from being the best stadium tour ever I also managed to call our greatest ever manager the team bus driver. Oops!

Bill Nicholson, a true legend and a gentleman. I still have that autograph today.
By Clarky on Topspurs website

My only brush with the great man came last year when me and a mate were crossing the road outside the ground. I looked into an old Cavalier car that had stopped, and then did a double take once I realised it was Bill. Me and my mate started doing the old 'Nayim hero' thing waving our arms above our head in worship of the great man.

He just smiled, waved back and drove off, probably thinking: 'What a pair of idiots!'

I couldn't believe at the time he was driving this Cavalier – I thought he'd have a chauffeured limo from Spurs!
Tommyboy, Topspurs website

I stood within 10 feet of the great man. It was outside Enfield Town's ground for the Johnny Wallace benefit match. I was queuing to get in, and to my left was the glorious group of men around the legend that is Bill Nicholson. He was surrounded by Hoddle, Perryman, Chivers, Burkinshaw and Peters, and they were like children round their dad. Even with all those names around him, he stood out unbelievably. I kid you not, the aura coming off that man was immense.

No, I didn't speak to him but, my God – his presence was something I will never forget. I even sat eight rows behind him in the stand with all those great Spurs names around him. My little boy was with me and I told him he was the greatest Spurs man ever. He was only five or so at the time and he didn't take it in.
Jason Fernee

I used to have my season ticket in The Shelf, or East Lower, as it's now called, and me and my mates used to go to the Northumberland Arms before the game, which meant walking back through the school to get to our entrance. So every home game at about 2.15pm we would leave and, sure enough, as if by clockwork Bill would pull up in his blue Vauxhall Cavalier and get out of the car. He had such a glint in his eye and we all said hello to him and in his broad accent he would simply smile and say: 'Hello lads, we need a result today,' and would smile

again. I hope this story, small though it is, lets people know what kind of man Sir Bill was – a man of the people, for the people.
Steve R, Chingford

I met the great man in the school car park behind The Shelf before we played Chelsea in the FA Cup. We'd just demolished them 5-1 a few nights before, and I asked him how he thought we'd get on. He said he couldn't see lightning strike twice. After shaking his hand I twaddled off to see us get stuffed 4-0. He certainly knew his stuff.
Naylor, Topspurs website

I met him after the Plymouth cup game. He was a diamond to listen to a rabid, drunken, Spurs fan. I would have told me to f*** off!
Bazzer, Topspurs website

My dad has a great story of meeting him. After he heard he had left us in 1974, my dad, who had just moved from Edmonton to Sidcup, went straight up to White Hart Lane. Just as he got there, the good man himself just came out of White Hart Lane. He spoke to him, and about four others.

The next day in the paper, Bill Nick said that he loved the club, and then he went on to talk about five people that came to WHL to see him after they had heard he was leaving. He loved the fans the most of all.

I think he might still have that paper upstairs somewhere. I'll have a look round sometime soon.
Floyd, Topspurs website

In 1971 we played Villa in the League Cup Final at Wembley. After the game my pal and I waited outside the main area where the team bus was parked. At about 7pm the bus came out and stopped to acknowledge the few fans that were there.

Suddenly Bill Nick came to the door of the bus and said that we could come onto the coach and touch the Cup. There were just five or six of us – all schoolboys – and it is a memory I will keep forever.
Gins Twin, Topspurs website

After the League Cup Final win against Leicester in 1999, thousands were milling around outside when there was a sudden hush and the fans parted like the Red Sea and Billy and helpers walked through – amazing.
Polar, Topspurs website

League Cup semi-final, second leg in 1987 against Arsenal at WHL. I had to stand up to let Bill Nick get to his seat along the same row. Shook the great man's hand. Some spotty Gooner in the row in front earned himself a slap (not from me, I hasten to add) by turning to his mate and asking 'who the old geezer was?'.
Lish, Topspurs website

BILL NICHOLSON

The day I met Bill Nicholson is one I will never forget.

I was only an eight-year-old boy but, already, I knew who he was and had an idea of the incredibly high esteem in which he was held. The reason I knew this was my school mate continuously bragged about living next door to him, told me all about him, what he had achieved and most of all what a lovely man he was.

I asked if I could meet him one day when I was playing at my mate's house and Mr. Nicholson was more than happy to oblige. It was at that moment that I truly understood what supporting Tottenham Hotspur was all about. I hung on his every word, as I imagine all the great players who played under him did. He told me what a great club Spurs was and how proud I should be to support them and he did so without ever talking down to me or treating me like the child I was. Everything I have ever read or heard about Bill Nicholson since then has been backed up by my own personal encounter with him.

John Nicholson (no relation)

I was fortunate enough to meet and talk to the great man on at least three occasions. The first was back in 1982-83, when the club were first trying to sell the executive boxes and we held the FA Cup. Bill was surrounded by people all evening and he had words with everyone, signing autographs and having his picture taken on numerous occasions.

The second was in 1999 when we attended a testimonial dinner for Bobby Smith at Enfield Football Club's Starlight Rooms. Most of the Double-winning team were there that evening. I was fortunate to have my picture taken with Bill and a few months later met up briefly again. Despite his bad arthritis he signed the photo for me and it now takes pride of place in my home.

A truly great man the likes of which we at WHL will never see again.

John Pelley, supporter since 1959

I'd just like to tell you about one summer holiday morning, when me and my pal (we were 11 or 12) were at Cheshunt hoping to see various first team players in for pre-season training.

This day I will never forget, as it was the day that Bill Nicholson took time out of his busy schedule to cast a glance at us two, and say something so profound and meaningful, I can still hear his words now ....

*"OI, YOU TWO, GET OUT OF THE F****** GOALMOUTH!"*

Magic, I've never forgot it and I treasure the moment, I really do.

Martin Holleyoake, MEHSTG website

I first came over to England with my family from Guyana in 1962. We settled in the Tottenham area, and at first it was a bit strange, mainly because I was freezing all the time. Then I found out that it is was April and not even winter! My cousins had told me all about English football, and I knew that Tottenham was home of Spurs but, living where we did, I didn't have a clue how to get to the ground. One day, I just walked out of the house and went exploring. I don't know how long I was walking but it must have been at least an hour.

I was stopping and asking people where the ground was, and they seemed to be pointing me in the right direction, but I got the impression some of them were having a bit of a game with me. Eventually, however, I got to the front of the stadium and asked the man outside if I could go for a look inside. He seemed very official, quite frightening really, and said probably not. Just then, a group of people started coming out of the ground, and I assumed they were players – they looked as if they were. One of two of them smiled at me and said hello, one ruffled my hair, or what there was of it.

It was then that I heard an almighty roar, and I knew in the depths of my stomach what it was. My mother – a fearsome woman who you did not mess with. She had been looking all over for me, and had followed my trail to the ground. Either that, or she just guessed where I had headed for as I had often said I wanted to find it. She tore into me big time, and then this slightly older man came out and asked what the problem was. My mother, not knowing or caring anything about football, led off at him as well. God, I was embarrassed.

When it became clear that I was in the wrong, however, the older chap told me that my mum was right, and that I should do as I was told and not just wander off. He did his best to calm my mum down, but he really had no reason to. Eventually, though, she did calm down and walked me off to whatever fate was waiting for me at home.

It was only the next day, as I looked in the paper, that I saw the picture of Bill Nicholson and realised I had met 'The Man'. At school, I couldn't stop telling everyone that I had met him – some believed me, some didn't, but I couldn't care less. I have been a Spurs supporter ever since and my mum even came to a few games with me. Bill Nicholson was a gentleman in every sense of the word.

Claude, resident of Tottenham

I was once working at Tottenham for BT and was in the car park with my tools when a silver Ford Granada pulled in, backed up and hit a bollard. As I was only about 12 feet away I obviously heard it. I looked around to see an embarrassed, smiling Bill Nicholson looking back at me. He put a finger to his lips and said: 'Shhh – don't tell anyone, will you?' I just replied: "Of course not, Bill." It may have only been for a brief moment, but it was one I will never forget – Bill Nicholson spoke to me!

Steve Hayward

What the statistics don't tell you is what a great human being Sir Bill was. My only meeting with him came when I was about 18 and was watching the youth side at the old Cheshunt training ground one sunny Saturday. Stood on the earth bank alongside the small stand there, I was engrossed in the match and a voice asked me: "What's the score, son?"

Turning around while saying we were winning 1-0, I was faced with Bill Nick. I was a little bit lost for words and even more so when he asked: "How are we playing?" What was I to say? Me, a mere watcher of the game trying to inform a man who had managed a team to the Double, won European trophies and been in charge of two great Spurs side, as well as playing for one in the 50s.

Well, I mumbled a few callow observations and he thanked me for that, telling me he liked this player and that. But I never felt that he was talking down to me. It was more like chatting to an uncle than talking to a legend of the game, who you had revered for years. And that was his abiding charm. His humility. No airs and graces. No big 'I am'. Yes, just plain Bill Nicholson.

When managers nowadays appear to be bigger than the team and some bigger than the game, Bill viewed his job as just that. Something to be done and left behind him. Except he never could leave it behind, as he was 24 hours a day Tottenham Hotspur. Even when Spurs showed him the door and he moved to West Ham as a scout, his one and only love was Spurs. And when they called him back, he bore no grudge and simply came home.

Sir Bill made a rod for the back of every Spurs manager who followed him, but that success is what they should try and emulate with the club. What they might not be able to copy is the way he conducted his life.

Our sympathy is with his relatives at this time as they have lost a loving member of their family. Spurs have lost their most favoured son of all those who have been associated with the club.

But the world has lost a wonderful human being.
Wyart Lane, MEHSTG website

I was playing for my school side, St Thomas More, on the old pitches behind the East Stand. No-one really took any notice of the old boy watching us. The ball was going out of play and as I went to take the throw, I realised it was Bill Nick who had thrown the ball back. After the whistle he had a word for all of us, even the Gooners amongst us! He stood and signed every scrap of paper that was thrust at him. I think the stadium should be named after him. 'The Bill Nicholson Stadium' has got a nice ring to it.
Tim Cronin, Broxbourne, Herts

I went out with a girl in the late 60s who lived a couple of doors from Bill, and met him a few times though her mum and dad. I think I only went out with her so I might bump into Bill some nights after taking her home!

Then one day I was talking to Bill and had a bit of a limp from playing for a Sunday morning team, and Bill asked me what was wrong. I told him I had hurt my ankle playing on the Sunday and I would miss our cup final on the following Sunday, but Bill said to come to the ground the next day and he would get it sorted for me. I had treatment three days running and I played in the final on that Sunday, so I would like to dedicate that cup win to Bill all these years later.
Jim Darker

I met Bill three or four times. On the last occasion we were in the same lounge at The Lane, during the friendly match against DC United, which was used as the launch for the Tottenham Charitable Trust. He seemed so unassuming that I just thought I'd go up to him and strike up a conversation. After I'd introduced myself,

I told him what a pleasure it was to meet him. The thing is, it was only a week after I'd met Margaret Thatcher, and in the past I'd also met Henry Kissinger, but Bill was something else.

I had met these two world figures but I got a bigger impression from meeting Bill. That was endorsed by the fact that, just a year after his testimonial against Fiorentina, here he was being presented to the crowd on the pitch at half-time, and he got the biggest standing ovation I have ever heard. What was upsetting for me was the fact that, as he came on with his walking stick, part of me wondered deep down whether that was the last time he would stand on the pitch at White Hart Lane. Afterwards, I went up to him and asked him how it felt, and he just replied: 'Fabulous, absolutely fabulous.'

In the lounge that night were some real Tottenham people – Klinsmann, Gascoigne, Hoddle, Ginola – but it was still Bill that stood out for me in that crowded room. It's easy to over-dramatise since his death, but I would have said the same thing at any other time – he WAS Tottenham.

Another occasion, around 1997, I was on my way to the ground and Bill used to leave his car in the playground of Park Lane School. I was walking along with him and we got chatting about how my dad used to watch all the great sides of his, and what struck me was the enthusiasm he still had whenever he spoke about those teams...Dave Mackay, Danny Blanchflower, John White...he pointed out that at the time, all those great players were on a maximum wage, and they were just normal people. But he added that so much had changed in the modern game so quickly and, although he seemed to live in the hope that the true spirit of the game would somehow come back, deep down I think he knew it wouldn't. He said that it's a different game today – that players look at the game differently, and that it all seems to be about money. I was amazed that Bill still had so much to do with a game that had changed so much from the one he played and loved, but he obviously kept an eye on football.

Daniel Wynne, spokesman of the Tottenham Supporters' Trust

Chapter 12
The Lighter Side of the Man

*"Jimmy Pearce and I were sitting together one day, when Bill looks at Jimmy
and says: 'If you had Pratty's heart and he had your skill, I'd have two bloody
world-beaters on my hands'."*
John Pratt

*It was always said that Jimmy (Greaves) was so important to Bill, that if you
wound Jimmy up, you wound Bill up. Phil Beal, however, couldn't resist a wind-
up, and one day at training before we were due to have a team-talk, Phil put
sneezing powder on Jimmy's shoulder. All the while Bill's trying to get his
message across and Greavsie is sneezing like mad. Bill was sorely tempted to tell
Jimmy to sort himself out, but he didn't know what the rest of us did.*

*Even worse than that was one day before a match, Beally had some laxative
sweets, but only every third one was loaded. The rest of us knew it, apart from
Cyril Knowles, who would always be there if anything was on offer. 'Can I have
one?' was probably Knowlesy's catch phrase.*

*Anyway, true to form, Cyril takes the sweet and the rest, as they say, was misery.
He was glued to the bog for ages, and Bill was fuming. To his dying day I don't
know if anybody ever told him who had set Cyril up, or even if anybody had, but
it would have been interesting to see how he reacted.*
John Pratt

*I had been getting it in the neck a bit from some of the sections of the crowd at
Spurs but Bill expected his players to be men, and as we all know he said that the
crowd paid our wages and were entitled to have their opinions. So one day, before
I was due to play my first game at Old Trafford, I asked him what I could expect.
He replied that it would be just like playing at Spurs, except that up there 55,000
people would hate me, whereas at Spurs it was only 45,000!*
John Pratt

*I'd been playing out of my skin for quite a while, and around that time there were
quite a few players heading towards a hundred quid a week, so I thought to myself:
'Why not?' I walked up to Bill's office, knocked and in I went.*

*"Bill," I said to him, "I think I should have a raise. I reckon I'm worth a hundred
pound a week."*

*Bill remained unaffected by this challenge to his authority. "What makes you
think that, Jonesy?" he said.*

"Because I'm the best winger in the world," I replied, and if the papers were to

be believed, I had a good argument.

"Well," said Bill, "that's your opinion, Jonesy, not mine. Close the door on your way out."

He never mixed with us and was loathe to give praise, but once he patted me on the back and said: "Well done, Jonesy."

I replied: "Blimey, Bill, you said well done."

"Yes," he said, "but remember, Cliff, a pat on the back is only two feet away from a kick up the a***!"
Cliff Jones

A few of us hadn't seen Darkie around for a while, and someone asked Bill if she was under the weather. He had that sort of look on his face – you know, half grin, half scowl, and he says: "No – she's banned."

It turns out that every time Darkie went to a game recently, we lost. So Bill told her to stay at home!
Maurice Norman

John Pratt saw the lighter side of Bill Nick.

During the arrangements for Bill's first Testimonial in 1983, he was sitting in on a meeting with the eight-man committee in the old office at the front of the West Stand. It had dragged on for quite a while, and I needed to get home. I had a 45-mile drive back to Maidstone.

"Bill," I said. "It's been great, but I really need to be getting back now."

"No, stop and have another drink," he replied.

"I can't," I argued. "I've got to drive home, and it's a long way."

"Just one more, Ken – that'll be all right, surely?"

I was dumbfounded. "Why weren't you like this before?" I asked him.

"Like what?"

"This," I said. "All these years I've known you, and you were always such a miserable b******!"

"I'm not miserable," Bill replied. "I'm dour. It said so in the papers."
Ken Jones

Bill was a big believer in team spirit, and if that meant letting the lads have a few wind-ups, he'd go along with it. We were in Portugal, due to play Vittoria Setubal, and we were in the hotel having a meal. This waiter brings one of those silver *serving trays up to me – you know, the things with the lids – and says: "This is from Cyril Knowles – your fish dinner." When I took the lid off, there was just the fish's head and the bones. I thought, right mate. I always warned Knowlesey that if he ever got me, I'd get him back with interest.*

Later on, we were walking around the fishing harbour, and I saw this stall with loads of fresh fish, and I bought a load. I managed to get the keys to Cyril's room, and shoved the fish under his pillow. He used to room with Pat Jennings, and from what I can gather, most of the night was spent with the two of them trying to work out where the God–almighty stink was coming from.

The following day, Bill was walking past me in the hotel and he just had this sort of knowing smile on his face, and then he winked at me without saying a word. He knew all right.

Phil Beal

Bill, of course, was this simple man who lived the spartan life, with no great feelings for shows of materialism, wasn't he? Well, maybe. In the early 60s, Bill used to drive around in this very basic Ford – I think it was a Poplar, or an Escort or Prefect, something like that. Well, one day it was parked in the car park at White Hart Lane, when in comes Dave Mackay in a shiny red Jaguar, and parks it next to Bill's car, which then appears to be shrinking by the second.

The following day, Bill rolls into the car park – in a silver Granada!

Dick Moss

Chapter 13

To us, he IS 'Sir Bill'

It was in the latter part of 2001 that a rather odd occurrence took place. Quite independently, two individuals who had no idea of each other's existence decided to embark on a campaign to get Bill Nicholson's achievements in football honoured in the form of a knighthood. These completely separate campaigns took shape within a few weeks of each other, and both were quite simply the brainwaves of people who had tolerated the foot-dragging by the establishment for long enough when it came to recognising true merit.

Bill, of course, had already received an OBE from HRH The Queen Mother at Buckingham Palace – and for an ordinary working class lad from Yorkshire, who was by his very nature quite understated, that would probably seem to be quite sufficient. Indeed, when Bill got wind of the knighthood campaigns he was genuinely touched and flattered but, in true Bill Nick style, couldn't really see what all the fuss was about.

After all, he had only been the first manager to win the League and Cup Double in the 20th century, the first boss of any British side to triumph in European competition, along with a further five trophies along the way.

He had been with the same club from his teens, quite often putting in 16-hour days, running his beloved club from top to bottom, ensuring that the players and staff under his guidance conducted themselves in public impeccably, whilst all the time playing football with flair and passion but within the rules of the game.

He was only the man who had been largely responsible for elevating the level and prestige of English football forever, but who had also put a club from a small suburb of North London on the football map of the world. No big deal, Bill would think.

If Bill was much too modest to seek royal approval of his outstanding achievements, there were others who felt differently.

One such person was found under the unlikely name of Harry Hotspur, a pseudonym for someone who was quite content to set about the task of setting up a website which was to draw attention to the glaring injustice of Bill's lack of regal bling, whilst all the time maintaining his private life . . .

Like all Tottenham fans, I was full of admiration for Bill Nick and all that he had done for the club," says Harry. "For quite some time I had wondered why he hadn't been honoured with a knighthood, like so many of the country's other great men of football.

One Saturday near the end of 2000, I was watching Sky TV's Soccer AM and heard mention of a group of Leeds fans who were campaigning for a knighthood for John Charles. I thought that if their campaign could get enough publicity to get on TV, then there was no reason why a campaign for Bill couldn't do the same.

Nobody else seemed likely to do it so I decided have a go myself. I don't think I even planned it to be a campaign back at the start – I just thought I might start an online petition to get some support going for some kind of initiative. So I put up an extremely poor one-page website and invited people to sign the petition. Publicising it on several popular Tottenham websites got the ball rolling and signatures started coming in.

Word soon started to spread and a friend who was involved in setting up the Tottenham Trust mentioned the campaign in a meeting with the club's chairman Daniel Levy. Levy had no hesitation in offering the club's full support and from that moment on gave me any help I requested from the club. He appointed Press Officer John Fennelly as a kind of liaison officer between the club and myself. Fennelly was absolutely superb and did everything I asked of him, and more.

Contacting the press and asking for publicity raised the profile of the campaign further. Sadly, many journalists were more interested in writing about Beckham's latest hairdo than one of football's all-time greats, but quite a few were willing to help and did articles on Bill and the campaign. I also managed to get a couple of mentions on Soccer AM.

I found out about another Tottenham fan – John Hayes – who was also campaigning for a knighthood for Bill, so I contacted him. We decided it would be wise to team up and combine our efforts. We have since become good friends.

I never had any grand plan for how the campaign would go – I was new to this sort of thing and was really just making it up as I went along! It would just be a case of thinking of new ways to get publicity, then finding ways to get that accomplished. As the support for the campaign grew it got easier, as I had a wider circle of people whose brains I could pick and whose help I could enlist. Getting Tottenham fans to help wasn't hard. Such was the respect for Bill, I only had to mention his name and the response was always: 'How can I help?'. The fans were superb, and their support was crucial.

Petitions, with several thousand signatures, were sent in to the relevant government department but these were not successful. I started to realise how the honours system worked. I believed it was a bit of a closed shop and I felt our petitions were being overlooked – or rather ignored.

I managed to enlist the help of a fairly senior person in the government, hoping that he could exert some behind-the-scenes influence for Bill's case. He worked very hard and even managed to get Minister for Sport Richard Caborn to personally nominate Bill. The Minister for Sport's recommendation was ignored by the honours department, who chose instead to honour Arsene Wenger and Gerard Houllier. It was then that I became disillusioned with the honours system. I felt I was banging my head against a brick wall, and there's only so long you can do that before it starts to hurt.

Obviously, I carried on trying but from then onwards, I felt we were unlikely to be successful. My feelings about the honours system were eventually proved to be true when the government admitted the system's methods were outdated and would be overhauled. Sadly that overhaul didn't come in time to enable Bill to receive the honour we all know he deserved.

However, I do feel the campaign achieved a lot – mainly in the way it raised awareness of Bill. He had always been so modest about his achievements and never sought publicity or praise for himself. We shone a spotlight on him again, reminding us all – as if we needed to be reminded – what a great man we had in our midst, and just how much we owed to him. It also brought him to the attention of the younger generation of Tottenham fans, who may not have known much about him.

Harry Hotspur

A few miles away, in rural Essex, John Hayes had similar thoughts of his own...

It was the year after Alex Ferguson was knighted. I thought that Bill, for what he achieved in his many years at Spurs, deserved similar recognition, especially as, being a child of the 50s, I did actually see his teams play. He was not only a great manager, but also a great ambassador for Spurs and football. I felt sure that I, an ordinary member of the public, should try and do something about it.

I sent off to the nominations department of the Home Office for the official nomination forms. I filled them in as I thought would befit such a man, together with a couple of letters backing the nomination. Once I had sent those letters off, I thought that it might be wise to write off to many other famous people and ask them to submit letters through me to help the nomination through.

Later that year, I heard of Harry Hotspur's campaign and we got together through the MEHSTG website and joined forces, hoping that the two different approaches would carry greater weight.

John Hayes

John enlisted the help of Ron Henry, left-back in Bill's legendary Double-winning side. Ron managed to somehow get a letter of nomination signed by all the surviving members of the double side, and that weighty document was sent to the nominations unit of the House of Commons.

The widespread appeal of the Knight Bill campaign is evident by some of the names who were prepared to become involved. Several were ones with obvious Tottenham connections. Glenn Hoddle, then manager of Southampton, wrote to the nominations unit to lend his support, as did Terry Venables, Gary Mabbutt, Gary Lineker, journalist and self-confessed 'Irritant of the Year' and avid Spurs supporter Richard Littlejohn. And from the club itself, chairman Daniel Levy. From quite early in the campaign, it was evident that the current regime at Tottenham considered that Bill's standing within the football community, and society at large, deserved their whole-hearted support.

Not quite so obvious were other figures from the football establishment who were keen to right the wrong. Football knight Sir Bobby Charlton placed his considerable clout behind the campaign, as did former England manager Graham

BILL NICHOLSON

Taylor, former head of the Premier League Richard Scudamore and former head of the Football Association Adam Crozier.

One of the even less obvious supporters was former Arsenal goalkeeper Bob Wilson. Now chairman of the London Soccer Coaches' Association, Bob had fond memories of Bill's fabulous side of the early 60s and, in spite of his obvious Arsenal connections, felt more recognition was due. A more in-depth analysis of Bob's views on Bill can be found in the 'Media's Final Page' chapter of the tributes section.

A cynical view of the world of Westminster would suggest that politicians usually don't get too wrapped up in sport unless there are votes involved, but from the tone of the following letter, it is clear that Bill had supporters in high places who had no political axe to grind...

I certainly supported the move to get Bill a knighthood, and wrote to the Honours section. I knew Bill when I worked with the apprentices on their education 'life skills' programme in the 80s and found him to be someone who cared deeply about each lad on the 'books' at Spurs. It seemed amazing that he had not been honoured and I found, when Sports minister, that many decent well deserving people seemed to have missed out on an appropriate honour. He was definitely one such person.
Kate Hoey MP, former Minister of Sport

Fellow Members of Parliament, Tony Banks (an avid Chelsea fan, but everybody's entitled to one mistake in their life), and Tottenham MP David Lammy (thankfully, a Spurs man) were right behind it from the off. In fact, when Banks sent Harry Hotspur an email endorsing the campaign, he could not resist ending it with: "Good luck for next season, and thanks for the six points!"

But time, as they say, was not on Bill's side. As he approached his twilight years, the need for more publicity gained momentum, and a couple of articles appeared in the club magazine *Spurs Monthly* urging readers, especially younger Spurs fans, to find out more about Bill's achievements and to get active. It is uncertain whether such an approach had the desired effect, but judging by the amount of signatures collected at the end of the campaign shortly after Bill's passing last October, it might have. There were over three thousand.

The media was called into action as well. Quite apart from having the campaign mentioned on Sky TV, national radio station TalkSPORT agreed to lend their support, ably supplemented by the views of their presenter and ex-Spurs man, Alan Brazil. The views of many of Fleet Street's (or is it Wapping's?) finest on Bill's merit for a knighthood can be found in the 'Media's Final Page' section.

But surely the most glowing testimonial to Bill's standing as one of the game's elder statesmen came in the form of a letter, undersigned by all 400 members of the Football Writers' Association, stating in their own eloquent words the injustice of the situation. Bill, it has to be said, was one of those managers who, unless you were one of the fortunate few who knew how to 'read' him, could be a journalist's nightmare. He was taciturn, not given to expressive rolls of dialogue in the mode of Clough, or the sharp one-liners of Bill Shankly; so the fact that, to a man, the industry chose to endorse Harry Hotspur's and John Hayes' campaign is proof enough that if you shout loud enough, and if the cause is just, you *can* make a difference.

Unfortunately, in many people's eyes, it will always be to the detriment of the honours system that Bill did not live long enough to see the fruits of so many people's labours. People such as Bill Nicholson are surely a national treasure, and should be treated as such.

Harry Hotspur now has an excellent website devoted to the life of Bill Nicholson. Entitled 'The Bill Nicholson Way', it can be found at www.thfc1961.fsnet.co.uk

 · DAVID LAMMY MP
House of Commons
London SW1A 0AA
Member of Parliament for Tottenham

Tel: 020 7219 0767
Fax: 020 7219 0357
www.davidlammy.co.uk

Mr D Spooner
The Nominations Unit
Ceremonial Branch
Cabinet Office
Ashley House
2 Monck Street
London
SW1P 2BQ

Our Ref: 010306

17 October 2001

Dear Mr Spooner

I am writing to you both in my capacity as a Member of Parliament and as a fan of Tottenham Hotspur Football Club. I am aware that your office has received a nomination for a Knighthood for Bill Nicholson O.B.E. and would like to add my name to the nomination.

Bill Nicholson enjoyed a successful career as a player, winning a cap for the national team and the League Championship in 1950-51 despite losing half of his career to the war, during which time he was a member of the Durham Light Infantry. Having retired from playing the game, Bill became manager of the Tottenham side and became the first manager in the twentieth century to win the league and cup double. He then went on to enter the history books as the manager of the first team to win a major European trophy. Not forgetting numerous domestic cups won under his guidance.

Bill Nicholson has been a faithful servant to Tottenham Hotspur Football Club for all but one of the last sixty-five years (excluding the war) and to this day does not miss a game. He has been a true ambassador to the game and should be rewarded for his services. Now aged eighty-one, time is surely against him, I only hope that his efforts are recognised during his lifetime.

Yours sincerely

David Lammy
Member of Parliament for Tottenham

PART 4
THE KING IS DEAD –
LONG LIVE THE MEMORIES

Chapter 14
Irreplaceable

"Change and decay in all around I see,
O thou who changest not, abide with me"
From the hymn *Abide With Me*,
sung at Bill's memorial service,
Sunday, November 7, 2004

It was the day that every Spurs fan hoped would never come but on Saturday, October 23, 2004, Bill finally said goodbye to his beloved Spurs forever. As news of his passing spread, it suddenly began to dawn on all of us that a tangible part of our soul had been lost, and the words from that old song *You Never Know What You've Got Till It's Gone* never rang truer. Even youngsters who had previously only understood that Bill was 'an ex-manager' suddenly began to realise just what this modest, unassuming man had done to elevate the profile of Tottenham Hotspur to world status.

On that fateful Saturday, Spurs were to entertain Bolton Wanderers at home. As one might expect, the mood was very low-key. Before the Premiership game, images of Bill and his legendary achievements were shown on the Jumbotron screens at either end of the stadium, and it will be forever to the credit of not only our own fans but also those of Bolton Wanderers that the minute's silence observed that afternoon was absolute – you could hear a pin drop. After that, and as blasphemous as the idea may have been to Bill himself, the result was largely an irrelevance. For the record, Spurs lost 1-2.

The following day, I took my 13-year old son Matt down to The Lane to pay our respects. It was obvious that the club had been expecting this day for some time – Bill, after all, was very frail in his last few days – but even allowing for that, they deserve a massive pat on the back for the fantastic job they did and the wonderful display they put on, which was done with impeccable taste and professionalism. Spurs have received a lot of flak in recent years from the media but when they get it right, they get it very right, and this was one of those instances. Bill would most definitely have approved.

The same could be said of the tribute service for Bill, held on Sunday, November 7, 2004 at White Hart Lane, also organised by Daniel Levy's wife. Players old and new turned up, along with thousands of Tottenham fans of all ages.

There were speeches made by Cliff Jones and Jimmy Greaves, back at The Lane for the first time in several years. Some of the anecdotes about Bill must have drawn a wry smile from the ranks of players watching. On the screen, images of the golden days of the early 60s brought back wonderful memories for many of the older fans present. Hymns such as *Abide With Me* and *Jerusalem* added to the sense of occasion.

Providing poignant recollections of the great man, Bill's players from the 70s were represented by Steve Perryman and Martin Chivers. Glenn Hoddle and Gary Mabbutt, two legends of the 70s and 80s, brought a modern perspective to the day's proceedings.

The day was completed by the releasing of 85 white doves, each one symbolising a year of Bill Nicholson's life. There were few in the sizeable crowd that day who remained untouched by what they saw and heard.

The following is a record of those traumatic, yet uplifting few days as recorded by Spurs players and fans at The Lane, in fanzines and on websites. They are Bill's people, and these are their thoughts...

I was brought up in a household of Tottenham supporters. I married a Tottenham supporter and we have passed that tradition and love for Spurs onto our three daughters. When I went into the ministry, I began serving in the Parish of Chigwell. Unknown to me, just around the corner to our vicarage is the Tottenham training ground. It seemed only natural to me that as well as caring for all those in my parish, I should also care for the Tottenham boys. It was through my offer to be available to the team, to support them in any way I can, that my name remained on file.

When Tracey Levy telephoned me and asked if I would be available to take part in Bill's memorial service, there was only one answer. Sunday, November 7 was a special day for me and for thousands of others who had the privilege of knowing Bill Nicholson, whether personally or through his contribution to Spurs. It was a great day for me and for the fans at White Hart Lane. I couldn't add or take away from the many tributes that were received from around the world and also from home. Also meeting ex-Spurs players is something that will always be very special to me.

Many people do go through life with outstanding gifts and qualities but the greatest gift you can give is of yourself. As a fresh faced 16-year-old Bill's life was changed through Spurs and the club was changed through Bill. He gave himself faithfully and with integrity to his beloved Spurs. And I believe that part of the reason he has become such a legend is that he possessed those rare qualities of loyalty and passion for all that he was involved in as well as his game. It never left him. He remained focused and committed to playing well, managing well and to win well.

It was a wonderful day for thanksgiving for such a gentleman's life, for his family and friends and for the loyalty of the fans, who still continue to keep that sense of pride alive. Bill made a huge difference to other people's lives. I never met him personally, and yet like many others I feel that I did know him. White Hart Lane remains a very special place to be. Thank you to all who work there for their welcome and their spirit.
Reverend Toni Smith, St. Winifred's Church, Chigwell

Chapter 15
The Fans Speak

Bill Nicholson - a Hammers tribute

In the 60s people used to go to watch Tottenham. That chant that the Man United fans used to sing at away games in the late 90s about: 'You're only here to see United' or whatever it was – that was actually true for Spurs in the 60s. No matter where they played the gate would go up (and by a huge amount), because people wanted to watch possibly the best (and certainly the most entertaining) team that the British game has ever seen. People talk about Arsenal now but in my opinion they didn't come anywhere near to providing the same entertainment that the Spurs team in the early 60s did. That was all down to Bill Nicholson and his view that the paying public were the most important thing in football. More important to him than winning a game even.

I am not ashamed to admit that in the 60s, depending on our own fixtures, I used to sometimes go to watch Tottenham (as did fans of all the London clubs – and from much further afield too) and they were poetry in motion. In Greaves they had probably the best goalscorer I have ever seen, bar none, and in Blanchflower probably the best midfielder – he used to try things on the football pitch that no other player would even dare to think of. And not only that, but they used to come off nearly every time as well. Add to that probably the hardest footballer I have ever seen in Dave Mackay, who could also play the game as well as any skilful player, and you can start to see why they were so good. Nicholson really did put together a team where the name of every player just rolled off the tongue – in fact back in the early 60s, I would say that most football fans in the country could name every player in that Spurs team. It's hard to comprehend now but that's how revered they were.

Had Bill Nicholson never got involved at Spurs they would not have enjoyed the 'big club' status that they have always maintained, even though since the early 90s their fortunes have changed considerably.

I was lucky enough to meet Bill Nicholson several seasons ago when we were playing Spurs at White Hart Lane. He was walking to his seat in the East Stand (apparently he used to refuse a seat in the directors' box as he liked to sit with the real fans). I shook his hand and told him that even though I was a West Ham fan and my family always had been Hammers, he was probably the man I held in the most esteem, football wise. Not only because of the delightful football that his team played but also because of his incredible loyalty to the club that he loved, even when they hadn't always treated him with the same respect. He thanked me for my words, said he had enormous respect for West Ham and the way they have always tried to play the game and basically said that Tottenham were so deeply ingrained in his heart that he would always love them no matter what. I replied: "Bill, you have that the wrong way round. It is YOU that is so deeply ingrained in the heart of Tottenham; it is YOU that will always be loved by them, no matter what."

I will certainly be going up to White Hart Lane this week to pay my respects to possibly the greatest football manager of my lifetime. I will leave a West Ham scarf and probably shed a tear or two – not because he died in unfortunate circumstances as he had a good, long life but simply because the game has lost a true great. How he wasn't given a knighthood, I'll never know.

RIP 'Sir' Bill Nicholson...if only you'd been a Hammer.

Matt C, MEHSTG Website

William Edward Nicholson OBE
A Fan's Homage to 'Mr. Tottenham Hotspur'
It is better to fail aiming high than to succeed aiming low.
And we of Spurs have set our sights very high,
So high, in fact, that even failure will have in it an echo of glory.

How many times in a lifetime are we subjected to the grossly overstated, and no more prevalent than at the sad passing away of yet another sporting star?

This person is great, that person was great, with the broadcaster of doom simply wallowing in rambling, overblown and unwarranted eulogies.

It would seem, in British football, that nothing more than a consistent crosser of the ball is hailed 'the best in the world', and that an accurate free-kick exponent is quickly lauded as 'world class' – regardless of whatever the earth's population has to offer.

Similarly, our thirst for ripping out jugular veins for the merest of fault is legendary. Oh for a distant age, where over-reaction and excessive exaggeration were yet to emerge. For a world immersed in so-called 'reality', surely none of this could be real.

I met Bill Nicholson but twice in my life, yet his doctrines and philosophies will follow me to the grave. This was no mere football manager, but a teacher, a leader, a profound thinker, and a man for whom the word 'dignity' was personally crafted from stone.

Make no mistake – Bill was no soft touch, and certainly not the kind 'uncle' figure that his later pictures portrayed. He was tough, uncompromising, and at times, ruthless. Whereas others were more complaisant, and complacent, Bill Nicholson demanded consistency, effort and battling qualities in equal measure. A tough task-master, he also called for skills with style – winning without grace was simply off the menu.

Yet for a man of few public words, Bill's sporadic, yet infamous quotes will live on in my mind, especially the one about entertaining the fans. If only other football managers felt the same way.

This was a true man of the players, a man of the times and, more importantly, a man of the people.

My first 'meeting' with him was many years ago, as part of a visiting party to early 70s White Hart Lane, with its wooden trimmings, its long-gone, crescent-shaped crossovers that perched on the perimeter fencing, and its semi-seated banks at each end of the stadium.

That was 'our' stadium. The White Hart Lane that will live in the memories of many grey-templed fans, and the place where most of our dreams were played out – those lucid, golden dreams of 'glory glory' nights, the great European journeys, and the culmination of our playground efforts coming to pass. Now they seem but ghosts from a bygone age; Blanchflower to Henry, Henry out to Jones, Jones knocks a cross in to White, who finds the path of Smith, and goaaaaaaaaaaaaal. Or should I say, the inevitable...

But Bill Nicholson didn't simply preside over one team. In his reign at The Lane, he built two – both strong, both crammed with character and, more importantly, both kings of style and entertainment.

And there he stood in front of me. A legend; staring down at the gaping, entranced teenager, who harboured little sense, but enough to know he was in the company of someone special.

Their names roll from the tongue like old friends; the players, the coaches, the trainers, the characters who made White Hart Lane a place of fantasy. A place to leave your troubles behind for two hours of fairy tale, passion and awe. You know them too. You witnessed what they did for us, and you know the high expectancy they've weaved in to the fabric of everyday Tottenham life. Now our shoulders are burdened forever.

Every coming season expectant, and with dreams of Nicholson's glory, and the soaring mountains he climbed. Yet those successes are now shrouded in the mists of the past; every win, every victory with style, every cup held aloft, every ghost of heroes past mere memories. But if we've learned anything from our brief moment in time, it must be thus; that the body has passed on, but the ideals, the thoughts and the standards must survive.

Like the passing on of the earth to the next generation, Nicholson's word should be allowed to grow, to be nurtured by a new breed of followers, and to pass in to future folklore intact, providing a legacy for those that come after us.

Our 'reunion' presented yours truly as a forty-something adult. A new career granting me access to the portals of the modern stadium as an eager and amateur(ish) new scribe.

Busting with questions and enthusiasm, those festering childlike feelings of awe returned, rendering me speechless, once again in the great man's company.

I wanted to ask so much; to find out the thoughts behind his actions, to understand the reasoning behind the man, to know what made that great brain tick and drove it on – but nothing. Nothing flowed during my second chance meeting with the icon who had styled my childhood. The man who had enticed me to Tottenham Hotspur above all others, and the man whose philosophies bought sanity to a world that had long gone mad.

"What are you looking for?" he gently asked.

"Inspiration," said I, as if he hadn't provided enough of it already.

BILL NICHOLSON

It was not a rude response on my behalf, just that his presence and the shock of it made me stumble for the correct words. My head wanted to burst. It was Bill Nicholson. Bill Nicholson the icon. Bill Nicholson the man who turned my Spurs into kings. Yet I could offer nothing to him, minus a few short grunts of communication that got lost in the ether. I wanted to thank him. To pass on my appreciation for all that he'd built. I wanted to keep him rooted to the spot for as long as it took. I wanted to drain his mind of replies to my still unanswered questions.

And so it was time to move on. To find my previously intended target, interview him and be on my way, But, understandably, it rankled that I'd missed a golden lifetime opportunity that I'd always regret

The journey home was long. Short in distance, but long in the world of missed chances. Had the great Bobby Smith, or the mercurial Greaves missed from such range, surely they'd have been lost to obscurity!

I wanted to tell everyone that I'd just met God. I wanted to scream at the top of my voice that I'd just met 'THE' Bill Nicholson. Yet inside I shrank, knowing that, with a major opportunity spurned, I'd never get the chance again. Yet before I'd concluded my work, Bill guided me to the correct part of the stadium. He spoke in tones that had enticed me, and millions like me, to White Hart Lane, with the flowing, flamboyant style that became his trademark – and with the reassurance that had guided hundreds of players throughout their careers.

Writing a book about Bill is not a simple task. With maximum respect, Bill was a wholly one-dimensional character. He was strong, 100% straight and honest, and as tirelessly hardworking as was humanly possible. To use modern day parlance, what you saw was what you got. There were few frills in his life, living in modest, convenient accommodation for most of his days, and expecting, and demanding much of all who worked under his umbrella. He did not court attention, did not conduct his life through newspapers or media, and could teach a lesson or three to those who do.

His achievements were in action, rarely in words.

But two questions remain, to date, unanswered.

It is easy to list the array of wonderful and staggering achievements in the man's life. That has been admirably covered by others more eloquent than I. But I wonder, one, what would have become of our beloved Spurs had he not arrived? And two, why the football world has universally turned its back on his achievements and played down his death in such a dismissive manner, or am I merely being over-sensitive to someone who meant so much to the lives of so many?

Bill was originally invited to trial for Spurs in 1936 having been spotted playing for Scarborough Working Men's Club by a northern-based scout. This is where the law of averages rule. What if the scout hadn't turned up, or Bill had been injured?

What if the game had been called off, and what if, what if, what if?

But in thankful acknowledgement of his induction, his playing career and subsequent managership, why, oh why, has the man not been knighted?

Why, in a world of awards given out like confetti, does the late, great, Bill Nicholson not get his due rewards? And this is where I came in.

The man is a true great. A bona-fide, 100-carat legend who will live forever in the hearts and minds of all who shared his life. He was the inspirational heartbeat of a community, a loyal and dignified talisman who only knew one way – The Bill Nicholson way.

Rest in peace, Bill, rest in peace...

Keith Palmer

We normally aim for some witty or pithy caption on our front cover, but it is neither necessary nor appropriate this time. We doubt that anyone reading this will be unaware of Bill Nicholson's enormous list of accomplishments during the 68 years he was associated with Tottenham Hotspur Football Club. We were going to say 'our club' but in this instance we should really say 'his club', for apart from the 18 months or so he spent scouting for West Ham in the mid-70s, after being harshly sidelined by the Tottenham directors when he resigned as manager, there can be few people in football who have been wedded to one club, so successfully, for so long.

Both our league championships had Bill centre stage, there were three FA Cups, two League Cups, two European trophies – but perhaps, even more significantly, the establishment of Tottenham as a European power – and all this employing both fabulous individual players mostly brought to the club by Bill and a brand of football that can never be forgotten.

The OBE Bill received in 1975 was scant reward for his true contribution not just to Tottenham but to football in general; he should have received a knighthood but they weren't handed out as liberally to football people in his day. The current regime at the club deserves great credit for the well-judged response to Bill's sad passing and the Memorial Service on November will be an emotional time for all of us.

And while there is always sadness when someone so loved dies, it should also be a celebration of a fantastic life that brought so much joy to so many. CaDD offers heartfelt condolences to Bill's family and friends for their far greater loss and to Billy Nick himself, wherever he now is, we say simply, thanks for everything.

Extract from Lead Article, 'Cock-a-Doodle-Do' November 2004

Goodbye, Mr Tottenham

On the morning of October 23, at 10.30am, I received a text message that simply said: 'Bill Nicholson RIP'.

By the time I left for the Bolton game, four more people had contacted me, all with the same sad message. Suddenly the match didn't seem so important.

I don't think the news really sunk in until I approached the ground and I realised that Bill Nicholson wouldn't be coming here any more. Then suddenly the game became significant as I thought how much Bill would have wanted Spurs to win – not just by a 1-0 Santini Special but with the style of attacking football he always served up to those fans lucky enough to go to White Hart Lane in the early 60s.

BILL NICHOLSON

Bill was a very dignified manager and his record speaks for itself. He made us the greatest club in the country. If it hadn't been for Bill I would have never supported Spurs. He bought the players I loved, whose names would decorate the covers on my school books (despite numerous warnings from my teachers).

When I started going to Spurs, Bill would often come across as an anonymous figure as he and Eddie Baily quietly made their way to the dug-out in front of the old West Stand. In those days, only the best was good enough for Tottenham and the team would do the talking for the manager.

It was a joy to visit White Hart Lane. My most personal memory comes from Sunday, April 14, 1991, a date none of us will ever forget. Before that semi-final I was nervous. It was a cold morning and I was trying not to let my mates see I was shaking. As we marched up Wembley Way, the first bit of Gooner-baiting began, but it seemed that the Gooners were more up for it, which wasn't a good sign.

At the top of the ramp the two sides clashed, but as we made our way through the chaos the crowd suddenly opened up and Bill Nicholson walked straight through. I rushed over and shook his hand, asking: 'Are we going to win today?' He gave me one of his smiles and said: 'Of course we are'. It was like meeting the Duke of Wellington before the battle of Waterloo. Suddenly I believed we could turn the Gooners over...and of course, we did.

White Hart Lane will never be the same without Bill. As a player and manager he brought pleasure into the lives of generations of Spurs fans. Like us, he loved Tottenham – and that's why we'll always love him.

God bless you, Mr Tottenham.
Angry the Yid

Extracts from 'Bill', CaDD 46

When CaDD started in 1994 we made a point of securing Bill as our first big interview, his suggestion to Melissa Oliveck that 'No-one's bothered about me any more' was as wide of the mark as he can have ever been. Later that season we were delivering another new issue to local newsagents when we saw Bill sitting in his car in a turning off Fore Street. We were just plucking up the courage to go and knock on his window to offer a free copy when we saw his wife Darkie emerge from the shop we'd just delivered to with a copy in hand. As she got in the car and gave it to Bill, he looked, we like to think, approvingly at it before driving off.

Shortly after Venables' sacking the year before, TISA held a 'rally' at the Sports Centre on the High Road. As Club President Bill could easily have taken the diplomatic line and kept quiet about the sacking but despite his outward modesty that wasn't Bill's way. He had, of course, signed Venables as a player and he still saw him, despite his faults, as a 'football man'. We'd offered an invitation but weren't sure he would attend.

As we began the meeting we became aware of interest turning rapidly to the door at the back. It took him nearly 10 minutes to walk to the platform, such were the number of people who wanted to shake his hand, and the standing ovation continued throughout that time. He later gave an impassioned address in support of his former player, interrupted numerous times by thunderous applause. Being able to shake his hand in thanks afterwards was a moment I'll never forget. Through most of the 90s he was similarly greeted at every Tottenham plc AGM he attended and, despite being consigned to a side table, he was always the person most in demand at the end.

That one man could be responsible for so many great memories for so many people is a fantastic epitaph and Darkie and his family should be immensely proud in their sadness that Sir Billy Nick was that man. Thanks for everything Bill. Truly the Greatest Spur of them all.
A C Spur, Topspurs website

His legacy is to have left forever something that all Spurs teams and staff should aspire to: that is to play football in a correct, honourable and entertaining manner.
He is the reason – though I have only started to fully understand this now – why I love this club. The ideal of Tottenham Hotspur FC has been moulded in his image, and let us hope that one day in the future we will be able to look on a Spurs team and say that it can match those that he so brilliantly created.
Greaves, Topspurs website

Bill
May your dreams fill the air above us.
May your passing be the spur for us to end the hurt.
May your spirit fill those in charge with courage and strength.
May we again see the dark clouds lifted and a glory glory night return.
May we again walk through the hallowed turnstiles with pride and joy and be served a feast fit for a king that was once Bill Nicholson.
Stefan, Topspurs website

I stood with my daughter for the minute's silence and even she at only seven-years-old understood the enormity of the situation. Brought a tear to my eye knowing that we'll never see the likes of him at our beloved Tottenham again and that my children will never know what it was like to support a club as successful as we were whilst Bill was in charge.
God bless you, Bill, you've earned a rest.
Beer Keller, Topspurs website

It's down to you, Bill, that I support this great club . . . I thank you, old fella.
Naylor, Topspurs website

On the BBC's 606 board Arsenal fans are being very respectful, posting on the Spurs board there. A testament to a man who embodies everything that is Tottenham.
ParkLaneCrew, Topspurs website

BILL NICHOLSON

From all at Cumbria Spurs – you will never be forgotten.
Mr.Tottenham Hotspur R.I.P. and THANK YOU for the memories.
CA2Yid, Topspurs website

From across the miles my thoughts are with the family and friends of this great man.
RIP Bill
Oz, Topspurs website

Just simply the best, and thanks for that '67 Cup win, my very first Spurs moment ... that I will remember forever.
Jurgenthegerman, Topspurs website

This is the worst day in my life as a Tottenham supporter. I'm sitting here with tears in my eyes. RIP Bill Nicholson.
Jacques, Norway, Topspurs website

RIP Billy Nick. Thank you for your 68 years with us.
Alexm, Topspurs website

RIP Sir Bill. My thoughts go out to his immediate family, and his worldwide family of Spurs fans everywhere. I met him out of the blue when I was 12 at The Lane and he was so kind and had such an aura that I was in tears afterwards. A sad day.
Dunphy, United States, Topspurs website

The greatest and the end of an era. Very sad, but also very proud. We were the greatest and NO-ONE can take that away from us.
Spursyid 61, Topspurs website

I've just read the awful news and realised that one of the most influential people in my life has just passed away. If Sir Bill hadn't built a team as successful as Spurs of the 60s, I probably would never have been a Tottenham fan.
In these days of fickle loyalty, Sir Bill showed us what it is to be faithful to one club, through thick and thin. A lesson to all those money-grabbing, lazy prima donnas who wear the cockerel today.
As we say on hearing bad news in Hebrew, 'Baruch Dayan emet'.
Sir Bill to us, despite what the authorities might think. I just hope that your passing is reported as much as Brian Clough's was. Say hello from us to Danny and Cyril up there with you.
Davidgranny, Israel, Topspurs website

RIP Bill Nicholson – the embodiment of dignity.
Hans Ulrik, Denmark, Topspurs website

BILL NICHOLSON

Farewell Oh Good and Trusted Friend

All the world's a stage
And all the men and women merely players.
They have their exits and their entrances,
And one man in his time plays many parts,
His acts being seven ages.
Sir Bill played all but the first part as a Tottenham man. What a man.

No words of mine will do justice to his contribution to the Tottenham cause.
The entire Tottenham family will mourn his loss, in particular his immediate family, and while our thoughts are with them today, this is not a day for sadness rather a time to rejoice in the memory of Bill.
Ar Dheis Dé go raibh a anam
Doc, Ireland, Topspurs website

During a lifetime of unequalled dedication and loyalty to Spurs (and to Spurs fans), Sir Bill brought unprecedented pleasure to those of us fortunate enough to be standing on the terraces in the 50s, 60s and 70s. Well done, Sir Bill. You reached the heights but you always remained a Spurs fan. You were always one of us and you never left us or let us down.
Few others in football have done so much for so many, without receiving due recognition. Bill is undoubtedly 'Mr Tottenham' and he is certainly 'Bill Nicholson OBE'. However, we Spurs fans have all done what the Crown regrettably failed to do – we knighted him.
'Sir Bill Nicholson' he always will be.
Roger Powell, Sydney, Australia

RIP our friend, our leader, the thing that makes THFC so great.
We should consider making a final gesture to Sir Bill, perhaps renaming the stadium in his honour.
I think there should be something everlasting about this great man.
Unbanned Bob, Topspurs website

Just because a club has all the best players doesn't necessarily mean they'll win all their trophies . . . but it's better than having bad players.
After a week of glorious sunshine here in NZ, I wake up today to grey skies and drizzle . . . and the sad, sad news.
Bill, after watching your first game as manager in the 10-4 win over Everton you got me hooked on Tottenham. I thank you from the bottom of my heart. RIP.
Bill Nic, New Zealand, Topspurs website

Mr Nicholson, at last Heaven has the manager it deserves. Heaven's gain is the human race's loss. Move over ,Mr Clough – the Governor's coming...
Noodles, Topspurs Website

About two years ago, I took the tour of White Hart Lane, when Sir Bill suddenly arrived at the reception area. I felt instantly that this was my only chance to get a picture together with the legend. A Swede had the same idea a few seconds before me, and when he was finished, I had my son Even take a picture of me and Bill. I didn't get the chance to talk much to him because the others were already gone, but it was a great moment and a fond memory for me. It's sad that he has passed away but I hope his passing is a symbolic new start for our beloved club.
Svein K. Johansen, Rørvik, Norway

That Sunday after the Bolton game was quite surreal. I went along to The Lane with my younger brother, where we signed the book, then went to look at the tributes left by the pitch. The music that was played – I was told by one of the groundstaff that it was an unused piece from the third Lord Of The Rings film – was really haunting, and summed it all up perfectly. On that screen were slow motion clips of some of Bill's finest moments in his years at Spurs, and it was only then that you realise just how much he had achieved with us. I had been at White Hart Lane on enough occasions when the temperature had plummeted – ice and snow on the pitch was not always a barrier to a bloody good game – but that day, the ground seemed as cold as I had ever known it. I suppose if you believed in these things, you could say that the ground itself seemed to understand what had happened…it was as if it knew Bill was gone. I certainly did.
Andy S, Buckinghamshire

The 649, 647 or 627 trolley bus took us from Galliard Road along Fore Street to the stop before White Hart Lane. The one with the black painted shop front that stood in front of you as you stepped off the bus. Was it a stationers?

Then the walk along Fore Street (or had it become Tottenham High Road by then?) Left turn up Paxton Road, and round the back to the 'family enclosure' entrance.

Was Bill Nicholson there then? This pre-pubescent youngster was too busy looking at other things. The Spurs band, the two penny 'programme', the cloth caps, the way the human waves surged down the terracing when something exciting was happening on the pitch. Just like the tide flowing up the beach, it never quite ebbed back as far because those bodies balanced on the back step rushed forward to take up the gaps created. Just like a packet of cornflakes, the contents of the terracing would shake down during the course of a game.

Another thing that fascinated me was the way people who fainted during the game were passed over heads, across the sea of cloth caps and outstretched arms that looked like a colony of hydra, to the front, where the St John Ambulance people were on hand. Nine times out of 10, once sitting on the orange shale at the pitch-side, the patient would make a miraculous recovery and watch the rest of the match from there!

I remember seeing Ted Ditchburn and Len Duquemin, and the last of the amateurs to play in the first division, winger George Robb, but I don't remember the manager. People came to support their team, not the manager.

BILL NICHOLSON

We moved soon after I started at senior school. Our new house was just behind Edmonton Green. In theory we could have walked the three or four miles to the Spurs ground from there. In practice, the easiest transport was by train from Church Street to White Hart Lane station and then a short walk past Cliff Jones' butchers shop to the ground.

These were the years I remember the best, when 'Nick' was putting together the Glory team. Dad didn't always get home from work in time for us to make the match on a Saturday but we watched most midweek games. Dad's boss was a long-term season ticket holder and had seats very near the directors' box in the old stand. Sometimes, when he was away, dad was allowed to use them and I would have to put on smart clothes and be on my best behaviour as we made our way though the posh entrance and into the best seats. It was a great view, but where were the really funny 'wags' whose one-liners used to have the Paxton Road end in stitches almost the entire match?

I liked John Hollowbread, but Bill Brown was a far better keeper. Later, Pat Jennings was The Best. Bill Nick certainly had an eye for a keeper. Baker, Henry, Hopkins and Norman were about the best stoppers around at the time. They talk of the likes of Nobby Stiles, but Mel Hopkins was as aggressive as any. I was excited to hear that Stan Matthews was coming down to play in the Blackpool team. Stan was well on in years at the time and Blackpool were in the second division. It was a Cup match. Stan got the ball early on and there was an expectant hush. Hopkins mowed him down in a scything thigh-high tackle, giving away a free-kick. Ten minutes later exactly the same thing happened again. Matthews didn't touch the ball for the rest of the match. It wasn't Wenger or Ferguson or even Shankly or Revie who invented the theory that results are built on steel as well as silk.

I loved Bobby Smith and his bustling runs and the talents of the waif called John White, but I also enjoyed the honest toil of little Tommy Harmer and then Les Allen. When Bill signed Jimmy Greaves I was mortified. How could he treat Les so? I was one of the boo boys who saw Greaves as an interloper and 'big head'. How dare he spend so much time during a game just standing around and not chasing after the ball? How lucky could one man be? It seemed that whenever the ball ran loose, there he was, unmarked, to stick it in the net. Lucky bugger! What about all those REAL players who were doing all the work?

It might have been his scissor kick into the top corner from the edge of the box as Spurs annihilated Plymouth Argyle 5-1 in a Cup replay that won me over, or I might finally have eventually realised that genius makes it's own rules.

If the three backs were the steel and the forwards were the polish, then who did that leave? The head and the heart of course! The head in the shape of Danny Blanchflower. Not the nicest man in the world they say, but he went up in my estimation no end when he became the first and possibly only person to tell Eamon Andrews where to shove his red book when invited on to This is Your Life! Anyone with the balls to do that has to be good!

Perhaps he preferred to let the brain and the left boot do the talking. It seemed as if, even in the most frenetic of matches, there was an area around him where, if the ball entered, things moved into slow motion. He put his foot on the ball, looked all around, had time for think-music, and then pushed the most exquisite of passes, always to an unmarked man. All the time this was going on, the rest of the players seemed to be just frozen in time; garden gnomes, as Danny the gardener tended his flowers.

If Danny was the head, then where was the heart? Huff, puff, here he comes! One thing you could always be sure of. Within 30 seconds of a match starting, the front of Dave Mackay's shirt would have mud all over it. I never saw a game where this didn't happen. He was part-labrador, chasing, retrieving, running, wagging his tail and dropping the ball at his masters' feet. Then he was part Rottweiler, fierce, aggressive, strong, courageous and unshirking. Heaven help anyone who invaded his space without permission. He was part mother hen, shepherding and protecting his brood and making sure they were always out of danger. Finally, he was part stallion as he charged forward into the fray with bullocking runs and a fearful kick.

I was 16-years-old in 1961 when Spurs entered the European Cup for the first time. I saw all the home legs and the atmosphere was electric. Whatever the team had conceded during the away legs was always simply swept aside at White Hart Lane in a wave of emotion and 'Glory Hallelujah's'...all except Benfica.

The Silver-Spooners had Hamlet, Swan Lake and Pagliacci, but nothing could compare with the classic evening served up that night. Plenty of heroes; they were the ones in white. Three villains; they were the ones in black. Not a bad supporting cast; Eusebio, Germano, Torres...and a sixty-five thousand strong heavenly choir.

Every emotion was explored to the full that evening. Who says cloth-cappers don't appreciate classic tragedies? Not a dry eye in the house as the curtain came down and the audience filed away, drained. The difference was, this was no fiction. It was real-live drama: Only a game?

There were many changes as I continued to follow the fortunes of the Lilywhites. Alan Gilzean, Mike England, Alan Mullery, Martin Peters and many more. All top stars themselves in their time.

I'm not a master of football tactics. Reading books on the game as it was played then makes it clear not many were, and that includes managers. Maybe he was among the first of the English managers to introduce such things, but for me, what Bill Nicholson did was what all the best chefs in the world do. He kept it easy, kept it simple and used the finest ingredients he could find.

His status as a legend for me is all about being able to spot the talent, work out the right blend and get more out of the whole than the sum of the individual parts. And the magic of the man is that he didn't do it once but over and over, without the ever-open chequebooks of the over-blown, over-hyped managers of today.

How it hurts to see Arsenal ruling North London. Why is this so? If it is all about money, then at what stage did the dreaded Highbury rivals have it over Tottenham? Is it a coincidence that it seemed to be around the time Bill left? Could it have really been just the one man who stood between Lilywhite success and being swamped by the red and yellow tide? For me, the going up the road of Campbell was the final straw. I wonder if he is on more than the £60 a week

BILL NICHOLSON

Greaves was when he signed for Spurs!

The likes of Ferguson, Wenger and Mourinho grab all the headlines these days, but they are now just the front men for armies of administrators. I don't think we will see the likes of Nicholson, Clough, or Busby again

John Berry, Perth, Western Australia

Being a fan for 60 years, I met Bill a few times, and he always had time to talk about THFC. Next to his lovely wife, it was the love of his life.

The last time I met Bill was last year, in the car park inside the ground. I had the 1961 replica shirt, with most of the Double-winning team's autographs on it, and although Bill had difficulty writing, he wrote his name on the shirt. It took him about 10 minutes but, God bless him, he finished it. I have collected many autographs over the years, but that is my most treasured one, which will stay in my family forever.

God bless you, SIR BILL – nobody will ever match your loyalty to one club ever again. R.I.P.

Eddie Wright

Bill Nicholson and Brian Clough were vastly different characters, yet they were both products of their times and are inextricably identified with football's yesteryear. Nicholson was the old-fashioned one-club man – an association stretching to 60 years – and continued to live in a small terraced house in the centre of the Tottenham community for the duration of his life. Clough took two unfashionable, provincial clubs to glories previously beyond their wildest dreams. Neither is likely to find a compare in the modern game. One wonders, too, whether Clough's approach to man-management could have worked in this era of agents, inflated salaries and inflated egos to match.

I had the privilege of being at White Hart Lane on Saturday, thanks to an offer from a friend made sometime earlier. It was an occasion when the game (against Bolton) became incidental, secondary to the higher object of paying last respects to a revered figure. The impeccable tributes and the dignified minute's silence were the lasting memories of a sombre occasion.

No doubt the kind of scenes I witnessed on Saturday were replicated at Forest and Derby following Cloughie's death. At all three clubs, the occasion also represented an opportunity to remember and reflect upon past glories, as yet unsurpassed.

But beyond each club, respects have been paid to these legendary figures across the land. Undoubtedly, because these were both characters – albeit as different as chalk and cheese – appreciated across the land. Clough, in particular, was loved as much for his ability to come up with the brilliant one-liner as for his undoubted achievements in managing football teams. But they were mourned not just as individuals, but for what they represented.

Indeed, this has been an opportunity for sentimentality, a chance to remember a period that so many see as a golden age of football, and to mourn not just the passing of two former managers, but also the passing away of an era.

I've always suggested that the magic of those olden days has increased as they have drifted further away. Let no-one tell you that those days were perfect. There are footballers who played in the past who must scratch around to make a pitiful living today. There were scars upon the game left by hooliganism in the 70s. And for all the romance of the terraces (I would still stand if I could), they could be unpleasant places on occasions.

But whilst that may be true, more pertinent is the general lack of a feel-good factor within football today. The era of the Premiership has brought a higher standard of player, thanks to the influx of top class foreigners, and has brought modern, clean stadiums and games beamed into houses across the land. But it has also led to the dominance of money, to a predictable league without soul, vast wages and vast expenses which have been passed onto fans.

Manchester United, Arsenal and Chelsea operate a cartel at the top of the league. There is an impenetrable league of three from which the Champions will emerge.

Any future challenge, if it ever materialises, will come from one of the other wealthy clubs currently just below that elite. It will not come, as Brian Clough's teams did, from a previously unheralded team who barely flicker on the national consciousness just now. There is no story in football. A book can be filled with the most beautiful prose but without a story to sustain it, it will not make for a classic bestseller.

It wouldn't be so bad but for the cost. It currently costs £40 to watch Chelsea, and £35 for an away fan to have the privilege of sitting in a dilapidated shed at the away end of Selhurst Park. A day out at the footy, with a programme, a pint or two and something to eat, will cost an adult £50 at the very least, once he's got himself there. Then there is the trickle down effect, which results in us paying £20 a game at Burnley, and the rest besides on many away days.

Often, for what? Inherent in football is the possibility of disappointment. Invariably, to sit in a meek atmosphere where you can hear the shouts of the participants. Frequently to leave unfulfilled, after another uninspired afternoon in a new, soulless out of town stadium bedecked in corporate logos.

Where the players can act without grace or dignity, and form an unseemly scrum around the referee after every decision. Players who then earn vastly inflated sums of money and scream their own self-importance from the tabloid press that fauns to them, but who are the icons of an increasingly footloose industry, where players and managers are gone in the blink of an eye.

As a culture of cynicism has built up amongst careworn supporters, so has a yearning for a mythical by-gone golden age. Of course, that isn't to suggest that dedicated football fans are on the verge of giving up on the game, and going somewhere else. We are wedded to our club, and the game is a massive part of all our lives.

But after the boom of the late 90s, which masked the unhealthy cancer eating away at footballs roots, reality is beginning to kick in. As a recent report in The Observer newspaper showed, attendances are beginning to slide. Not even Arsenal have sold out completely, including the away end, this season. Travelling fans in particular have found other things to do with their Saturday afternoons, or Sunday evenings, or whichever time TV has deigned that the game should be played.

Money, dissatisfaction at the coldness of the authorities, and the frustration at the attractive but insubstantial fare on offer, have combined to place fans close to the brink. The deaths of two venerable old figures within the game have brought that starkly into focus. Amongst the reminiscences of the radio phone-ins up and down the country is a stark truth: football is lost, dislocated from its truth. We'll still be there, but with how many others?
Richard Oldroyd, Clarets Mad (Burnley FC) website

Because he was not flamboyant, nor outgoing, nor political, he did not gain favour among those within the corridors of power. He said what had to be said. Nothing more, nothing less. He did his job and went home. He did his job well. He did his job better than most. And he was 'Sir' Bill Nicholson. Maybe not in the Honours List, but in our hearts.

May you rest in peace and reap the rewards of the joy you gave to many.
Benny The Ball, MEHSTG website

I was shocked to tune into the radio and hear that Sir Bill Nicholson had died. Although I had not seen him this season, apparently he had been to some games, but his illness had got worse over the last few months and he had entered a nursing home. Bill had been very frail for some years but was always happy and humble and I think it was this that makes him more of a human being than some of today's supposed 'character' managers. The atmosphere at the game was odd. Like a family member had died but wanting the team to do well to show him that the Spurs spirit will carry on.

The result was not important and the whole day was all very sad. Shame his achievements were in a day and age when they were not recognised as being out of the ordinary rather than those of today, which are commonplace. Arsenal fans say that we won the championship in black and white (there being no colour TV back then), but that was when it was a proper game and when it really meant something. Not like today. Bill, if there is a Heaven, I am sure you will find success with a team up there. If not, you will be eternally remembered for what you did for Tottenham Hotspur on Earth.
Barry Levington, MEHSTG Website

Here was a man who had few equals in the history of the game. Actually that is not true. In 1961 he had no equals in the game in the 20th century. The Double, which was then the holy grail of English domestic football, had eluded all the best teams England had yet produced and was considered by many to be near impossible. Spurs under Nicholson not only won it, they cantered to the title with such style and swagger that all those old enough to have seen them still rate them as one of the very best English sides of all time.

Yet when Nicholson's side had won the FA Cup Final in 1961 to complete this groundbreaking achievement, this particular manager was not overcome with joy.

He felt they had not won it in the style of which they were capable. This reaction, confirmed by the man himself in his rare interviews, explains why he never again won the League championship. As the pragmatic 'win at all costs' approach took hold later in the decade, Nicholson found himself up against more ruthless, less principled managers who scorned the more attacking theories and were not afraid to send teams out to stop the opposition playing, rather than picking a team to beat the opposition. Football, like life as the 60s wore on, became less innocent and more cynical and the likes of Revie's Leeds United prospered while Spurs became more a 'Cup Team', capable of beating anyone on their day, but lacking the necessary ruthlessness to kill off teams week in, week out. When the great Double achievement was emulated a decade later, even the most avid Arsenal supporter could not claim that Bertie Mee's team had achieved it with anything like the style of Nicholson's. But it was in the record books. Just like the teams that have achieved it since. But Nicholson got there first and that is something that cannot be taken away.

His amazing long link with Tottenham, which dated back to 1936, is unlikely to ever be repeated. The very fabric of all the club stands for and the vast majority of all of its finest hours had Nicholson's involvement either directly or indirectly stamped on them. This is a club that has only ever won the title twice. Nicholson played in the team that landed the first in 1951 and after retiring to become coach and then manager in 1958, was of course at the helm in that history-making season of 1960-61. The lack of adequate TV coverage at the time makes it hard for those not old enough to make an objective judgment on just how good this team was. Although comparisons between eras are often pointless, there is no doubt that this was a magical collection of players blended together by Nicholson through a mixture of shrewdness and intelligence rarely seen before or since. The following

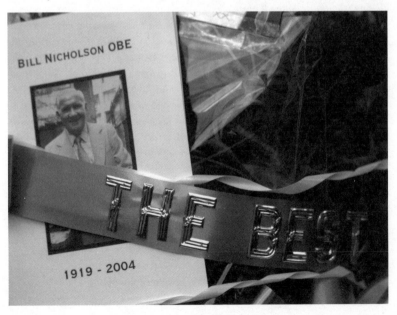

BILL NICHOLSON OBE

THE BEST

1919 - 2004

season Spurs retained the FA Cup having by now added Jimmy Greaves to the great Double team, but consider how close Nicholson came to an achievement that would, to this day, have probably earned him the title of the greatest British manager of all time. A highly unexpected defeat to eventual champions Ipswich in Easter 1962 was all that stood between them and a second consecutive Double. In the same month, Nicholson's team came within a whisker of beating Benfica and claiming a place in the European Cup Final.

The Treble, not achieved until 1999 by Ferguson's Manchester United, was almost within Tottenham's grasp 37 years earlier. Football is a game of 'if onlys'. The next season, 1962-63, did though see another memorable first – no British team had won a European trophy until Tottenham carried of the European Cup Winners' Cup that year.

A dynasty, like the ones built at Liverpool and Manchester United, should have been built at Spurs. It was not to be. Injuries (Dave Mackay being the most obvious), retirements (Blanchflower), tragedies (John White's death) and complacency from the Spurs directors meant that the standards set could not be maintained. New heroes were signed, and in most cases they would be excellent signings (Gilzean, England, Mullery, Chivers, Jennings, etc), but the new players and their manager had an almost impossible legacy to live up to.

Throughout the 60s Spurs remained a force, but they were never able to mount a realistic challenge again for the title. The FA Cup was won again in 1967, although this was the last trophy of that decade. The early 70s saw the cabinet doors open again three years in succession, but whilst the success was welcome, League Cup wins over Aston Villa and Norwich City in 1971 and 1973 were a long way short of the triumphs of before. Even a record-breaking second European Trophy in 1972 – the UEFA Cup – had some of the gloss taken off, as it was an all-English affair against Wolves.

The game had well and truly changed and it wasn't just opposing managers that had sacrificed principles that Nicholson was now up against. The culture of the 'celebrity footballer' was taking hold, although it was a long way short of the situation we know today. All the same, Nicholson found it hard to get the best out of players who did not always show the respect he deserved. Added to that was the well known culture of 'under the counter' payments in the transfer market. Rightly or wrongly, Spurs refused to be involved in such antics and it is therefore no coincidence that the 'star' signings started to dry up at Spurs. The name of Tottenham and Nicholson were no longer enough to attract the best.

Spurs were in decline by the time Nicholson conceded defeat to this new era. He still guided Spurs to the UEFA Cup Final in 1974 but the subsequent defeat and the violence on the terraces during that game rather summed up just how things have moved on. He finally resigned in September of that year after 16 years in charge and eight trophies won. Whilst he may have left behind a team that took several years to rebuild, there is no escaping the harsh facts for Spurs fans – in the 30 years since his retirement, the club has won only five trophies.

Quite why the Tottenham board chose to ignore Nicholson's advice that a 'dream team' of Danny Blanchflower and Johnny Giles was the best way of regenerating the club in 1974 is something the fans were never told. Quite how Nicholson's ties with the club were allowed to be severed and he ended up at West Ham as a scout is another question these men were unable to answer. The fact that they ignored his advice and appointed ex-Arsenal player, Terry Neill, speaks volumes for their judgment at the time.

Neill's successor, Keith Burkinshaw, ensured Nicholson returned to the club in a scouting/advisory capacity in 1976 and although he remained behind the scenes, Nicholson was responsible for identifying and brokering some of Burkinshaw's key signings. The Spurs team of the early 80s remain the only team to have come consistently close to matching the achievements and style of Nicholson's great sides of the past. The mismanagement of Spurs since the true glory days of the 60s by various boards of directors and ill-suited managers is a tragic collection of self-inflicted wounds that Nicholson must have found hard to stomach. His comment: 'If we are not in Europe we are nothing', remains true to this day.

The story recounted by Hunter Davies of Nicholson modestly struggling to take his seat at Wembley amongst the ordinary fans (and not in the royal box) before the 1999 League Cup Final, rather sums up how the club's traditions and pride were eroded over too many years by men who had no feel for the true spirit of the club. Here was the greatest man in the club's history fighting his way into the dilapidated old stadium like the other mere mortals, whilst directors and a chairman not fit to clean his boots, let alone lace them, were enjoying the pomp and glory in the royal box. The club's President, it's greatest manager, not to mention its most loyal servant, was apparently not worthy of VIP invitation. A shocking and shaming story that those responsible for should be ashamed of.

The great man lived long enough to be the first to be inducted into the Spurs Hall of Fame in March 2004. Just in time. Without Bill Nicholson, a Spurs Hall of Fame would have had few candidates worthy of the title. Thanks to him the name Tottenham Hotspur is famous the world over. Now that the man has passed away, it is up to the current custodians of the club to never forget Bill Nicholson. Never forget the standards that he set. Never forget the way he wanted the game to be played. And therefore never be satisfied with anything but the best.

It is one hell of a legacy – one that few have been able to live up to since 1974. Many have failed to even understand it. But it's a legacy Spurs fans can be proud and if Nicholson is watching from somewhere else, one he would not want to see squandered forever.
Chris Sadler, MEHSTG website

One of my earliest memories is of the FA Cup being paraded along the High Road on an open-topped bus in 1967. I didn't realise what was going on –, I was only five. I had never heard of Bill Nicholson, Jimmy Greaves, Dave Mackay, Danny Blanchflower, Bobby Smith, John White or any number of the outstanding players to pull on the lilywhite jersey. It wasn't until three years later, when my dad started taking me to The Lane, that I had any idea of who or what it was all about. It was, of course, the mighty Tottenham Hotspur, and meant players of the calibre of Martin Chivers, Martin Peters, Pat Jennings, Cyril Knowles, Alan

BILL NICHOLSON

Mullery and Alan Gilzean, all under the leadership of Bill Nicholson.

My cousins helped fill in my areas of ignorance. They lived in George Lansbury House along White Hart Lane, and I stayed with them occasionally. They showed me their scrapbooks and told me all I needed to know. Once indoctrinated, there was no turning back. I collected scrap cuttings of my own, my dad used to bring back broadsheet colour specials from the long-defunct London Evening News featuring the team. I cut out photos and stuck them on my bedroom wall. Spurs were everything to me. There always seemed to be something to celebrate and gloat to school friends over. Looking back now, it seemed such an exciting time.

Triumphs seemed to happen as a matter of course. Trying to hear what was happening in European matches on a barely audible transistor radio was a thrill. Then, in 1974, a few months after losing the UEFA Cup final to Feyenoord amid scenes of mayhem and violence, Bill resigned as manager of Tottenham. I was stunned. As a 12 year-old I had no real conception that managers of football clubs changed. Of course, players came and went, but the manager always stayed. I couldn't imagine Spurs without Bill Nicholson in charge. He was Spurs and always had been. Things could never be the same again. How could the club go on without Bill in charge? The club did go on, managers came and went – some good, most indifferent.

How could anybody ever hope to live up to the legend that had created the most beautiful football team ever to kick a ball in England? The sad truth is, nobody could.

I often fantasised that, whilst visiting my cousins, or visiting the graves of relatives in the garden of remembrance on The Lane, that, with Bill living nearby, I'd bump into him and get chatting about the club, the team and what was needed to return it to the top of the league. I'd ask him about his time as manager and how was he able to mould such feared yet beautiful football teams?

I never did meet him. The nearest I ever came was at a TISA meeting to support Terry Venables. The room erupted when he came through the door and he took the podium to the sound of wild applause and his name being chanted as if he was Jesus Christ himself. He said a few words. Quiet, unassuming and yet with the passion of a man who had the love of the club running through him like the letters in a stick of seaside rock. He WAS the club, and he was one of US. It amazes me now that when Spurs supporters talk of the glory years and of the Spurs Way, and of the tradition of the club, football journalists sneer and say that is all in the past. But now the great man has left us, they are using those very words to describe the club as if they somehow understand what it means to us. I despise them. They are a collection of two-faced, hypocrites. Where were they when supporters were campaigning for Bill's knighthood? Those who decide these things must surely hang their heads in shame for their criminal omission. And so now the club must look to the future without its greatest talisman. The signs are promising but we must be patient. The club needs us all to stand together for the sake of the memory of Billy Nick. He loved the club like one of us – we cannot let him down.

Farewell, Sir Bill. You'll always be in our heart.

Steve White, MEHSTG website

I have to say I felt that Bill should have been treated with the same respect as Brian Clough. However, it appears that only Tottenham held a minute's silence in his honour. I do not understand the logic of a minute's silence at matches as sometimes great football men are given the national respect they deserve and on other occasions they are not. Even though it is my natural inclination to shun everything Tottenham-related, it doesn't mean to say I can't appreciate a great footballing gentleman, nor does it mean that as a lover of the beautiful game I wouldn't give him his due respect. It would seem there is a grey area here as to who gets a minute's silence and who doesn't. Of course if there were a silence for every notable football legend that died during the week we would probably have one before every match. I suspect in the case of Mr. Nicholson it was because he was only an important figure to Tottenham fans and the older generations of supporters, such as myself, that he wasn't given a national send off.
Brian (Arsenal fan)

Chapter 16
Bill's Boys Say Goodbye

Bill was a good friend, a good player and a great manager. I had some of the best times of my playing career with Bill keeping an eagle eye on things.

He was so determined to make his Spurs side the best that sometimes he would be at the ground all hours of the day and night, long after the rest of us had gone home. Bill was the last of a special breed, and the game of football will miss him. So will I.
Tommy Harmer

I've often heard people talk about the great managers, and they talk about Shankly, Clough, Paisley, and rightly so – but Bill is up there with any of them. I don't know of anybody in football, either at the time or since, who knew as much or worked as hard as Bill. It was his attention to detail that stuck out at first, but then you got to see the real Bill – the man with complete loyalty to his players, but a man who demanded that they give nothing less than 100 per cent, every match.

Bill would have kittens trying to adapt to today's game. The players today are a different breed to our day – I know they have different expectations nowadays, but Bill would have probably asked more of them than many of them would be prepared to give. It's been well documented that Bill often wanted players to play for Spurs who would be prepared to pay for the privilege. Most people think that's actually a joke but he meant it. Bill regarded playing for Tottenham as the greatest honour a player could get, and he couldn't understand why players would want more out of the game such as material gain. It was just alien to him.

I found out about Bill going on that Saturday from the radio, although I had spoken to his daughter, Jean, the day before, when she had told a few of us that he was in a bad way and to expect the worst. Even though I knew what was coming, it was still like a hammer blow. Bill had been like a father to many of his players down the years, and if anything of him is to be passed on to future generations of players and supporters of Spurs, it's that there should be a bond between the fans and the club. Bill, don't forget, lived in the Tottenham area for most of his life, and he had a great sense of community. He felt that the club was part of that community, and the two went hand in hand. It's an idea that he was always taking great pains to instil in his players, and we never forgot it. We'll never forget Bill, either."
Cliff Jones

This whole 'dour Yorkshireman' thing has been blown out of all proportion with Bill. I preferred to think of him as down to earth. He was good company when the mood took him, and if you wanted to talk football, Bill was your man. There was nobody with a wider knowledge of the game – Bill was one of THE top managers of the last 50 years.

He wasn't one of the 'hair-drier' type managers when things went wrong – I'd never seen him lose it completely, but I guess the closest he came was when we were leading Aston Villa 5-1 at half time, and we took our foot off the pedal a bit. Many managers would do that, you know, keep what we've got – but Bill wanted maximum effort all the time – he would never settle for 5-1. He was right, of course. Villa came back at us and the game ended up 5-5.

You have to feel quite sorry for managers who have been at Spurs since Bill, because he isn't just a hard act to follow – he is an impossible act to follow, and it must have been quite difficult for each of them.

I was in Scotland on both occasions when Bill and Brian Clough died. The press had peppered me with phone calls – it seemed that no sooner as I had put down the phone, than I was answering it again. I guess it was to be expected – they were very different characters but in their own way both men were geniuses and were also the heartbeat of their clubs – completely irreplaceable.

Bill was absolutely straightforward. When he said something he meant it – he would never go back on his word. He never let us forget we were out there to entertain the public. He was 100% honest and 100% Spurs.

I'll miss him terribly.
Dave Mackay

Sometimes I used to go past the club late at night and Bill's office light would still be on – he was just devoted to the club.

Big men make big decisions, and Bill was a big man. As much as he loved every one of his players like a son, he was totally committed to doing what was best for Tottenham Hotspur, and when the time came to replace people, he would always do what he had to. Nobody I knew resented him for it.

I was in Toronto visiting my son when I got a phone call from my daughter telling me that Bill had died. I was very upset, even though it was quite well known that he hadn't been a well man for some time. I can honestly say that Bill Nick and Tottenham gave me some of the best days of my life, and I will forever be glad of that. I don't regret a single moment of it.
Terry Medwin

I'll be forever grateful to Bill for giving me my chance at Spurs. I'd only ever spoken two words or so to Jimmy Anderson, and felt that I was being overlooked. It was Bill who ran the club then, anyway, and when he took over, he was ready to give anyone a go. He knew us all better than Jimmy did.

There were so many great players at the club, many of them brought in by Bill, that it was always going to be difficult to break in. But whenever I did get a chance, I always gave it my best shot and I think Bill appreciated that.

He was a difficult man to communicate with sometimes. I can remember us drawing with Newcastle, and Bill got us in the dressing room and slaughtered us.

BILL NICHOLSON

And yet another time, we had been beaten 5-1 by Manchester United and he seemed quite pleased with the way we played. You just never knew. But he always demanded 100%, and you made sure you gave it. Nobody wanted to get on the wrong side of Bill, that's for sure.

I was actually an Arsenal fan before I signed for Tottenham but that changed straight away after. Playing under Bill was an honour and a privilege, and I had 11 wonderful years.
Eddie Clayton

I refused to believe it when I got the phone call on that Saturday morning. I think it was somebody from the press who called me, and I sort of said, as much to myself as anybody: 'Bill Nick dead? Don't be bloody ridiculous.' But of course it was true.

Bill was proof that you can be thorough, unbending and even hard as a manager but still be a gent. Remember, he was a working class lad from a family of nine children, so he came up from the bottom. With an upbringing like that, you're going to be a bit of a tough nut.

One thing I always tell people about him was that if he ever dropped a player, he'd take them to one side and tell them to their face, but so they would be the only one to hear. He never wanted to humiliate anyone. There are many managers today who just put up the team sheet and then hide, but that was never Bill's way. The game has lost someone really unique.
Maurice Norman

My wife and I were travelling back in my car from visiting our son in Derbyshire, We were having the journey from hell, and were detouring through Enfield when my mobile rang. We were only crawling along at the time, so I answered it. It was Gary Richardson from the BBC, and he asked if I could spare some time to have a quick chat with him.

*I can remember saying: "Not now, Gary, I'm having a bad time in traffic and it's p****** down with rain." He went on to say that surely I'd want to comment. I said: "On what, exactly?"*

It was then that he told me that Bill had gone. I turned to my wife and just said: "Bill's dead." There was a stunned silence between us. I put the mobile down and neither of us said anything for a few minutes.

Bill was one of the greatest blokes, if not the greatest, that I've ever worked for. He firmly believed we should be paying to play for Spurs.

We have all lost part of our history.
Jimmy Greaves

Bill was a Yorkshireman, like me, and I'd say he was pretty typical. If he'd got it in his head that the grass was blue, there was no point trying to argue otherwise. With Bill, though, he was right so often that it would be a good idea to stick your head out of the window and check just in case!

Bill was a one-off in some respects, though. His ideas on coaching were years

ahead of his time, and even nowadays you see things being taught that he used to use with us at Spurs. Anybody who was at White Hart Lane for his memorial service will realise that he will always be thought of as the biggest influence on Tottenham Hotspur – and the fans will never let it be forgotten.
Terry Dyson

A lot of Bill's ex-players came back to White Hart Lane 1n 1984 for the launch of his autobiography. We had all been sitting round in small groups, chatting about old times, that sort of thing. Then Bill realised that somebody wanted a photograph, so he just stood up and said: "Right lads, photo-call!" and you know what? All these grown men, some quite long in the tooth by then, just stood up like a load of school kids and did exactly what he had said!

That just shows the way Bill could command respect from his players, but it was coupled with a deep regard for the man. I can't see the game producing any more like him.
Peter Baker

I hadn't spoken properly to Bill since the 1991 FA Cup Final. We'd met at Spurs occasionally, but it's difficult there because everybody wants to talk to him and you get a bit here, a bit there. At the Forest game, he was his usual self – so engrossed in the game, you couldn't work out what he was thinking or what he was feeling.

It was always strange with Bill, but when I was a player some days he'd walk by you without even noticing you, and others he'd be quite open and chatty. Somebody suggested to me that maybe it was because sometimes he was so wrapped up in the running of the club, like he had a thousand and one things going on inside his head, that he'd be off somewhere else. That would make sense, I suppose.

Bill was Bill, and everybody respected what he stood for.
Frank Saul

Some of Bill's former players stand in silent tribute to him at the home game v Bolton Wanderers.

BILL NICHOLSON

To be a great manager you must have the respect of the players and Bill certainly had that.

What I admired most about him was the way he trusted players. He treated us like adults and we responded to that.

Bill got together some great players like Cliff Jones, Terry Dyson and Les Allen and we moulded perfectly. We could not have wished for a better team or a better manager.
Bobby Smith

Bill always used to say to all of us: "I don't much care what you do off the field, just as long as you get it right on the field." But that wasn't strictly true all the time, because Bill did take an interest in his players – and I took an interest in Bill later on.

At home, we used to grow lots of our own vegetables, and I'd often take them up to Bill and Darkie when they still lived in Tottenham. Bill's pride and joy was his lawn – only a small strip of grass in his back garden, but he wouldn't even let people walk on it! So when he got a bit older, and found it a bit much, I'd give it a trim every now and then. It seemed like the least I could do.

It's funny, but when all that was going on in the 60s, with the trophies just coming one after the other, you sort of got used to it. It was as if it was just everyday life. But now, looking back, I look at what we did and I think to myself: 'Blimey – did we really do all that?' It just seems so unbelievable now.

Bill was so much a part of Spurs that you look around and wonder where and when there will ever be anybody else like him. Of course, there won't be.
Ron Henry

He could be a right so-and-so when he wanted to be, but that was just down to him wanting the best for Tottenham and the fans. There are plenty of managers around nowadays who might treat players harshly but maybe only for the sake of looking good when they go for another job. With Bill, you knew he wasn't looking any further than the next game.

Winning the Double is something that most players never get close to in their careers. Thanks to Bill, I can say that I did it.
Les Allen

It's sad when anyone you like dies, but even more so when they've done so much for you – as Bill did. He brought me down to Spurs from St Mirren, and he showed a lot of faith in me as a player. I guess if there's any consolation to be had, it's that he led a great and long life, but it's still the passing of an era.

Bill had so much to offer the game. It was criminal that, after he resigned in 1974, all that knowledge seemed to be lost forever. I'm sure Bill could have done a real job, maybe with another club or even with an England manager, because his knowledge of international football and tactics was legendary.

I'd just finished playing golf when I came in and heard the news on Sky. I

couldn't actually make the words out but I saw old Tottenham people being interviewed and they were showing images of Bill in his prime, so I knew. He was something special.
Jimmy Robertson

I'd just had a hip operation, and it was extremely tender. When I received an invitation to go to Bill's memorial service at The Lane, my first inclination was to say yes without question. But then I thought about it, and came to the conclusion that it would have just been too much of a risk at the time. One knock and I'd have been back to square one.

Bill? When people in years to come talk about the 60s, and the name of Bill Nicholson will be mentioned, people should remember what he achieved not just for Spurs, but for football as well. He was as much an icon of the time as anybody I can think of. I was asked if the current Arsenal team was the best I had ever seen – I said no, Spurs in 1961 were even better.

Bill was a wonderful, lovely fella who I will miss as lot, and it's a great shame I couldn't get there.
Terry Venables

I was at home when I got the call from Martin (Chivers) telling me about Bill going, and I have to admit there were tears. I'm not an over-emotional sort of fella usually, but Bill treated all his players like family and, no matter what he said about any of us down the years that may have seemed a bit harsh, we all felt the same about him. I was gutted. I called Steve Perryman shortly afterwards, and he was floored by it as well, although most of us knew it wasn't far off because he was in a bad way for quite a while. In spite of how I got treated at times by certain sections of the crowd at The Lane, the fact is that Bill picked me for a hell of a lot of his teams over the course of seven or so years, so that's all the endorsement I need on my playing career.

A part of Tottenham Hotspur died that day – and it was a good part.
John Pratt

Bill was an unbelievable winner, he loved to be winning things. He had a great knowledge of the game and a photographic memory.

Bill was a perfectionist and his Double side was the nearest thing to perfection in football so far. There were a lot of good managers about in his day and Bill was as good as any.
Alan Mullery

Bill was a great manager who wasn't afraid to make hard decisions. I had played a few games for Spurs but all of a sudden I got a bit of a run in the side during the UEFA Cup campaign of 1974. I was quite young at the time, and it would have been a bit of a risk putting a relatively inexperienced kid in at the deep end like that. But Bill just did it.

I was on my way to Norwich for a game against Everton with Keith Burkinshaw, who was working for the FA at the time, when his phone rang. It was his wife on the line, and I took it because he was driving. She told us that Bill had gone that morning. It was a bit of a shock to us both, I can tell you.

I had some great times playing at Tottenham, and I'll always be grateful to Bill and Spurs for that.
Mike (Matt) Dillon

I don't think that there will ever be anyone like him again. He was a perfectionist. To me he was all what Tottenham is about. He was simply . . . Bill Nicholson.
Martin Chivers

Bill's daughter, Jean, phoned Chiv on Friday night, the 22nd, when I was round there, and told Martin the news. It hurt like hell. I will always remember Bill as the man who took a chance on me, even though he had doubts over my strength. I got into nearly all Bill's teams. The two Martins – Chivers and Peters – are hosts in the Bill Nicholson Lounge at Spurs on matchdays, and they always introduce me as: 'Phil Beal – the first name on Bill's team sheet'. I was one of the few players who Bill would give praise to occasionally – because he probably recognised that I would give everything I had, week in, week out – and that was what he wanted from his players. I didn't realise at the time that the other players knew it, but they do now and they still wind me up about it. I can think of worse things in life than getting praise from somebody like Bill.

How the man never got a knighthood is beyond me. He is right up there with the other greats – Clough, Shankly, Busby, Revie – and Bill Nicholson.
Phil Beal

Bill Nicholson was totally dedicated to Tottenham. He was the first person to arrive in the morning and the last person to leave at night.

It was as much about a respect for the man himself than anything else that took me to Spurs.

He had a great knack of being able to find players who would fit into his side. He would encourage us to go out there and play the way we have been brought up to play, which was good for me because I was used to a similar style to Spurs while playing at West Ham.

Bill was a major servant to English football and a fantastic man. It was an honour to serve under him.
Martin Peters

As a manager, Bill was often at his best when things weren't going too well. He'd get you in at half-time, and lay it right out in front of you, what you were doing wrong, and what you could do about it. And although it's been said many times before, it was his honesty that most people found endearing about him. With Bill, if he told you not to worry about things, it was because there was nothing to worry about, not because he just wanted to change the subject.

I got along well with Bill, because I was the kind of player who would give everything, and he responded to that. I think as a manager he sort of had a soft spot for players who played their hearts out, and I guess it's because they remind him of how he played himself.

The last time I saw Bill was at Tottenham – it might have been about five or six years back. To be honest, I remember him that way, and I'm pleased about that.

Bill was a real influence on me when I was manager of Wales. Many of the things that you heard and learned at Cheshunt were passed on, and will be for some time to come.

Mike England

Bill and I had our ups and downs during my time at Spurs but that shouldn't take away from the fact that I thought very highly of him, and I respected him. Strangely enough, we got along a lot better after I left the game. I don't know whether it's just the fact that the years mellow you, or whatever, but it's true.

I hadn't seen Bill since Cliff Jones' 60th birthday bash – it had been about six years ago. I wish it hadn't been that long but you can't turn the clock back.

Roger Morgan

I had 12 years as a Tottenham player under Bill Nicholson and could not have wished to play for a better manager. I can still hear his wise words in my head when I am out on the training ground as a manager myself today.

I was also brought up at Tottenham to train with the ball on the ground and continue to use many of Bill's methods.

Today's players won't go far wrong if they do things his way.

Joe Kinnear

When you thought of Tottenham you thought of Bill Nicholson.

It was not exactly a secret that Bill had been quite poorly for some time. Martin (Chivers) had been keeping us all up to date with what was going on, because he lived quite near to Bill up at Brookman's Park, and had been visiting him on a regular basis. Not that it made things any easier when we found out – Bill was like a father to me, and he was probably the biggest influence on my life, let alone my career.

When Martin rang me and told me that morning, it was the saddest of days.

The memorial service at Tottenham on November 7 was wonderfully done. The club, and in particular the chairman and his wife, deserve a lot of credit for the way it went. Releasing the doves at the end was special.

Pat Jennings

It was on that Saturday morning that Martin Chivers rang me at home and broke the news. Oh, but it was a sad day.

I attended the memorial service at White Hart Lane and was also at Bill's funeral. It's strange, but even there we all found something to smile about. Before I had signed for Spurs, Bill's wife Darkie had made it well known that I had been

her favourite player – she liked my style, and when I eventually joined the club, the rest of the players had picked up on that and said that it was actually Darkie who had signed me, not Bill. This had carried on throughout my career at White Hart Lane, and even at Bill's funeral. Darkie had been very frail – it seemed to have hit her hard – but she still managed a smile when the lads started ribbing me. They were a special bunch of players, led by a very special man.
Ralph Coates

He had the total and undying respect of all the players and staff associated with the club. He ate, drank and slept Tottenham Hotspur.
Barry Daines

I had the pleasure and privilege of playing for 10 years under Bill Nicholson. He was without doubt a great manager, but also a great man. He was also an ardent supporter of Tottenham Hotspur.

His passing was a great blow not just to Tottenham in particular but also to football in general.
Alan Gilzean

The main reason I signed for Spurs was the honest approach of Bill Nicholson. He came across as straightforward and truthful and that continued throughout my career playing for him.

Bill was always fair and never lost sight of the fact that the players should do their best for themselves, the club and most of all the fans. He pushed the barriers and continually raised the standards. You could never rest on your laurels with Bill.

That grounding has stayed with me throughout my career. It was an honour to work for and with him.
Steve Perryman

I was only at Spurs for three or so seasons but I learned so much in those days. It makes me a bit puzzled when people say that Bill wouldn't be able to get along in today's game – the idea that he used to run everything in the club from the team selection, to the transfers, to the hot-dog stands, is a bit alien today, or is it? Wasn't Sir Bobby Robson doing much the same up at Newcastle until recently?

There are aspects of the game that have changed, but Bill was good enough to have adapted. Maybe not to 'player power' but, tactically, it's still 22 men and a ball.

I was a Spurs fan as a boy growing up in Walthamstow, and it was a dream come true when I got to sign for Spurs under Bill. He seemed a lot more relaxed as he got older. It was as if he had a chance to sit back and take a good look at what he had achieved, without the worry that he had to go back and do it all again the next day. He was one of the very best.
Dennis Bond

I was training with the youngsters up at Spurs Lodge that Saturday, when somebody came up to me and said that Bill was dead. I couldn't believe it, so I went and checked. Sadly, of course, it was true.

Bill had turned this club into the greatest club in Europe, if not the world. Now, I realise that we haven't exactly been able to maintain that over the last few years, but we will get back there one day. We're on the right tracks.

Bill took the push-and-run style of the side he played in back in '51 a stage further. Every year was quality at White Hart Lane, with the Benficas and the Dukla Pragues. He elevated the club to a household name, and I hope that will never be forgotten. Hopefully Spurs will get back to where they belong.
Jimmy Neighbour

The Jumbotron screen at White Hart Lane says it all.

Chapter 17
Tributes From The Game

I was fortunate to meet Bill when I was a young impressionable manager at Aberdeen and it was through a great mutual friend, Jim Rodger. Jim was one of the great journalists of his time and a truly good man. Bill was Godfather to Jim's daughter Joyce and had the same trust in Jim as I had. Nonetheless, when I knew I was to meet the great man I was quite nervous. I had a million questions I wanted to ask him but never got any over my lips, simply because he was so ordinary and down to earth and all he did was talk about football. There was no need to ask anything, Bill was giving me everything I could ask for – his time and knowledge; it was a fabulous day.

In assessing Bill's career as manager of Tottenham Hotspur we think of class and beauty. The pass-and-run style of the late 50s and early 60s will remain in people's minds forever. Just think of that Double-winning team, Blanchflower, Mackay, White, Greaves, Jones – the names just trip off the tongue.

It is one thing to achieve but another level to do it with class and Bill achieved that distinction with great honour and dignity, and, importantly, it never changed him. As the years rolled on and I was ensconced in my position at United, I always looked forward to seeing him, he never passed you without a conversation, on football of course.

There have been great men in all walks of life and Bill was one of them, and it was a pleasure just to have met him.
Sir Alex Ferguson CBE

He was not only one of our great football managers but also one of our great coaches. Solid, honest and totally reliable.
Sir Bobby Robson

It is impossible for me to sit in judgement of Bill Nicholson – I was only 16 in Bill's last season in management. But Nicholson's 16-year reign as Tottenham manager hardly needs an assessment. He was simply the best, and his record speaks for itself.

When I first arrived at the club, he commanded such respect that we were all in awe of the great man. If we saw him coming along the corridor we'd all rush out of his way. He was like the headmaster at school. He would come along to watch the youth team in the morning when I was playing. Whenever he turned up it was a huge incentive to do well and impress him. I heard a story that Bill was tempted to throw me into the first team at the beginning of his final season when things were not going too well. Obviously, he decided against it but I'm not sure how true it was that he considered giving me my big chance then.

In my view, Bill Nicholson WAS Tottenham Hotspur, and everything the club stands for emanated from Bill who installed the foundations. The success he brought the club was phenomenal. Bill Nicholson was on a par with other truly great managers of his time like Bill Shankly and Sir Matt Busby – they are all legends. Because of that it must be difficult for any manager to step into their shoes.

Bill was the manager throughout the club's most successful period and I've always had the highest respect for him and for what he achieved.

Bill always remained totally dedicated to Spurs. He had presence, he knew what he wanted, he knew how his team should and would function. He established the traditions of Tottenham Hotspur Football Club. He played for the great push-and-run side and then took it on himself to achieve all that he did. He was the cornerstone of the club. Indeed Bill had it all.

Glenn Hoddle

Bill Nicholson was the man who brought me to Tottenham, so I have a lot to thank him for.

I have the utmost respect for what Bill achieved throughout his career, and for what he did for Tottenham. He was responsible for bringing the glory, glory days to the club, and his Double-winning team of the 1960s is the one people always talk about, and the one the fans always want Tottenham teams to emulate.

Bill will always be a legend. He had that same incredible aura that Bill Shankly and Sir Matt Busby had. He was respected throughout the whole country not just for what he achieved, but also for the way he had done it.

Bill lived a life which revolved around Tottenham Hotspur Football Club. Nobody had a bad word to say about him because he was a gentleman. He was respected not just for what he achieved, but also for the way he had did it.

Gary Mabbutt

It was always a privilege meeting Bill Nicholson because he had such an aura about him. He had an incredible knowledge of football and everyone in the game knew and admired him for what he achieved at Tottenham.

He set high standards and established a tradition at Spurs that will live on for a long time to come. The word legend is used too freely but that's what Bill was. He was simply the best.

Jamie Redknapp

I started getting involved in coaching in the early 80s under Ian Greaves, Jim Smith and Maurice Evans at Oxford United. This interest often took me to the London area clubs on scouting missions, where I would often bump into Bill. I had rookie status in this department of the football world at that time but it never stopped Bill giving me his time.

He would have the right word or some very important advice in response to my ever-inquisitive questions. I remember on one such occasion at a Luton Town

game, Bill suggested in a wonderfully warm way that I should make sure I take a day off each week to be with my family, adding that this would benefit the football club by keeping the brain fresh for the training ground. This from a man who gave all his time and his life to building truly great teams for Tottenham Hotspur FC. I will never forget those pearls of wisdom that have been a great help in managerial jobs at Walsall and Bristol Rovers.
Ray Graydon

I never played against any of Bill's sides but I always knew about Tottenham from my time watching as a child.

He produced teams that were so good and so brilliant and his achievement of being the first manager to win a European competition with a British club was fantastic.

I knew the status of the man and the status he held at this club. I remember them as a kid and how great Tottenham were at that particular time.
Sam Allardyce, speaking on the day Bill died, Spurs v Bolton (23/10/04)

It was Steve Perryman who had phoned my wife to say that Bill had died, and she rang me. I was shocked, because I had seen him at a club function about a year before and he had seemed quite well. I honestly had no idea how ill he had been.

Bill's advice and willingness to help had been invaluable to me when I first joined Spurs. He knew the club from top to bottom, and that's why I had brought him back. He is the kind of man that football really misses nowadays – a no-nonsense, straight as a die man who told you what was what. A lot of people in football today don't have the courage of their convictions, but Bill would stand by everything he said. It'll be a sad day for football when the last of his breed has gone.
Keith Burkinshaw

Bill was one of the most successful managers of all and I was privileged to have worked closely with him for many years.

He was a typical Yorkshireman – not exactly cavalier in his ways – but players always knew where they stood with him. One of Bill's great strengths was his organisational ability, being thorough and planning properly. He was a one-off.
Eddie Baily

Many reams have been written regarding the statistical achievements of Bill's reign at Spurs. He was down to earth, blunt, tough but fair; and an exceptionally hardworking and knowledgeable man. His wonderful work and achievements for Tottenham will not be equalled.

Bill expected the players to do the job they were paid for, to play with movement and style and with harmony. For 16 years that harmonious rhythm was the personification of Tottenham Hotspur. They set standards and Bill won great accolades for the way he conducted his outstanding orchestra.

I think we can safely say that Bill Nick served and enjoyed his time 'on the grass' when football, as portrayed by Tottenham, was a game to grace White Hart Lane and all other famous English and European arenas.

Who will ever forget his push-and-run Spurs side? None of us who were lucky enough to see them will ever forget them.
David Pleat

When I was a student at Loughborough College between 1960-63, besotted by goalkeeping and the game of football, I was dazzled by the Tottenham Hotspur that Bill had created.

Only two clubs previously – Preston North End (1888-89) and Aston Villa (1896-97) had achieved the coveted League Championship and FA Cup Double.

Many years elapsed until, in 1960-61, Spurs, playing far more league games – 42 – ran away with the championship and became the first team in the 20th Century to lift the two principal domestic trophies in the same season.

The football Bill's side played was so stylish that none of the nine other Double-winning teams, before or since, have come close to matching it. They remain one of the teams who've had the biggest impact upon me as a coach, along with the Busby Babes, Brazil 1970, Holland 1974, and Arsenal 2003-04. All but Holland were triumphant and all providing entertainment beyond the rest, when it came to passing, movement, possession and eye-catching goals.

The dignity and sense of fair play Bill Nicholson extended was witnessed by me first hand in 1969. I was in Arsenal's goal during an utterly disgraceful League Cup semi-final at White Hart Lane in which fists replaced football and local pride spilled over into violence and the law of the jungle. We beat Spurs 2-1 but towards the end of the game I took an outrageous challenge from a Spurs player which could have ended my career. Immediate medical attention was needed which entailed my going through the Spurs' dressing room.

Pleasant greetings, as you can imagine, were not forthcoming. Bill Nicholson however followed me into 'casualty' and spent many minutes apologising and ensuring that I was only battered and bruised, not broken. I appreciated his calm and concern in the midst of a typical North London frenzy and from that moment, at every opportunity, as player or subsequent TV presenter, I would spend wonderful time with the great man.

Meeting his wife Darkie cemented a friendship for my wife Megs and me with the Nicholsons. He was a gentleman, a genius, humble, caring. You won't find anyone with a bad word to say about Bill. In the past two decades, in my capacity as Chairman of the London Football Coaches' Association, our annual dinner was made so special for all guests by the joint appearance of Bill and his old adversary, Arsenal manager Bertie Mee. After Bertie's death, Bill would turn up and, on being announced, there would be the same response year in, year out. No-one received a standing ovation of such magnitude as Bill Nicholson.

Everyone with a love of football will miss him. Happily that familiar smile and the black and white images of his great team will never fade away.
Bob Wilson, Chairman of London Football Coaches' Association

BILL NICHOLSON

It was a privilege and a pleasure to work under Bill for all those years. I know everybody says the same, but he really was a wonderful man. I never tire of recalling the times when Bill would come down to watch the boys' team playing, and what never failed to amaze people was how animated he would get – far more than at Spurs games. You'd see him urging them on, almost 'kicking every ball', and showing his exasperation when a player would choose the wrong option. Occasionally he had to be reminded by the sports master, Mr Mackay – no relation – that these were only kids! That teacher was the only person I can ever recall telling Bill off. We would often sit in his office at Tottenham for hours on end and just talk football – anything and everything to do with it, but always football. He wasn't a showy or ostentatious sort of man – you'd never find Bill on the showbiz circuit, doing the 'film premiere' thing. It may have been quite vogue for sportsmen to do that in the 60s, but that just wasn't his style. It would have taken up too much of his football time.

Bill was so generous and keen to promote kids' football, that he often allowed the local schools to use the ball court at Spurs when it was free. When he was there to watch, they would have certificates made to present to the players who were deemed to be the hardest triers, and it often turned out to be the overweight boys with glasses and spots – the ones who traditionally get picked last in five-a-side in the playground. I don't know how many of those certificates are still around but I suppose they must be treasured possessions for their owners. Almost as precious were the looks on those kids' faces when they won their certificates – it was as if they were saying: 'what – ME?' You can't buy moments like that.

On one occasion, there was a game going on with the boys, when a booming Scottish voice called out: 'OK if I join in?' It was Dave Mackay. The boys, having managed to close their mouths again, agreed, only for seconds later to be joined by Danny Blanchflower – then Cliff Jones...

The rest of the Scotland team were watching from the gallery. There had been an England-Scotland fixture at Wembley the day before, and Mackay's team-mates were mercilessly winding him up. Dave, whilst taking care not to injure the lads, was nevertheless charging around like it was a Cup final – Dave Mackay never knew the meaning of 'half-throttle'.

Bill somehow got wind of this, and hit the roof. Spurs had re-arranged their Saturday fixture and were due to play it on the Monday – less than 24 hours away. Bill told Cecil Poynton, the club physio, to get down there and cut the game short.

Mackay's reply? 'F*** off – winning goal!' I could imagine Sir Alex Ferguson or Arsene Wenger's reaction nowadays, but I think Bill Nick later saw the lighter side of it all.

I can remember when Jimmy Pearce got picked for England Schoolboys. Jimmy was a graduate of Rowland Hill and, although a Tottenham-born lad, a few big clubs (including Spurs themselves) were very keen on him. Well, Jimmy had to go down to Lilywhites outfitters in London – quite prophetic, I suppose – to get his England blazer, which would cost £75. That, of course, was quite a princely sum in those days. When the school secretary went to settle the bill, the shop manager told him there was no need, because it had already been paid – by Bill Nicholson.

It transpired that Bill had been keen on Jimmy as a player since his very early days, and was as pleased as punch that his big chance had come. Jimmy needed no persuading to sign for Spurs after that.

Dick Moss, MBE (Connected to Tottenham Hotspur in some capacity or another for 24 years under Bill Nicholson and Keith Burkinshaw, Dick was also former Head Teacher of Rowland Hill School, Tottenham, which has close ties to the club. He was awarded the MBE in the 2005 New Year's Honours list for services to young people in North London.)

I knew Bill from our army days, and I always had a great regard for him. He was a very good player. I have very many happy recollections of playing with him and against him.
Sir Tom Finney

Bill Nicholson, like a few of us older players, lived through the change that seemed to overtake the modern game. He remembered the days when we had to fight for an extra pound per week – not like today, where 'superstars' are handed king's ransoms for doing things that should be their bread and butter. They often receive adulation and promises of riches that bear no relation to their playing skills. It is, in a sense, the passing of an era. The game will miss Bill Nicholson.
Jimmy Hill

I was deeply saddened to hear of the death of Bill Nicholson.

I have met many footballing greats but 'Mr Nic' stands right up there with the best of them. And I'll never forget the day when I was a 17-year-old lad and he stuck out his huge hand and welcomed me to White Hart Lane.

I was too young to know the entire history of the Tottenham Double-winning side but the feat is etched in every hopeful's mind.

It was there in the background the day I arrived at the gate to be signed by Peter Shreeves.

I waited nervously in the foyer and this gentleman walked towards me, held out his hand and introduced himself as Bill Nicholson. I was a lad from South London, Millwall were actually my team, yet here was a legend. Peter Shreeves was a bit busy so Bill said: 'Let me show you around while you are waiting.' He took me to the trophy room and spelled out the club's history and in passing mentioned the double-winning side.

He never boasted he was the manager and preferred to tell me about the great players in the side. But I always believed he should have got greater recognition for what he achieved. He should have been knighted for his services to football and being the first manager in modern times to win the Double.
Neil Ruddock

Everyone connected with football in whatever sphere, be they directors, officials, players, supporters or media, would have been aware of Bill Nicholson's achievements in the game, even though many of them would not have seen his teams in live action.

Bill was well schooled in the art of coaching and management by playing in the Tottenham teams of 1949-50 and 1950-51, who won the second and first division championships in successive seasons. Unfortunately, owing to an abundance of other talented players at that time he only appeared once for England, against Portugal at Goodison Park in May 1951; scoring with his first touch in the game.

I first met Bill when I was working for Crystal Palace and we played Tottenham in the FA Cup in season 1969-70. Having drawn at White Hart Lane in the original tie, we beat Spurs in the replay at Selhurst Park and Bill, who was obviously disappointed, hid his feelings and wished us well in the next round – but wasted little time in setting about reshaping his team as this match signalled the end for Jimmy Greaves and Alan Gilzean in the Spurs shirt.

Over time I was to get to know Bill better by serving on the South East Counties League Management Committee with him for many years. The League was for the youth teams of clubs in the south-east and many future household names started their careers in that league before going on to make their mark both on the domestic and international scene. Bill took a great interest in the youth set-up in this country and, during his later years whilst scouting for Tottenham, would often be seen on a Saturday morning at the training ground watching the youth teams before going off in the afternoon, to carry out his duties at another match; very often in the lower divisions and the non-league. He had of course been instrumental in bringing Gary Mabbutt, Graham Roberts and Tony Galvin to the club from such teams and who later proved stalwarts in their careers at Spurs. Of course I had the pleasure of working with Bill at Tottenham for many years and valued his guidance.

Peter Barnes, former Spurs Secretary

I was driving in my car when I found out that Bill had died. I'd heard all week that he'd been ill, and that it was simply just a matter of time. I'd been in touch with a member of his family for about the previous three or four weeks, and he'd been telling me that time was running out for Bill. Then, on the morning of the Bolton game, it must have been about ten-thirty, it broke on TalkSPORT that Bill had gone, and I just had to pull over. I'd never felt such a loss for anybody outside of my family.

Then at the ground, we saw the montage on the screen, which was obviously prepared in advance. And that minute's silence...I'm also the club's commentator for the videos, and I tell you I had to stop before the game and compose myself, because tears were running down my face. My eldest son, who was with me, asked if I was all right because he could see that I was visibly moved by it all.

Then, of course, we went back on the Sunday morning, and I remember all the tributes from other clubs. So many people seemed to realise that Bill put Tottenham right on the top of the football world.

Daniel Wynne, Chairman of the Tottenham Supporters' Trust

The death of the great Bill Nicholson has stunned White Hart Lane. The silence *that greeted the tragic news descended slowly and reluctantly on our famous old stadium as the magnitude of his passing devastated all that knew the great man.*

Even those of a younger age, who were only aware of Bill's legendary status but had not seen his sides play, will stop and reflect when told of his demise because each and every generation of Spurs fans knows chapter and verse about his deeds as player and manager.

To so many, Bill Nicholson WAS Tottenham Hotspur. Who could have known that the young boy who stepped off the train at White Hart Lane station as a 17-year-old in 1936 would go on to become such a giant in the club's history?

Bill's influence on this club can be seen by a look back at our history. Prior to his playing debut in 1938 we had never won the League title and had only won the FA Cup on two occasions. As a player he helped us win the Championship for the first time in 1951 as part of our great push-and-run side and when he took over as manager he really put us on the world stage.

Bill was all about the good things in the game. His teams played with bravado, style, skill and grace. His players performed with a flourish, entertaining all along the way.

After winning the illustrious Double in 1961 we played in the European Cup for the first time and then went on to break so many records.

By lifting the European Cup Winners' Cup in 1963 we became the first British club to win a European competition and after our UEFA Cup success in 1972 we later became the first English side to have played in three major European finals. We won the League Cup twice – again the first side to do so – and took our FA Cup winning record to five.

All was achieved with Bill at the helm during the most successful period in the club's history.

Bill's legacy was to create a Tottenham way of doing things. He set the example himself and proved that winning could be achieved with style. He was the rock on which this club was built and was an inspiration to us all.

Youngsters, listen when your elders tell you of the deeds of Bill Nick and his great Spurs teams. Because no description or mortal memory of those black-and-white days can ever do justice to the reality of a magical time in our history.

And the catalyst, as those glory days and nights cascaded into history, was Bill Nicholson. He was quite simply the corner stone on which the club's modern day reputation was established.

Bill loved the club and called it his life. And we all loved him.

It is so hard to accept that he is no longer with us because his shadow was so immense. We have our memories but they can never be enough.
John Fennelly, Spurs Press Officer

I have heard a great deal about Bill Nicholson and would have loved to have had the opportunity to talk football, and Tottenham in particular, with a man who did so much for this club. Sadly, that can never happen, to my great regret.

To achieve success on a regular basis and to play entertaining football is always my ambition but it is difficult to achieve. Bill certainly managed it because the

BILL NICHOLSON

fame of his Spurs sides spread way beyond these shores. It is clear that he was a great man because every Spurs fan loved him.
Frank Arnesen, Spurs Sporting Director

As a child growing up in Holland, I was always fascinated by the names Tottenham Hotspur and White Hart Lane. They were both so original that they really captivated my imagination.

So you will appreciate just how proud and thrilled I was when I took over as the club's head coach. And how fitting that White Hart Lane should be situated at the end of Bill Nicholson Way.

Everybody in football knows the name Bill Nicholson. He created a magical team at a special time in our history and the great deeds of his Spurs side as they conquered Europe were certainly noted on the other side of the Channel.

Sadly, I never met Bill but I knew of his deserved renown and was touched on arrival at Tottenham by the love that Spurs fans of all ages held for the great man. Looking at the record books subsequently illustrated fully just what Bill Nicholson had achieved.

I am proud to follow in his footsteps but also know that I have such a hard act to follow. Bill set such standards that his work can never be eclipsed, and nor should it be, but it is up to his successors to try because that is what Bill Nicholson would have wanted.

Indeed, people who knew Bill tell me that he set targets, not records. In other words he loved Spurs so much that he wants subsequent teams to get better with each passing year. He was not about Bill Nicholson; he was always about Tottenham Hotspur.

I can relate to that and be lifted by his dream. As I told supporters when I was first appointed as head coach, I want the same feeling that Bill enjoyed, the satisfaction when you retire of looking back at a job well done.

Frank Arnesen and Martin Jol at the memorial service to honour the man who all subsequent Tottenham managers have been trying to emulate...

The Press changed that sentiment to suggest that I wanted to be the next Bill Nicholson. As proud as I would be to achieve such a reputation, I did not say that. I know that there will only ever be one Bill Nick.

Bill's sad but uplifting memorial service at The Lane underlined so much about him and how he remains in the hearts of Spurs supporters. I sat there so impressed by the obvious respect his memory evoked. It was a poignant scene on that morning at The Lane but so much more the celebration of a wonderful life of a footballing man that the entire audience would have been touched by his genius.

That included our senior players. Many were new to the club, and some from abroad, but even without knowing Bill's legacy, they could sense that they were now at a special club that was once steered to greatness by an unassuming man who achieved world renown.

I share that high regard and, as the baton passes to me, feel humbled by Bill's success. But I also feel inspired.

Martin Jol, Spurs Head Coach

Bill Nicholson's contribution to this club can never be overestimated. This great man made Spurs a household name and gave it a global perspective that was never there before.

Yet for all his marvellous achievements and incredible status within the game, I stand here and think of Bill Nicholson the man. Because that is how I will always remember him.

As a warm, generous man who just loved to talk football with anyone and whose ready smile always put people at ease, despite the fact that they were in the company of someone who was quite simply a footballing legend.

But that in itself is so much a tribute to Bill. There were no airs and graces about him. He had a track record that was second to none in terms of soccer success but you could never imagine him ever changing or acting differently in any way.

True, he was always ready to talk about the old days but never from his own perspective. He was always a team man from his days as a player and that's how he stayed.

Bill loved this club and the Spurs fans – and our supporters loved him in turn. And although they did not bear witness, even the modern generation of Spurs fans appreciate his achievements because they can understand the magnitude of what he did for Tottenham Hotspur and the standards that he set.

The fact that Bill was involved as a player and manager in both of our league title wins is a special achievement on its own but there was so much more to come as the greatest period in our history cascaded into a kaleidoscope of success after success.

Bill did so much for his beloved Spurs that we must never let his legacy fade. He must be our inspiration as we strive to ensure that a new era dawns here at White Hart Lane.

And we go forward in the knowledge that Bill's spirit lives on in all that we do. Indeed, we know that Bill Nick will be there with us every step of the way.

Daniel Levy, Spurs Chairman

Chapter 18
The Media's Final Page

As Bill Nicholson strode purposefully from the dressing room one sunny morning in August 1959, clipboard in hand, his haircut severe enough to satisfy any sergeant-major, a group of Spurs players sat preening themselves on the grass at Cheshunt.

Their smugness was understandable. Two days earlier Spurs had opened a new season with a marvellous 5-1 away victory over Newcastle United. It was always difficult to win there, never mind by such an arousing margin.

But Nicholson hadn't come to praise his players. Armed with notes, transferred from the little metal-jacketed pad into which he was known to scribble furiously during matches, he ripped into them.

Bill Brown should have saved Newcastle's goal, Maurice Norman hadn't done well enough in the air. Danny Blanchflower was coming too deep for the ball. Dave Mackay was selling himself in the tackle. Would no-one escape? Cliff Jones thought he would. Cliff had scored a hat-trick so there was a smile on his face. It wasn't there for long.

"And as for you Jonesy," muttered Nicholson, "I do more work in my back garden than you did on Saturday." He hadn't been in his garden for a month.

It should now be abundantly clear that Bill Nicholson was never easy to please. The years had mellowed him, proof perhaps that the stresses of management can do much to transfigure a man's true nature.

But if, of his illustrious contemporaries, Matt Busby was more urbane, Joe Mercer and Bill Shankly more spontaneously passionate about their trade, no one has done more to nourish faith in the best team game on earth than the greatest of Spurs managers. Those of us who recorded Nicholson's historic deeds were inclined to reach for words that seemed to be appropriate. In print he was always dour, dogged and unyielding. After all he was never a sportswriter's dream.

On the other hand, Bill was always worth the effort. Beneath that intimidating exterior there was a true believer, a man who was determined that his teams should try to win in style. Sensing that winning in itself was not enough, he once said prophetically: "We must play the football the public wants to watch, rather than the football we feel we ought to play."

You see, for Bill Nicholson, it has always been, lovingly, a glory game.

There will never be another Bill Nicholson. Everybody has heard all the clichés, but there was more to the man than that. The most common word to be banded around is 'dour'. But this was a man with a taste for drama – you have to look no further than the signings of Greaves and Mackay. Clandestine meetings, telephone calls between three clubs, agreements that nobody would bid more than a certain fee . . . and of course, the grand gladiatorial entrances. It was pure theatre, and Bill seemed to revel in it.

The same applied to his teams. It is surely the greatest paradox in football that sometimes, players who display all the flair and guile in the world on the pitch produce teams that would put Speedy Gonzalez to sleep, while 'workmanlike' players like Bill can give us wonderful sides that set the pulses racing.

Bill Nicholson was a man who didn't let anyone in very easily. Whenever I had the job of interviewing Bill, he was usually quite forthcoming with his answers, as long as they were ones he was comfortable with. But there was often a point at which he would display signs of tiring of the conversation, and the trick with Bill was recognising that point and moving on.

Most people, when referring to Bill's achievements, cite the obvious – the trophies, the great sides, the marvellous European nights. But it is so easy to overlook the fact that he was innovative, forward thinking, and a master tactician. Although he was not officially Walter Winterbottom's assistant manager for the 1958 World Cup, Bill was sent to prepare a dossier on the Brazilians – the electrifying side of Garrincha and the emergent young Pele. With the help of Bill's know-how, England gained a very creditable 0-0 draw against the side that was to go on and lift the trophy. It is contributions like this to the advancement of football that will be Bill's gift to the game he loved.

I had known Bill as a friend for the best part of 50 years, and football has lost something special.

Ken Jones, journalist for The Independent, and former Chief Sportswriter of the Sunday Mirror

There has been nothing like the Glory, Glory Hallelujah nights at White Hart Lane as Spurs' first bid for European honours in the 60s. Crowds of 60,000 packed the floodlit arena and a passionate atmosphere was whipped up by the cheer-leaders circling the track.

Spurs had won the League and Cup Double in 1960-61 for the first time this century with style as well as convincing victories, and the whole of football looked to them to restore British pride after disappointing set-backs at club and international level in the 1950s.

British? Captain Danny Blanchflower was Irish, Scotland provided Dave Mackay, John White and Bill Brown, and Cliff Jones and Terry Medwin were Welsh. The formidable English backbone was to be reinforced in the new year by Jimmy Greaves.

Bill Nicholson was a major reason for the successes which followed. The meticulous way he "did his homework" as he put it, prepared everyone for not only the opponents and tactics but also the pitch, dressing rooms, training facilities, travelling, hotels, food and so on. He also kept the side on top by shrewd and costly injections of fresh blood – quality players like Greaves, Alan Gilzean, Terry Venables, Pat Jennings, Alan Mullery, Mike England, Martin Peters and Martin Chivers.

BILL NICHOLSON

In the period 1961-74 Spurs played against opponents from 16 different countries. Of 27 ties at home they lost none and drew only four. They took part in eight finals (three FA Cup, two League Cup and three in Europe) and won them all except the last against Feyenoord.

What a record and what vibrant nights at White 'Hot' Lane!"
Bernard Joy of the Evening Standard (1983)

To have the good fortune in youth to encounter outstanding teachers is one of life's most valuable advantages. Reading Natural Sciences at Cambridge University in 1953, I attended the lectures of that eminent zoologist Professor Sir James Gray, yet simultaneously I met someone who has been, the way events turned, an even more significant influence on my career. Bill Nicholson taught me, as they say, almost everything I know.

Although having played much representative senior schools soccer, I only began really to understand the game when, on mellow autumn afternoons, Bill came to coach the University squad – for him a labour of love, for only later did one learn that his fee, paid by the FA, barely covered his travelling expenses. It was an exciting, fascinating experience to be involved once or twice a week with a shrewd, clear professional mind: what Bill did above all for Cambridge, in an era which included several well known amateur footballers and cricketers such as Peter May, Mike Pinner, Jerry Alexander, John Pretlove, Bill Knightly-Smith and Reg Vowels was to simplify the game.

It was not so much the expertise he gave us – at 20 you are too old a dog to learn new tricks – but what he told us not to do, the way he improved our collective performance by giving us an insight into the secret of all successful professional sport, the careful repetition of good, sound habits, often invoked over toast and honey after training, round a gas fire in someone's digs.

He was then just emerging as a coach and manager of the future, who would come to be as respected within the game as Matt Busby. There has always been much more to Bill's philosophy on the game than merely the correct text book. As a player and then as manager of possibly the most colourful and exciting club side in English history, he has believed in and always taught the wider fundamental virtues: that you can only take out of anything as much as you put in, that honesty is something which must extend to your contribution to your team, that talent does not absolve you from responsibility.

.There are few managers if any who have made a more profound contribution to the history and success of one club. Inadequate though he may at times have found our skills, we at Cambridge were proud and privileged to have had the opportunity to play under the guidance of such a man – who has always been willing to give more of himself than was due, and expected the same of others. Without him, Tottenham would not stand as it does today. Such is his modesty, I doubt if he himself realises the truth of that.
David Miller of The Times (1983)

I should like to take this opportunity to record some of the things Bill discussed with me or that I saw from watching his magnificent teams of 1959 to 1963. Much of what he taught seems unfortunately to have disappeared from a lot of today's tactical ploys as exhibited in his sides. These included the use of the short corner, with the receiving player along the goal-line, close to the kicker, in order to avoid any offsides. The switching of flank players to confuse full-backs. The centre-forward standing between the centre-half and one of the full-backs so creating a marking difficulty. The long throw-in to the goal line (perfected by Mackay to Smith, then Gilzean especially for the flick-on to Jimmy Greaves). And finally, now revived by Van Nistelrooy but perfected by Martin Chivers, the concept of standing behind the central defender – again, making marking both difficult and awkward.

Words of wisdom given in an interview for this magazine of yesteryear included: "Habits learned whilst young whether good or bad will be the first things to manifest themselves under pressure", and "Give the ball and go, then support it and never stand back and admire your pass."

I have been prattling for years about the need to get all sections of the game together and on one never to be forgotten Sunday in the late 70s, Bill Nick, along with the late Jackie Goodwin, for the coaches, and Ken Aston and Stan Lover, for the referees, attempted to do just that in front of a large group from each of those groups. To this day I have never heard of that experience being repeated, more's the pity.

Bill will always hold a special place in the hearts and minds of LFCA members and we are proud to say that we honoured him during his lifetime especially at our annual dinners over many years. It was intended to produce a special edition of this magazine in his memory but it was felt that by the time it was published it might have been too late. Nonetheless it is never too late to remember him both as a sportsman and a gentleman.

Ken Goldman, Editor, The Journal of the London Football Coaches Association

Nicholson – the soul of a poet and a love for the beautiful game

On a May evening in 1961, Danny Blanchflower looked back on nine months of rare achievement. The Tottenham team he captained had become the first side in 70 years to win the League and FA Cup Double. In doing so, they had played with a style which was almost without precedent in the English game.

Danny understood the significance.

"We've had what Bill Nicholson, in one of his more passionate moments, might call a pretty good season," he said.

Nicholson, who has died at the age of 85, was not given to overstatement.

As a stereotypical Yorkshireman, he spoke as he found. He disdained frivolity and empty show, and he never could understand football people who wanted to see their faces on television or their names in headlines. A stranger might easily have mistaken him for a dull man, but the stranger would have been wrong.

For Bill Nick, as generations of his players knew him, was one of the finest football managers the British game has produced; fit to keep company with Paisley, Busby, Shankly, Stein and the great men of that glorious tribe.

He joined Tottenham as a player in 1936 and he never really left them. He played

BILL NICHOLSON

in *Arthur Rowe's mould-breaking push-and-run team in the early 50s, when he won his solitary England cap – scoring with his first touch in international football in a 5-2 win over Portugal at Wembley – and the experience made him a fervent believer in the beauty of the game.*

For that dour exterior concealed the soul of a poet. Nicholson wanted the game played beautifully, with a proper respect for its spirit.

There were other trophies, but it was the manner of victory which lingers in the memory.

Spurs played it beautifully, because Nicholson insisted that there was no other way. It served his purposes to preserve his dour public image, yet in private he would speak entrancingly about the game he adored.

He lived simply and plainly, but his head was full of glorious dreams; dreams which players like Blanchflower, Dave Mackay, Cliff Jones and the rest had enacted all those years ago.

Ten years after his Double-winning team broke up, Nicholson looked back wistfully.

'Maybe I didn't realise it then,' he said, 'but it was sheer pleasure. I loved it. Most of all, I loved talking with Danny: talking and arguing. He always made me laugh. I don't half miss it now.'

Almost as much as football will miss Bill Nicholson.

Patrick Collins, Mail On Sunday

Tears for the man who will forever be Mister Tottenham

Tottenham 1 Bolton 2

On a wet afternoon in north London, thousands yesterday paid tearful respects to Bill Nicholson, whose football teams could warm the heart on the coldest of wintry days.

Outside the main entrance at White Hart Lane, fans came quietly to lay their floral tributes to the man they called 'Mr Tottenham'. On the guard rail others knotted their scarves or scribbled a homily to Nicholson, whose name was synonymous with Spurs for 60 years.

On the diamond screen inside the ground, nostalgic black-and-white clips from Nicholson's teams brought to life the legend of men like the late Danny Blanchflower, the elegant, eloquent Ulsterman who advanced captaincy to a level David Beckham could not understand; like Dave Mackay, a hard, smart defender; like Bobby Smith, a raging bull of a centre-forward.

In the stands middle-aged supporters wiped away a tear or two and told their sons of the days when Tottenham's cockerel crowed loud and proud over the land. They reminisced over the Double team of 1961 and remembered the European trophies Nicholson's vision brought them, the Cup Winners' Cup in 1963, the UEFA Cup in 1972.

And they cheered as the screen filled with film showing the white double-decker bus ferrying some of Nicholson's heroes along the Tottenham High Road with another haul of silverware.

Down on the pitch, some old Tottenham players had gathered to pay their own respects to Nicholson.

Pat Jennings showed he still carries himself like a guardsman. Mel Hopkins and Tommy Harmer, who played for Nicholson more than 40 years ago, were there with men from a later era, like Ralph Coates, Martin Chivers, Martin Peters, John Pratt and Phil Beal. Paul Gascoigne stood next to Jennings as a minute's silence was observed without a sound.
Malcolm Folley, Mail On Sunday

Mr Tottenham deserved a knighthood

Bill Nicholson never did get the gentle tap on the shoulders necessary to assume his rightful place among football's knights.

Yet events at White Hart Lane yesterday showed he was touched by something more – a genius for lifting spirits so that even the most dismal, murky afternoon might appear touched by magic.

If the fans left defeated, the memory of Bill Nicholson meant they were not downhearted. They made their way into the bluster and drizzle hoping for a brighter future, and for a leader who would one day restore the glory, glory to Tottenham Hotspur. They left hoping for the second coming of Bill.

In 1961, Nicholson's Tottenham became the first post-war team to win the Double, setting records that remain unbeaten.

Their run of 11 straight wins from the start of the season stands in the top flight, as does their 31 wins in 42 matches. Nicholson set a standard for entertaining, flowing football that many claim has never been surpassed – even by Arsene Wenger's Arsenal after 49 games without defeat.

Many of the messages attached the missing 'Sir' to Nicholson's name. There is still great resentment in this part of London that his achievements have not been recognised in the manner of Sir Alex Ferguson or Sir Bobby Robson.

Sadly, having finished as a manager in 1975, too much about Nicholson is undervalued or forgotten. He was one of only four men to win a Championship medal as a player and manager with the same team

Nicholson, 85, had been ill for some time and passed away yesterday surrounded by his family.

Tottenham had prepared for this sad event and the footage broadcast on giant screens at the ground was emotional and inspiring.

Every now and then we heard from the great man, his memories, his philosophy.

Midway through, spontaneous applause broke out and lasted until the words 'Bill Nicholson 1919-2004' filled the screen. Yet one could not help but think there was a little something missing.

Double winner Cliff Jones conceded as much. He said: 'There was a strong campaign for him to be knighted and I am amazed he wasn't. He did so much for the game and the club. He drilled into us that the most important thing was the club and its fans and I would put him alongside greats like Bill Shankly, Matt Busby, Brian Clough and Ferguson.'

A pity that was not appreciated yesterday, when the devotion of fans tying brand new replica shirts to the gates, was undermined by the surliness of current Spurs

BILL NICHOLSON

coach Jacques Santini, who refused to add his own tribute after watching his side fall to Bolton.

In his defence, Santini might not initially have understood Nicholson's importance.

Some things cannot be lost in translation, however. Like the fact Santini would not have such a big club to manage were it not for the old man on the screen. To be told this and still stay silent was just rude. Once again, Nicholson deserved better.

So if the current coach is in need of proper perspective, it is to be found on page eight of the match day programme, where Tottenham's triumphs are listed.

In all, there are 16 trophies – and nine involved Nicholson (eight as manager, one as player).

A fan's banner said it best: Sir Bill Nicholson – Mr Tottenham.

At least somebody knew, at least somebody understood.

Martin Samuel, News of the World

Nicholson's gift was to celebrate the artistry of the game

You know how you get tongue-tied in the presence of people who, without being aware of it, have changed your life for the better? Thus it was that I stuttered thanks to Bill Nicholson for the memory of his Double side, whose sense of style shaped my love of football. What a privilege it was to meet Nicholson. It was in March this year, on the night he became the first occupant of Tottenham Hotspur's Hall of Fame, amid the adulation of a packed banqueting suite at White Hart Lane and with all but three of his history-making players (the late Danny Blanchflower and John White, and Bill Brown, ailing abroad) in attendance. Emboldened by his gentle manner, I asked what he thought of Arsene Wenger's all-conquering Arsenal. 'Oh,' he said. 'I think they're pretty good. Don't you?'

That was it; he was getting on a bit. But what do fancy words matter next to the beauty of teams such as Nicholson's, or Wenger's? Precious few are worthy of mention in the same breath. When it comes to football with elan and swagger, these sides, created in North London a few miles and a few decades apart, would be on any short-list. For me, it is a short-list of two. There have been sides as effective, terrific-to-watch sides built in Liverpool, Manchester and elsewhere, some with more impressive rolls of honour than Nicholson's or (thus far) Wenger's. This is not the time for argument; it is a question of personal taste.

Nor are the pros and cons of whether Nicholson should have had a knighthood suitable for quantifying. All we, his most fervent admirers, would say is that Nicholson was set apart by his courage, which applied to both the aesthetic and the ethical, and his perfectionism. At the dinner held in his honour, Cliff Jones, that lightning-quick, ridiculously brave and thrilling winger, confirmed that the often-grumpy Nicholson hated players intimidating referees. He would scathingly tell his men: 'You don't even know the rules, you lot.' And he taught them the importance of entertainment. 'We trained to provide attractive football, in small groups, always with a ball, making little triangles and patterns. We had a great commitment and a manager who told us the most important people were the fans

– they had to have value for money.'

He even chastised his men for the performances that completed each part of the double! So, when Spurs got the benefit of his capacity for taking pains, so did football. Bill Nicholson was a true hero of the game. I'd have given him a dukedom.

Patrick Barclay, Sunday Telegraph

Farewell to a true gent

At Capital Radio we gave yearly football awards – such as player of the year, young player of the year etc. We also gave a Bill Nicholson award every year, for a fan or club secretary or someone like that who deserved recognition.

We got more votes for that award than anything else. And I am sure that is because it had Bill's name attached to it.

Bill Nicholson stood for an honesty and integrity that is sadly disappearing from our game.

He truly was one of the greatest English managers of all time.

We'll miss him.

Jonathan Pearce

Glory Man

The author of the classic book on Bill Nicholson's Tottenham of the 70s salutes a manager who was guided by army days . . .

I met Bill Nick by chance at Wembley in 1999 at the League Cup Final, Spurs against Leicester. I was walking up those awful concrete steps towards turnstile G when I heard a group of lads ahead of me shouting out someone's name. It wasn't Gee-no-la, Gee-no-la, which was what all Spurs lads were shouting in 1999, but a name I couldn't work out at first: 'Billy Nicholson'.

I eventually caught up with him, struggling to hold on to a railing, pausing for breath, helped by his younger daughter. He was 80 that year, but being very brave.

I said hello and took his arm, while his daughter took the other, and we managed to get him to the top of the steps. Before making his way to his seat, he said he wanted the lavatory. I said I'd take him, which was a struggle with the usual Wembley squalor. I feared he might get trampled on, but little groups of Spurs fans recognised him, made a magic circle for him, let him pee in peace.

We chatted a bit about old times as I led him to his seat. It was one of the ordinary ones, just beside mine, for ordinary Spurs fans. I asked why he wasn't in the royal box, or at least with the directors in their plush quarters, after all he had done not just for Spurs but for British football.

"Oh," he said with a thin smile, "they forget things."

I spent almost two years in the early 70s hanging around Billy Nick and Spurs, writing a book, although in my mind it was a year in the life of a football team, anywhere, any time. Brian Glanville, then as now one of our leading football experts, said I wouldn't have a chance getting access at Spurs.

They had an unhelpful, old-fashioned board and a dour manager. In Bill's own autobiography, a few years later, he said he didn't know who had given me permission.

He certainly wouldn't have done, if asked.

Nobody did. I just hung around. In the end, Bill let me join in pre-season training and be present in the dressing room during games (a privilege no outsider has had since). At moments of high emotion, I feared I might get chucked out and I thought: 'Well, if I lose the book, I'll have had the experience'. Strange that I got away with it, but I felt I understood his rigid, puritanical, northern background. And I learnt to keep out of his eye-line. He was a product of his age and class, one reason why there won't be another manager like him. Everything has changed, from diets and wages to the psychology of management.

He had six years during the war as an army PE instructor and his wife, Grace, always known as Darkie, said he lived his life as if he'd never left, imposing iron discipline at work and at home. 'When I've ironed his shirts, he inspects each one. If any is not right, I have to do it again.'

He and his assistant, Eddie Baily, lived and breathed army metaphors. A game was a battle, players were urged over the top, bayonets came out, you got in at 'em. On a trip to Bristol once, to watch the reserves, he drove me in his car and I managed to get more than the usual few grunted words on his theory of man-management.

'In the army I spent six years handling people. I've discovered that it's best to tell people there's always a bit to go, that they must try harder, that they can do better.'

By then, that theory wasn't quite working, especially in his handling of Martin Chivers, England's best centre-forward of the early 70s. He was doing it for England, but not for Spurs. Nicholson was clearly failing to motivate him. Chivers would sulk, hulking in the dressing room, while Bill raged. He didn't throw things, or tantrums, but his fury was obvious. Chivers was probably the single biggest problem in Bill's long career. Years later, when Chivers retired, they were great friends. Chivers' character seemed to change totally.

Bill was of his times in his coaching methods. I can hear Alan Gilzean in training getting a bollocking for bringing the ball down on the front of his boot instead of trapping it underneath, as Bill had been taught in the 30s. He made the youth team re-do its official team photograph – two boys had hair longer than he approved of.

He was against women coming anywhere near football, wouldn't let Darkie or his two daughters ever go to a game. "When he comes in from a match," said Darkie, "I can't tell from looking at him whether they've won or lost. Me or the girls, we're up in the air if we've heard Spurs have won, all excited and shouting."

On the day he was made manager in 1958, he never rang his family. It had happened just a couple of hours before a game against Everton, whom they beat 10-4. When he got home, he still didn't mention it.

He'd never wanted to manage, preferring to coach, but felt he had to take it, or a new manager would sack him. And he never had a contract, then or later. Impossible to imagine today. Even on his Sundays, he would go in to the empty stadium and do some work. His home, a modest semi, was a 10-minute walk away. At his older daughter's wedding, Darkie heard a noise beside her and thought he was coughing. "Then I saw the tears. He couldn't stop. He kept on saying: 'I never saw her growing up'."

In his glory, glory years at Spurs, the directors believed he could walk on water. Once managers fall or fade, memories grow thin, as I saw at Wembley in 1999. But the fans will never forget Bill. And the board eventually did make him president.

Even named a little street after him. So he will live on, in memory as well as on the map...

Hunter Davies

(Hunter Davies: 'The Glory Game' was first published in 1972. An updated edition is published by Mainstream.

Chapter 19

Bill's Legacy

So the great man has gone, and we, his extended family, have to pick ourselves up, dust ourselves down, and carry on. Bill would have insisted on nothing less.

Much has been written over the course of the last few years about Tottenham Hotspur, and the apparent obsession of its fans living in the past. I prefer to think of it as revisiting the past, and with the greatest respect to 95 per cent of British league clubs, if they had a past like Spurs they would be more liable to do the same. The simple truth is, sometimes you have to look to the golden years of a club's history to capture the essence of what they stand for, what they are.

It's no coincidence that clubs like Wolves, Burnley, Stoke, Sheffield Wednesday and others who are currently outside the comfort zone of the Premiership still think of themselves as sleeping giants. They are steeped in history far more glorious than many of the clubs currently in the top flight, and those lessons will have been passed down from father to son several times over. Whether they are right to think that way is open to personal opinion, but in the case of Tottenham Hotspur, several regimes have tried to recreate those wonderful times and have not only failed, but have received little but vitriol and scorn for their trouble. Some, of course, have simply seen the opportunity to balance the books, but in the modern world that is not as distasteful as it sounds. The harsh reality of life in modern football is that there are too many clubs chasing too few fans, and the old argument that clubs have to 'cut their cloth' accordingly holds some weight.

But there is more to the ethos of 'The Tottenham Way' than the pursuit of silverware, although God knows it would help. It is also about making the game a spectacle again, about sticking to very simple values and expecting those under your wing to do the same. It has nothing to do with providing lip service to those who want instant thrills or even instant success – but everything to do with a long-term belief that what you are striving for is both sustainable and worth sustaining. The easier way to look at it is to suggest that, had Bill not taken the step all those years ago to take over from Jimmy Anderson, Tottenham Hotspur may well have been just another club with a vaguely successful past that lived in the twilight world of the lower divisions, with its fans seemingly happy to revel in what was, and not what could be.

It is perfectly understandable for younger Spurs fans to believe that the kind of days their grandad burbles about over the sherry each Christmas will never come again. Yet football is, as one of our favourite sons is often keen to remind us, a funny old game, and if we look maybe 10 or even 20 years into the future, who knows where the journey of discovery that is Tottenham Hotspur will take us?

As we now watch the likes of Chelsea, Arsenal and Manchester United lording it in the Champions League, it would be wise to remind ourselves that a few short seasons ago, Leeds United were in the semi-final of that very competition, and yet nowadays they look forward to six-pointers with Gillingham, Cardiff City and Plymouth Argyle. Even Nottingham Forest, twice winners of the ultimate prize in European football, are now in serious danger of dropping into the third tier of English football. In short, just as football can change quickly, it can change back even quicker.

As Spurs supporters, we all live in the hope that one day, one wonderful sunny day, another side in Spurs shirts will emerge from the shadows of the mighty teams that Bill built in the 60s and 70s. Most of us who remember those days cling to the belief that the law of averages must fall in our favour one day. If that is to be the case, one thing is certain – no amount of future domestic success, no amount of future European glory, no avalanche of plaudits from football's elite, will deflect from the fact that the blueprint for any future success was laid by the hand of William Edward Nicholson all those years before.

So what if, given the will, the resources and the luck that all successful clubs need, Spurs find themselves one day challenging once again for the ultimate prize in football, and are eating at the table of the high and mighty? If, one day, the unthinkable should happen and a Tottenham Hotspur team lands the trophy (albeit in a different form) that was cruelly and unjustly denied to us in 1962, what would Bill be thinking as he looks down from his position in the ultimate directors' box?

I would suspect that a small part of him would be saying: 'Yes, they did well, but that number four should have squared the ball for that second goal'. I also feel that an equally small part of him would be comparing those players to his beloved Double side and running the rule over them accordingly. I am sure, however, that as a Spurs captain finally holds aloft the greatest prize in European football, the best part of him would be surveying the glorious scene with a huge grin, whilst in his broad Yorkshire brogue uttering something like: 'About bloody time, too!' For as Bill himself so eloquently put it…

"It's been my life, Tottenham Hotspur, and I love the club."

Bill Nicholson OBE, 1919-2004

Bill's Record

Bill Nicholson as a Tottenham Hotspur player

Season	Football League	FA Cup
1938-9	8	-
1946-7	39	2
1947-8	38	5
1948-9	41 (2 goals)	1
1949-0	39 (2 goals)	3
1950-1	41 (1 goal)	1
1951-2	37 (1 goal)	2
1952-3	31	7
1953-4	30	6
1954-5	10	-
Total	**314 (6 goals)**	**27**

Bill as an England player

Bill played once for England (May 19, 1951), at right-half against Portugal at Goodison Park. He scored the first goal with his first kick of the match in a 5-2 victory.

Bill Nicholson's honours as Tottenham Hotspur manager

1960-61	Football League champions
	FA Cup winners
1961-62	FA Cup winners
1962-63	European Cup Winners' Cup winners
1966-67	FA Cup winners
1970-71	Football League Cup winners
1971-72	UEFA Cup winners
1972-73	Football League Cup winners

Tottenham Hotspur's playing record under Bill Nicholson

	P	W	D	L	F	A
Football League	667	306	164	197	1208	922
FA Cup	67	39	15	13	160	72
League Cup	34	20	8	6	62	32
Europe	55	36	8	11	141	60
Total	823	401	196	227	1571	1086

Tottenham Hotspur's League record under Bill Nicholson

Season	Pos.	P	W	D	L	F	A	Pts
1958-59	18th	42	13	10	19	85	95	36
1959-60	3rd	42	21	11	10	86	50	53
1960-61	1st	42	31	4	7	115	55	66
1961-62	3rd	42	21	10	11	88	69	52
1962-63	2nd	42	23	9	10	111	62	55
1963-64	4th	42	22	7	13	97	81	51
1964-65	6th	42	19	7	16	87	71	45
1965-66	8th	42	16	12	14	75	66	44
1966-67	3rd	42	24	8	10	71	48	56
1967-68	7th	42	19	9	14	70	59	47
1968-69	6th	42	14	17	11	61	51	45
1969-70	11th	42	17	9	16	54	55	43
1970-71	3rd	42	19	14	9	54	33	52
1971-72	6th	42	19	13	10	63	42	51
1972-73	8th	42	16	13	13	58	48	45
1973-74	11th	42	14	14	14	45	50	42

Bill as England Under-23 coach

Date	Venue	Opposition	Result
19/5/57	Sofia	Bulgaria	2-1
26/5/57	Bucharest	Romania	0-1
30/5/57	Bratislava	Czechoslovakia	0-2
31/5/67	Athens	Greece	0-0
3/6/67	Sofia	Bulgaria	1-1
7/6/67	Ankara	Turkey	0-3
25/09/57	London	Bulgaria	6-2
16/10/57	London	Romania	3-2
24/09/58	Sheffield	Poland	4-1
15/10/58	Norwich	Czechoslovakia	3-0

Bill's Wartime Playing Record

Season	Team	Opponents	Date	Result
1939-40	Hartlepools	Darlington (H)	30/03/40	3-1
1940-41		No playing record		
1941-42		No playing record		
1942-43	Sunderland	Huddersfield (H)	26/09/42	1-3
		Huddersfield (A)	3/10/42	2-2
		Bradford Park Ave (A)	10/10/42	2-4
		Bradford Park Ave (H)	17/10/42	2-1
	Tottenham	Portsmouth (A)	24/10/42	0-1
	Fulham	Portsmouth (A)	07/11/42	1-1
	Middlesbrough	Newcastle (A)	21/11/42	0-3
		Gateshead (A)	5/12/42	0-5
	Sunderland	Middlesbrough (H)	16/01/43	7-0
		York City (A)	23/01/43	0-4
		Newcastle (H)	6/02/43	3-3
	Newcastle	Middlesbrough (H)	10/04/43	4-0
		Huddersfield (H)	24/04/43	0-1
		Gateshead (H)	26/04/43	3-1
1943-44	Newcastle	Bradford City (A)	28/08/43	1-2
		Bradford City (H)	4/09/43	3-2
		Bradford (A)	11/09/43	0-1
		Bradford (H)	18/09/43	2-1
		York City (A)	25/09/43	0-2
		York City (H)	2/10/43	1-1
		Huddersfield (A)	16/10/43	1-1
		Sunderland (A)	6/11/43	2-4
		Middlesbrough (H)	11/12/43	1-1
		Sunderland (H)	27/12/43	4-2
		Sunderland (A)	1/01/44	0-3
		Gateshead (A)	29/01/44	3-1
		Middlesbrough (H)	12/02/44	4-1
		Darlington (H)	19/02/44	2-0
		Hartlepool (H)	11/03/44	3-0
		Sheffield United (H)	8/04/44	3-1
1944-45	Darlington	Huddersfield (A)	30/09/44	2-1
		York (A)	7/10/44	0-2

		Hull City (H)	28/10/44	7-1
		Gateshead (A)	11/11/44	3-1
		Bradford (A)	18/11/44	3-0
		Sunderland (A)	09/12/44	2-6
		Middlesbrough (H)	23/12/44	5-2
		Sunderland (A) (Cup)	06/01/45	1-1
		Sunderland (H) (Cup)	13/01/45	3-2
		Middlesbrough (A) (Cup)	03/02/45	1-0
		Hartlepool (A) (Cup)	17/03/45	3-0
		Newcastle (A) (Cup)	24/03/45	1-2
		Newcastle (H) (Cup)	31/03/45	0-3
		York (H)	02/04/45	7-3
		Gateshead (H)	07/04/45	2-4
		Gateshead (A)	14/04/45	4-3
		York City (H)	28/04/45	2-2
		Hartlepool (A)	05/05/45	0-2
		Middlesbrough (H)	09/05/45	5-3
		Hartlepool (A)	21/05/45	5-0
1945-46	Tottenham	Fulham (A)	09/03/46	1-1
		Fulham (H)	16/03/46	1-3
		Plymouth Argyle (H)	23/03/46	2-0
		Plymouth Argyle (A)	30/03/46	1-0
		Portsmouth (A)	06/04/46	1-0
		Portsmouth (H)	13/04/46	2-0
		Charlton Athletic (A)	17/04/46	0-1
		Nottingham Forest (H)	19/04/46	3-2
		Newport County (A)	20/04/46	4-1
		Nottingham Forest (A)	22/04/46	2-0
		Newport County (H)	27/04/46	1-0
		Coventry City (A)	04/05/46	1-0

Bill's Signings

Player	Year in	From	Fee (£)
Les Allen	1958	Chelsea	20,000
Bill Brown	1959	Dundee	16,500
Dave Mackay	1959	Heart of Midlothian	30,000
Tony Marchi	1959	Torino	20,000
John Smith	1959	West Ham United	20,000
John White	1959	Falkirk	20,000
Len Worley	1959	Wycombe Wanderers	Not known
Frank Saul	1960	School	n/a
Jimmy Collins	1961	Lugar Boswell Thistle	Not known
Jimmy Greaves	1961	AC Milan	99,999
Ron Piper	1962	Arsenal	Not known
Phil Beal	1963	School	n/a
Laurie Brown	1963	Arsenal	40,000
Derek Possee	1963	School	n/a
Jimmy Robertson	1963	St Mirren	25,000
Alan Gilzean	1964	Dundee	72,500
Pat Jennings	1964	Watford	27,000
Cyril Knowles	1964	Middlesbrough	45,000
Roy Low	1964	School	n/a
Alan Mullery	1964	Fulham	72,500
Keith Weller	1964	School	n/a
John Collins	1965	School	n/a
Roger Hoy	1965	School	n/a
Neil Johnson	1965	School	n/a
Joe Kinnear	1965	St Albans City	Not known
Steve Pitt	1965	Corinthian Casuals	Not known
Terry Venables	1965	Chelsea	80,000
Dennis Bond	1966	Watford	20,000
Roy Brown	1966	School	n/a
Mike England	1966	Blackburn Rovers	95,000
Martin Chivers	1967	Southampton	125,000
Tony Want	1967	School	n/a
Peter Collins	1968	Chelmsford City	5,500
Ray Evans	1968	School	n/a
David Jenkins	1968	Arsenal	55,000
Roger Morgan	1968	Queens Park Rangers	110,000

Terry Naylor	1968	School	n/a
Jimmy Pearce	1968	School	n/a
Ken Hancock	1969	Ipswich Town	7,000
Steve Perryman	1969	School	n/a
John Pratt	1969	School	n/a
Roy Woolcott	1969	Eton Manor	Not known
Jimmy Neighbour	1970	School	n/a
Martin Peters	1970	West Ham United	200,000
Ralph Coates	1971	Burnley	190,000
Barry Daines	1971	School	n/a
Phil Holder	1971	School	n/a
Graeme Souness	1971	School	n/a
Ray Clarke	1972	School	n/a
Matt Dillon	1972	School	n/a
Terry Lee	1973	School	n/a
Chris McGrath	1973	School	n/a
Neil McNab	1973	Morton	40,000
Keith Osgood	1973	School	n/a
Alfie Conn	1974	Rangers	140,000
Chris Jones	1974	School	n/a

Bibliography

1966 And All That – Geoff Hurst – Headline Book Publishers, 2001

A Biography of a Visionary – Dave Bowler & Danny Blanchflower – Victor Gollancz, 1997

An Autobiography – Pat Jennings – Collins Willow paperback, 1983

Behind Closed Doors – Irving Scholar – André Deutsch, 1992

Cloughie – Brian Clough – Partridge, London, 1994

Cloughie - Walking On Water – Brian Clough – Headline Book Publishing, 2002

EX magazine – published by Football World

Glory Glory – My Life With Spurs – Bill Nicholson – MacMillan London Ltd, 1984

Greavsie – Jimmy Greaves – Time Warner, 2003

Matt, United and Me – Jimmy Murphy – Souvenir Press Ltd, 1968

Let's Be Honest – Jimmy Greaves – Pelham Books, 1972

Pegasus – The famous Oxford and Cambridge soccer side of the fifties – Ken Shearwood – Oxford Illustrated Press, 1975

Ron Atkinson – A Different Ball Game – Andre Deutsch, 1992

Soccer At War – Jack Rollin – Willow Books, 1985

Spurs Again – Ralph L Finn – Robert Hale and Co, 1971

Spurs Go Marching On – Ralph L Finn Robert Hale Ltd, 1963

Spurs Monthly – published by MPress (Media)

Spurs Supreme – Ralph L Finn – Robert Hale Ltd, 1961

Stiles After The Ball – Nobby Stiles & James Lawton – Hodder and Stoughton, 1993

Still Crazy – the authorised biography of Joe Kinnear – Hunter Davies – André Deutsch Ltd, 2000

The Essential History of Tottenham Hotspur – Bob Goodwin – Headline book publishing, 2001

The Final Score – Brian Moore – Hodder and Stoughton, 1999

The Glory Game – Hunter Davies – Mainstream Publishing Co (Edinburgh) Ltd, 1972

The Glory Glory Nights – Cockerel Press, 1986

The Jimmy Hill Story – Jimmy Hill - Hodder and Stoughton, 1998

The Way It Was – Sir Stanley Matthews – Headline Publishing, 2000

Time On The Grass – Bobby Robson – Arthur Barker Ltd, 1982

Venables – Terry Venables & Michael Joseph – The Penguin Group, 1994

Winning Isn't Everything: a biography of Sir Alf Ramsey – Dave Bowler – Victor Golancz, imprint of the Cassell Group, 1998

Yours Sincerely – Ron Greenwood – Willow Books, 1984

Acknowledgements

When I was first approached to write this book, as a life-long Spurs fan I jumped at the chance. The idea that I could finally get to pay homage to the great Bill Nick was enough – but the possibility that I could be speaking to, and even meeting, players who had previously existed as two–dimensional images on my bedroom wall as a kid was mind-blowing. If this was work, I thought, put me in for overtime.

I had no way of knowing, however, quite how much goes into a project of this kind. With that in mind, untold thanks must go to:

My wife Carol, without whose invaluable help this book would have been completed much later and in a secure unit somewhere.

John Pratt, the first player I interviewed, and the font of all knowledge. John, you can have your phone back now. And thanks for the beer.

Publisher Tony McDonald, for his advice, patience and help, and his colleagues at Football World, Danny Francis and Susie Muir.

Empics and Action Images, for their photography.

Neale Harvey, for some very useful phone numbers.

Harry Hotspur, for his know-how and being a generally all-round good egg with some top-notch Spurs literature.

Daniel Wynne, for his input and contacts.

John Fennelly, for his help and advice.

Ashley Weller, for putting up with my daft emails.

Andy Porter, Spurs historian.

John Hayes, for more input and contacts.

Kevin Saban, for his contacts and buying me beer when I needed it most – and for being my best mate.

Chris Moy, for words of encouragement, knowing people, and being my nephew.

Tim Crane, for his help with news research.

Peter Ward, for putting me in touch with people who know people.

Morris Keston, for knowing everyone in the Western World.

Tony Maitland, for trying.

All at Montrose FC, for their help in finding 'Gilly'.

All at the National Football Museum, Preston, for knowing much more than I do.

Kevin Storey and the Durham Light Infantry Association, for trying as well.

Jim Duggan, for running the best damn website around.

Also, the following websites and fanzines to which I am eternally grateful:

Topspurs, My Eyes Have Seen The Glory, Glory Glory Net, Ozspurs, Splodgy, Clarets Mad (unofficial Burnley FC), Toffees Mad (unofficial Everton FC), Red Issue (unofficial Manchester United FC).

Colonel Sanders, for feeding my family when my secretary didn't have time to cook.

All the staff, players, ex-players, ex-managers and countless fans of Tottenham Hotspur FC who have helped so much with the content of this book. Also, let's not forget the late Ron Burgess and Bill Brown, two of Bill's former White Hart Lane colleagues who have sadly passed away in recent months.

To the Nicholson family – for their input to this book at a difficult time.

And finally...to Bill Nicholson OBE...Sir, I thank you just for being part of my life for all those wonderful years.

The Author

Born in 1956 in Kentish Town, North London, Steve Hale is a life-long Spurs supporter who currently combines his career as a freelance writer with working for parcel carriers UPS. He has previously written over 30 feature articles for the official Tottenham Hotspur magazine, Spurs Monthly, and has had short stories published.

Steve saw his first Spurs game in April 1966, when he was taken to White Hart Lane by his elder brother. The experience obviously left a mark on him, as did Bill Nicholson, and when the opportunity arose to put his admiration for the Spurs legend into print, Steve needed no pushing. "It was a dream come true," he says. "And a once-in-a-lifetime chance which I wasn't about to let go."

He has plans to begin writing screenplays and has said he aims to get one completed before Spurs win the Premiership – that way he says he feels under no time pressure!

Steve is married with two children and currently lives in Barkingside, Essex.